D0426444

SONG AND ACTION

SONG AND ACTION
The Victory Odes of Pindar

Kevin Crotty

THE JOHNS HOPKINS UNIVERSITY PRESS
BALTIMORE AND LONDON

This book has been brought to publication with the generous assistance of the David M. Robinson Publication Fund.

The Johns Hopkins University Press, Baltimore, Maryland 21218
The Johns Hopkins Press Ltd., London

Library of Congress Cataloging in Publication Data

Crotty, Kevin, 1948–
  Song and action.
  Originally presented as the author's thesis
(Ph.D.—Yale University, 1975)
  Bibliography: pp. 161–67
  Includes index.
  1. Pindar—Criticism and interpretation. I. Title.
PA4276.C7 1982 884'.01 81–48180
ISBN 0-8018-2746-9 AACR2

 # Contents

≋ Preface ≋
and Acknowledgments

The present study, a distant relative of a doctoral dissertation submitted to the faculty of Yale University in 1975, seeks to continue and extend the ground-breaking work of Elroy L. Bundy on the traditional character of the epinicians of Pindar. Bundy argued that scholars had built up a fundamentally misleading portrait of Pindar as a difficult, abrupt, and willful poet who felt compelled to insert irrelevant expressions of his private interests into his odes. Bundy insisted that Pindar was an encomiastic poet through and through and that the difficulty he presents for modern readers is essentially due to our ignorance of the conventions and the repertoire of stock motifs that Pindar manipulated, or "orchestrated," in order to give praise to the victorious.

Bundy and Schadewaldt before him mapped out a number of the conventions from which the epinician poet draws in order to make his songs, arguing that before we can understand the odes of Pindar, we must acquaint ourselves with the epinician genre in which he worked. Pindar emerges from Bundy's work as a thoroughly "traditional" poet, in the sense that he worked completely within the considerations of the genre and included within his poems nothing that was irrelevant to his genre-imposed role as *laudator*.

Bundy's monographs have proved to be very fruitful, but they suffer from two limitations. First, they do not give adequate scope to the individual, special genius of Pindar. This has been pointed out by a number of scholars who have used Bundy's insights but tempered them with a healthy respect for the scintillating originality of Pindar's art. Second, Bundy's work does not fully convey the scope of the traditionality of the odes. The encomiastic motifs and conventions seem to be taken by Bundy as ultimates. The purpose of my book is to look beyond these and to find in the poems the deeper, less obvious layers of tradition.

Bundy's work is reminiscent in many ways of Milman Parry's, for Parry, too, insisted on the traditional character of the Homeric poems. Homeric studies—in particular, the debates between the "analysts" and "unitarians"—were hampered by the failure to appreciate the traditional character of Homeric language and the consequences of this for the composition of the epics.

The "formula" occupies a position in Parry's work on Homeric language roughly analogous to that occupied in Bundy's work by the encomiastic motif. Both represent the traditional building blocks—received, not invented by the poet—from which he makes his poem. The formula has been notoriously difficult to tack down in a definition, however. Parry's own definition ("a group of words which is regularly employed under the same metrical conditions to express a given essential idea") has been several times modified. The general tendency of these modifications has been to loosen the definition in order to account for several similarities among different expressions that are noteworthy and significant, even though the expressions themselves may appear, at the purely dictional level, fairly remote.

The essential difficulty in defining the formula seems to be the traditional character of every aspect of the poems: the heroic epithets, the sentence construction, the scene types, the stories told, the cultural presuppositions and patterns. While the *aoidos,* or singer, of the Homeric songs undoubtedly had a repertoire of fairly fixed expressions that aided extemporaneous creation of dactylic verse, it is nonetheless difficult to uproot and separate such expressions from the broader themes of epic song and the even broader concerns of archaic Hellenic culture from which the themes and, ultimately, the expressions derive.

The critical responses to Parry's work on Homer are similar to those prompted by Bundy's work. Some scholars have sought in various ways to show that the system of formulaic expressions available to the "singer of tales" does not preclude individual creativity, while others have tried to ground formulaic expressions in the culture, by tracing the connections between the special, formulaic apparatus of *epos,* and the society and vision that fostered the poetry.

The present study is analogous to the latter of these approaches. My object is not to deny Pindar's singular genius; rather, I attempt to come to grips with the strangeness (for us moderns) of the victory ode and to illuminate the reasons why the praise of athletes was deemed a proper subject for poetry. I seek to do this by considering the significance of victory, retribution, friendship, return (*nostos*)—all of them pervasive motifs in Pindar's epinicians—in other products of Greek culture: other poems, myths, civic institutions, and rituals. To style Pindar as a "traditional" poet may evoke an image of a poet who manipulates, mechanically and with a minimum of thought, a number of predetermined motifs, appropriate for encomiastic purposes. This, however, is to restrict "tradition" artificially to literary motifs, without considering their sources in the warmth and urgency of human experience.

My purpose is not unlike that of those scholars who try to rescue Pindar from the more mechanical aspects of Bundy's description by stressing the poet's personal creativity, thus presenting the odes as worthwhile and genuine products of the imagination. My goal is much the same; only the strategy is different. I have traced several "encomiastic motifs" back past the confines of a literary genre and tried to show their roots in a rich tradition of thought about the mortal person, the proper means of disposing one's limited life, the means by which death-bound, struggling individuals may band together to form community and so afford some protection against the flux and unpredictability of the world.

For instance, victory as a combination of joy and toil (*olbos* and *ponos*) is a staple topic of Pindar's epinicians. Yet it would be wrong to ignore the backgrounds to this antithetical mode of conceiving victory, and the way in which such a presentation of victory relates the epinicians to other kinds of poetry—epic, lyric, and tragic, themselves suffused with traditional elements and traditional concerns. In chapter 1 and the excursus to it, I shall spend a good amount of time arguing that such an antithetical vision has influenced the structuring not only of Pindar's odes, but also of other examples of the archaic lyric; the structure is intended to bring out both members of the antithesis, and to ensure that the song does justice to the complexity of the world it describes.

Again, Pindar regularly describes his odes as "payments" or "just returns" of the athlete for his victory. This may very well be a hardened, purely literary fiction; it is doubtful that a victory in fifth-century Greece that went without song represented a glaring injustice. It is well known that Pindar's sense of the "obligation" to praise victory was not sufficient to prompt him to compose an ode unless he had been well paid to do so. If the motif ended as a poetic fiction, however, it surely did not begin as one. Recompense and straight dealing are pervasive themes in early Greek poetry. The vast action of the *Iliad* is predicated on the hero's wrath at not receiving his proper *time*, or honor, from his fellow warriors; Hesiod undertook his *Works and Days* when he felt that his brother Perses was attempting to deal crookedly with him.

In chapter 2, I will study the connections between recompense and praise, and the importance of these for the maintenance and stability of the community. A consideration of book 8 of the *Odyssey* should illuminate the significance of these themes in the odes. Furthermore, praise is so closely tied to retribution that it can be compared in many particulars with the means of dispensing justice. To demonstrate this, I have included a section on the *Oresteia* and have tried to show not only the striking similarities between the social uses of praise and of justice as conceived by two archaic authors, but also the surprising resemblance of the poetic structures each employed to express the nature of praise and of justice. Throughout chapter 2, I compare the epinicians to the works of other poets as a way of locating elements in the epinician program that participate in the broader streams of Greek culture and may indicate how the literary genre of epinician poetry has its origins in those streams.

If the ode is just retribution, it is also a pledge of friendship between *philoi.* The *philotēs,* or friendship, of poet and athlete is a standard topic in epinician poetry, one that allies it with other kinds of lyric—most notably symposiastic and erotic verse. An investigation of *philotēs* illuminates not only the connections between epinician and other forms of lyric but also the connections between lyric song and the ties binding members of a community. Pindar presents the *philotēs* between himself and patron in a variety of lights and, if we bear in mind the full complexity of this *philotēs,* we are afforded an insight into the archaic understanding of human society and how it is maintained. In chapter 3, I pursue these arguments and try to expand my investigation of the connections between epinician poetry and archaic perceptions of the community.

The motif of *philotēs* in the odes and the symposiastic and erotic elements employed by Pindar in his discussions of *philotēs* are much more than literary commonplaces. Friendship, the fellowship of the table, and amorous union are the concerns of an important group of Greek myths, and the comparison of myths and epinician poetry will be important in both chapters 3 and 4. There my approach to Pindar's mythic narratives will have an orientation different from that of numerous recent studies, which show, by means of repeated words and themes, the relevance of the narrative to the surrounding poem. I will be more interested in Pindar's narratives as means of establishing a connection between the special literary products of his particular talent and the continuing, traditional concerns of Greek culture, as these may be glimpsed in its myths.

One of the most striking and beautiful features of the traditional, archaic perception of man and his world is the awareness of the limits of all human perception, and the limits on all mortal attempts to erect an orderly, predictable world. A lack of dogmatism, a broad tolerance seem built into this vision of mortal life. Thus, even when Pindar reflects back on the traditional Greek stories and "corrects" them (most notably, in *Olympian* 1) or comments on their incongruities (as in fr. 169, "*Nomos ho pantōn basileus*"), he does not necessarily uproot himself from that tradition. Throughout the odes, moreover, Pindar stresses the circumscribed validity of human distinctions between good and evil, and while he praises the victorious, he makes it clear that the victorious and the defeated are not utterly distinct. The high hopes of the man now buoyed by victory may easily be dashed by a defeat, and what most distinguishes victor from loser—that is, the gods' benevolence—lies outside the control of the individual. The epinician, then, is of a strictly limited validity, and if the praise is to be true and genuine, the ode must confess its own limitations. The victory song cannot secure immortal life for the victor, nor can it distinguish absolutely between the victor and those he has defeated.

The limitations of the victory song, and, more generally, of human societies will be investigated in chapter 4, although some preliminary observations will be made in chapter 1 as well. In chapter 4, I treat the odes as a means of securing the successful return home (*nostos*) of the victor from the games, and I compare several myths about victorious athletes who were not welcomed by their townspeople and became exiles. I argue that the epinician is a means of renown and honor accorded by the community; it is distinguished from heroic cult, a means of renown and honor accorded by the gods and imposed on the community. The epinician thus represents a particular kind of *kleos,* different from the other kind and incapable of affording the victor the same prerogatives. I hope to show not only the limitations of victory song but to indicate again the way epinician poetry and, more generally, acknowledgment participate in a coherent traditional structure of perceptions about mortals, their accomplishments and their societies.

To show more clearly the connections between the epinician genre and other products of archaic Greek culture, I needed analytical terms of sufficient generality to be valid for a wide range of material, yet specific enough to be enlightening. The notions of *praxis* (action) and its concomitant *pathos* have seemed best suited to my purpose. They are useful not only for what the athlete does but for what the poet does. More generally, athletic competition in the odes seems to be a paradigm for all human actions that aim at some good. The offering of tribute thus becomes an occasion for reflections on the reasons why people act, the world upon which they act, and the reaction of the world upon them.

Moreover, the terms *praxis* and *pathos* serve to show the considerable connections between victory and tragedy (see chapter 1). They also help one treat the relationship between the moral vision of the world (wherein one "suffers" in due proportion to what one "does") and another vision, wherein one's *pathos* is not determined by one's actions and is often disproportionate to it.

While *praxis* and *pathos* are Aristotelian terms, I believe they lend themselves naturally and easily to the elucidation of archaic poetry. Their usefulness in this regard has been shown, for example, in the studies of John Jones, *Aristotle and Greek Tragedy* (London, 1962) and James Redfield, *Nature and Culture in the Iliad* (Chicago, 1975), both of which have influenced the present work.

The translations of Pindar are my own, although I have been happy to have nearby the fine new translation of the odes by Frank J. Nisetich (Baltimore, 1980). In citing Greek names, I have used the Latinate versions for authors, localities, and mythic heroes and kept closer to the original Greek spelling for the names of athletes. My text throughout has been that of Bruno Snell and Herwig Maehler, 5th ed. (Leipzig, 1971). Citations of the scholia refer to the edition of A. B. Drachmann, *Scholia Vetera in Pindari Carmina,* 3 vols. (Leipzig, 1903–1927).

Finally, this book has been difficult to write. I would like to thank Victor Bers, Sheila Murnaghan, Vasily Rudich, Gordon Williams, and, especially, Thomas Cole, all of whom provided encouragement and criticism. A deeply appreciated grant from the Morse Fellowship Committee at Yale enabled me to complete the manuscript.

SONG AND ACTION

1

The Ode as *Praxis*

In his epinician songs, Pindar praises the victor partly by attempting to illuminate the significance of victory in human life. The odes are replete with aphorisms on the conditions of mortal existence and how the athlete's victory (or, more generally, any excellence) relates to these conditions. For example, in the opening verses of *Nem.* 6 we read, "One is the race of men, one of gods; but from a single mother we both take breath. But keeping them apart is all allotted power; for the one is nothing, while the brazen heaven remains in its secure seat. Still, we bear some likeness to the immortals in mind or nature—although we do not know, by day or night, toward what goal fate marked out for us we run" (1-7).

Pindar describes the mortal race by a series of opposing propositions. Gods and men are kin, since both descend from Gaia, or Earth, their common mother. On the other hand, the two are utterly separate from each other. The gods have no shackles on their power; they live securely and blissfully. The perfection of their existence is epitomized by their freedom from death, whereas death epitomizes the insecurity and frustration that are an inescapable part of mortal life. The safety of the gods' heavenly place is set against the "nothingness" of humanity.

This pessimistic conception of the fleeting, vain character of human life must not be divorced from the fact that gods and men are bound by kinship. Our proximity to and distance from the gods are both true, simultaneously. Pindar stresses this by adducing another pair of propositions that seem to exist uneasily with each other. Our minds are like those of the gods, for the *nous* can enjoy something of that foreknowledge which is the gods' prerogative (cf. *Isth.* 1.40). However, the powers of the human mind are never sufficient to clarify the ultimate uncertainties of mortal life, and so the mind also suggests distance from the gods.

If the individual mortal is compounded of strength and weakness, a similar complexity can be seen at the level of the family and its fortunes through the years. In the verses immediately following those quoted above, Pindar turns to speak of *to suggenes*, the innate mettle or worth

1

of a family. "The innate" is compared to "grain-bearing fields, which give by turns, now abundant life to men from their plains, and now, ceasing, seize their strength." The image of the field is a recurrent one in the odes and describes the checkered fortunes of a clan, which has an illustrious career in some generations and a less brilliant career in others. Pindar uses the image, for example, in *Nem.* 11.37–43, and there says, "Thus fate (*moira*) leads on the mortal tribe." The alternation of fortune is not a simple "fact" about this or that family but is one of the constituent elements of the human condition. As such, this alternation of good and bad times resembles the mingling of opposites (kinship with the gods and distance from them, the mind's wisdom and its ignorance) with which Pindar begins his ode. Time reveals in successive fashion the timeless oppositions that shape mortal life. Victory and loss alike are subsumed by "the innate" in humans.

This oppositional mode of description was common in Greek thought from the earliest times. It shaped not only Pindar's descriptions of human life but also pre-Socratic accounts of the world and its origins, and it continued to exercise an influence on Plato and Aristotle as well. The oppositions structuring the thought of poets and philosophers may well derive from the observation of polarities in nature—for example, "right-left," "male-female," "light-darkness." Such polarities are symbolically rich and came to be associated with religious notions; thus "sky-earth" suggests "Olympian gods–chthonic gods" and also "gods-men."[1]

One of the clearest examples of this oppositional mode is to be found among Pythagorean accounts of the structure of the world. Some Pythagoreans argued, Aristotle tells us in the *Metaphysics,* that there existed ten principles (*arkhai*), which they arranged in two columns of cognates: limit and unlimited, odd and even, one and many, right and left, male and female, resting and moving, straight and crooked, light and dark, good and evil, square and oblong. In the same passage, Aristotle refers to Alcmaeon of Croton, who said that most things in human affairs (*ta polla tōn anthrōpinōn*) go in pairs of contraries—for example, white and black, or sweet and bitter, good and evil, great and small.[2] The world as we know it derives from this ultimate duality, and the objects of our experience evince the original oppositions.

The mortal condition is presented as subsuming both members of an opposition. Men are both wise and ignorant, both similar to the immortals and dissimilar. The complex interplay of these oppositions is visible in human activities. The athlete, heir to a tradition of family excellence, undertakes the rigors and uncertainties of competition in one of the national athletic festivals. There he finds his *aretē* and resolution pitted against those of other athletes. If he should win, this results, to be sure, from his superior strength and determination, but not entirely so.

There is an element of chance in competition, since the gods, who exist outside of men's control, either grant or withhold victory. Pindar takes the difficulty of the contest, and the constraint placed upon the athlete by effort and competition, as signs of the gods' determining role in human affairs (*Pyth.* 8.73-78).[3] Victory is not an automatic function of the athlete's *aretē*. His actions may achieve or miss their goal, for reasons which cannot be confined to character or worth.

There is both a human and divine cause of victory, or, to put it another way, we can discern both active and passive elements in victory. The athlete actively seeks and achieves victory; he is then awarded or denied victory by the gods.

This view of human achievement and its modality is not Pindar's personal property. Albin Lesky has studied the causation of events as found in Homer and in Aeschylus; the description he offers of the complex of causes is strikingly similar to what we see in Pindar.[4] The characters in the *Iliad* and *Odyssey* can explain events in several ways: as caused by their own activity, or by the gods' will, or by a combination of the two. Hence, when Agamemnon claims that he mistreated Achilles because the gods visited *atē* on him (*Il.* 19.86ff.), this does not contradict an earlier speech, where he blamed his own folly (9.119). The fact that the gods caused a person to do something in no way mitigates the person's responsibility for having done it. Lesky's argument recalls Dodds's concept of "overdetermination" of causes in the epic, although the term "overdetermination" perhaps implies too great a division between the causes.[5] According to Lesky, there is "ein echtes Ineinander" of the different causes.

The scene of Hector's death provides another striking instance of this complexity. Zeus lifts the scales and Hector's *kēr*, or doom, sinks (*Il.* 22. 208-14). It is certain that Hector will die in combat with Achilles. This does not mean, however, that Achilles has no responsibility for killing Hector. Homer's objective narrative shows both Achilles' determination to avenge his friend Patroclus by Hector's death, and the timeless "rightness" of Hector's death; it reveals, as Cedric Whitman writes, "both the freedom and inevitability of action."[6]

Activity can with equal validity be described with reference to its mortal agent or to forces beyond the agent's ken, or again to both of these simultaneously. This type of causation, alien to our logic, has subtle but profound connections with the presentation of character in Homer, which again is at odds with more modern notions of the self and personality. There is a certain primacy of action, rather than character, in the epics. Action is not conceived in Homer as an outer expression of the hero's inner identity, which exists apart from the action and transcends it. Rather, one exists in his actions. Hermann Fraenkel has shown the

3

public, eminently visible nature of Homeric man.[7] The Homeric warrior is not a synthesis of his history; rather, he is that history itself. Developing Fraenkel's insights, James Redfield writes, "Homeric man, being objective, has no innerness. He expresses himself completely in words and acts, and is thus completely known to his fellows. He has no hidden depths or secret motives; he says and does what he is. Such a man is not an enclosed identity; he is rather a kind of open field of forces."[8]

What is true of Homeric man is true also of Pindaric man. The athlete, as presented in the odes, does not exist as an inner-directed being, an "ego," a unique personality who synthesizes experience. He is presented objectively. His actions—the competition in the games and his success or failure—express the athlete completely. In addition, however, these actions and their results express things other than the individual athlete: the forces that resist, abet, or somehow modify the individual's attempt. It would seem, then, that Aristotle's insistence in the *Poetics* on the primacy of action over character is as valid for Pindar and Homer as for the tragedians.[9] The artistic habit of focusing objectively upon the action, rather than upon the subjective state of the doer, helps us appreciate the many agents and forces shaping human life.

The athlete's activity, as presented in Pindar's odes, may be compared with the tragic action, as described by Aristotle. In the *Poetics*, Aristotle argues that tragedy is an imitation (*mimēsis*) of an action (*praxis*), not of human beings (50a16-17). Tragedy provokes fear and pity by presenting a coherent action in which a change (*metabasis* or *metabolē*) occurs (52a14-18). For Aristotle tragedy is a presentation of the mutability in human life, rather than the portrayal of a person who suffers. The action need not have a sad ending;[10] what is important is the change, or *metabasis*, whatever direction this change might take. So, in offering advice on the proper length of a tragedy, Aristotle suggests that it be of a sufficient length to show a change "to good fortune (*eutukhia*) from bad fortune (*dustukhia*) or from good fortune to bad fortune by events occurring in order according to probability or necessity" (51a13-15).

The *metabasis* is effected by *hamartia*, a misaim or error (53a7-12). This *hamartia* is explicitly distinguished by Aristotle from character traits of vice and depravity; that is, *hamartia* is not a "flaw" in the hero's character but a feature of the *praxis*, by which the action does not attain to its stated goal.[11] Oedipus the king undertakes to clean Thebes of the plague, and ends by revealing himself as a pollution and outcast. Agamemnon seeks to bring Troy to justice, and ends by miring himself hopelessly in bloodshed. *Hamartia* is the skewing of the subject's purpose; it is a quality of the action which shows the irreducibility of that action to the purposes of its agent. The "going awry" of the action

4

brings about the reversal of fortunes. The *praxis* becomes a *pathos;* "the doer suffers," as Aeschylus says in *Agememnon.*

In tragedy, the *pathos* must not be a just requital for one's *praxis;* the tragic effect resides in the disparity of what one does and what one suffers. Hence, in chapter 13 of the *Poetics,* Aristotle says the tragic hero must not be conspicuous for virtue or justice, nor again should his fall be due to his own vice (52b34–53a10). If a character is strongly marked as virtuous or vicious, what happens to him will either seem fair (the good rewarded, the evil punished) or foul (the evil man triumphant, the virtuous man ruined), but not tragic. The emphatic presence or absence of virtue creates an expectation, even a demand for just requital. If an artist confounds the expectation, his plot is dirty, polluted (*miaron*); if he fulfills the expectations, he will not provoke an emotional response of fear and pity.

The tragic effect is to be had, then, in situations where morality and the demands of moral sentiments are not at stake. Tragedy deals with the insufficiency of mortal resources in a world designed without regard for men's will or well-being. The important distinction in tragedy is not between good and evil characters but between the mortal and the immortal. The tragic plot, therefore, must deal with situations in which this insufficiency is shown; to portray such situations is something different from the foul, polluted (*miaron*) denial of justice and proper requital.

The *muthos* (plot) of tragedy, which is the coherent order of an action with a proper beginning, development, and conclusion (50b26–51a15), is comparable to the athlete's "story" of entrance into a contest, the competition, and the result. The athlete's *praxis* is not tragic, of course; it does not rouse fear and pity. However, victory and tragedy are alike in that both deal with an action, mingling *praxis* and *pathos,* through which a change in fortunes occurs. In neither is the *pathos* simply a reward for the character of the person undertaking the *praxis.* In both tragedy and victory, a mortal acts and is responsible for his actions, since these have been undertaken freely. However, the action is finally insufficient for the situation. In tragedy what the person experiences (*pathos*) seems out of joint with what he or she has done. This *pathos* is not a requital for one's actions; it "feels" like something imposed and passively received because it confounds what one has attempted. In victory, on the other hand, the person must be reminded that success, too, has a passive element; to believe that the person effects his success by personal worth is hubristic. The victory ode is meant, among other things, to show the similarity of victory and tragedy.

To claim that consequences are not determined by acts does not mean that the *pathos* is unconnected with the *praxis.* What people experience depends upon what they have done; human beings are in fact responsible for their actions and, to that extent, for the consequences of those actions. But the "responsibility" is different from that which a stimulus has for the response—that is, the person's actions do not wholly determine their effects. One is "responsible" in that he must abide by the consequences of his actions, even though these consequences could not have been foreseen.

So, for example, in one type of plot, a character decides to kill another, unaware that his "enemy" is in fact his closest kin (54a5–9). If the true state of affairs is not discovered before the deed is committed, the person is still "responsible" for killing the other, although the consequences are the opposite of what he would have wanted, had he known the full situation. The tragic effect of such a plot is due to the audience's perception that the character could not have known the situation. The audience sees how a crucial action is undertaken in ignorance. The plot exposes the disparity between human actions, undertaken to achieve some purpose, and the world upon which people act; this world is beyond their ken, ultimately, and is indifferent to their purposes.

The connection of *pathos* and *praxis* in victory is similar. The victory is impossible unless the athlete decides to compete and strains to win; the victory depends on his actions. On the other hand, the action does not earn the victory; it is not a just payment for what the athlete has done. Competition is like the situations depicted in tragedy, since both show the insufficiency of an individual's actions in securing what he wants. The athlete is pitted against other athletes, and no one can securely predict how the contest will conclude. The excellence of the athlete deserves praise, for the victory could not have been won without it; as Pindar stresses throughout the odes, however, *aretē* cannot guarantee victory. Excellence is a necessary, but not sufficient, cause of success.

Victory may be described as the fortunate conjunction of one's projects and divine benevolence; what the victor "suffers" or undergoes complements and concludes what he set out to accomplish. In the tragic action, conversely, we find a disjunction, whether fortunate or unfortunate, of *praxis* and *pathos*. (So, for example, one character on the point of killing another desists upon suddenly discovering who the intended victim is. Although the outcome is happy, still the person's project is confounded by circumstances; thus the story is an appropriate one for tragedy.)

The tragedian imitates an action by selecting an appropriate incident from the wealth of traditional stories and tailoring it so that it is suitable for dramatic presentation. He conveys the flux of mortal life pri-

6

marily through his plot. The epinician, on the other hand, makes use of narrative but is not primarily a narrative genre. The epinician genre had its own set of conventions involving praise for the victor and his family, naming of the victories, recounting one or more of the old myths. The victory ode is rooted in the present situation; unlike tragedy, it explicitly names its audience and addresses it. Rather than presenting in dramatic fashion a selection from the old stories, the epinician is itself an action, wherein the poet attempts to give just and adequate praise to the victorious athlete, and to confound the jealous.

Pindar regularly compares his activity to the athlete's, and his descriptions of his songs are notable for their emphasis on movement and activity. "I am not a sculptor, to work statues standing still upon their base. Sweet song! Go on every merchant-craft, in every small boat out of Aegina . . . " (*Nem.* 5.1-3). The poem is a javelin hurled (*Ol.* 13.93-95; *Pyth.* 1.43-45; *Nem.* 7.70-72, 9.55), an arrow shot (*Ol.* 1.112, 2.91-100, 9.5-12; *Nem.* 1.18, 6.26-27; *Isth.* 5.46-47). The song is "winged" (*Isth.* 5.63), and the renown it secures is an "unquenchable ray of good deeds" that "goes over the all-fruitful earth and across the sea" (*Isth.* 4.41-42). Pindar also regularly uses metaphors of the road to describe his odes. To cite only one from a large number of passages, Pindar says in *Pyth.* 4.247-48, "It is a long way for me to go along the beaten path. Time is short. I know a certain short path (*oimon*). I am the leader of many others by my skill." Metaphors of the chariot are also common. "Phintis, yoke up for me now the strength of the mules; hurry, so that I might drive on a pure road and come to the family of (these) men" (*Ol.* 6.22-25). The poem is also a boat, sailing to the ends of the earth (e.g., *Nem.* 4.69-70), often threatened by storms and winds (e.g., *Pyth.* 11.39-40, *Nem.* 3.27).[12]

The ode represents for Pindar an action complementing that of the athlete. The completed ode is the "victorious" conclusion of the poet's action, a *praxis* which shows the same ambivalences of activity and passivity as may be found in the athlete's career.

It is the purpose of the first chapter to clarify what may be meant by claiming that the ode is a *praxis*. My argument will center, for the most part, on considerations of structure in several of the odes. There can be traced in each of these odes a thematic development, which makes use of the formal rhetorical structures of the genre (e.g., opening praise, central myth, final praise) and encomiastic conventions (e.g., priamels, vaunts, prayers to the Muse, transitional motifs), but which cannot be reduced to these.[13] In the group of poems to be studied first, the opening part presents victory as the individual's accomplishment, the fruit of one's own excellence and determination. This presentation is countered

7

by another in which victory is shown rather as *pathos*. The closing verses effect a resolution of the clash and offer a final, embracing description of victory.

There is a kind of "thesis-antithesis-synthesis" pattern in these odes; their development has a dramatic character, in that we find a tension between opposing descriptions, followed by a resolution. The victory ode, I argue, is not monolithic; in these odes, at least, it can be shown to be an unfolding process, no part of which can be removed without doing injury to our understanding of the poem as a whole. The "unity" to be expected from the Pindaric ode is not the coherence of an essay (that is, discourse about a subject).[14] Rather, we must look for something like the coherence of an action. The athlete's endeavor and success, as well as the poet's effort and his completed song, bear a certain relation to the tragic plot described by Aristotle as a "whole," evincing a natural beginning, middle, and end.

A study of the varying descriptions of victory in the ode, the order of these descriptions, and their relationships to each other may also suggest new ways of thinking about the classification of Pindar's odes. A recent attempt at classifying the odes is based on formal, conventional features like the presence or absence of central myth, the length of the opening section, or the placement of the victor's name and the list of successes.[15] Without denying the usefulness of such a classification or wishing to supersede it, I would suggest that there are important connections among the odes that go undetected by such a method. So, for example, an ode containing an elaborate central myth may seem very like another ode containing no myth at all, once our attention is directed to the pattern of thematic development.

I do not attempt anything like a full-scale classification of the odes. It will be enough if I can show certain new ways in which the odes relate to each other. In a sense, any classification does injustice to the poems, since the connections among poems are supple, allowing, for example, greater or lesser complexity among poems of a single type. Moreover, different methods of conveying the nature of victory as an event mingling *praxis* and *pathos* are found in the odes; while distinguishing between these different methods is useful, the distinctions ought not to obscure the persisting vision of victory that the poems share and express, and the connections between different ways of embodying this vision in song.

Some odes, for example, rather than developing along the lines of "thesis-antithesis-synthesis," present the poet in the act of composing the ode. In this way they offer a quite vivid expression of the ode as an action, in which both active and passive elements exercise an influence. By virtue of conveying this mingling of opposite elements, such poems resemble those of the thesis-antithesis-synthesis type. It would be wrong

8

to obscure the resemblance by a rigid classification of the poems into distinct types. While I disagree with Fraenkel that "unity" is not to be found in the individual Pindaric ode, he is right to stress the coherence of the timeless realm of values that informs each ode and illuminates the significant event of victory.[16] What I present below is a suggestion for classifying odes in a way that may illuminate the profound, traditional vision from which the several odes spring.

I begin with *Ol. 12,* since it is brief and has been elucidated in some recent articles.[17] The ode, composed in honor of Ergoteles of Himera for his victory in the long-distance race, begins by invoking Tyche, or Chance, "the divine power which makes things happen as they happen (τυγχάνειν)."[18]

"I beg (*lissomai*) you, child of Zeus who gives freedom, protect Himera of the broad strength, Savior Tyche. For by you are the swift ships steered on the sea and, on land, rushing wars and the assemblies which bring counsel" (1-5). The control Tyche exercises over the world is emphasized here in a number of ways. Verdenius points to the distinction between *lissomai,* the word used for making the request, and *eukhomai.*[19] *Eukhomai* looks to an exchange; the supplicant reminds the god of past services in the god's honor and so seeks a return. *Lissomai* exhorts some one to do a purely gratuitous favor. The supplicant's subjection to Tyche, implied by the use of *lissomai,* is corroborated by several expressions of Tyche's significance. She is "savior"; her status as Zeus's daughter "emphasizes the fact that she is no arbitrary power but forms part of the world order governed by the gods." I have translated *kubernōntai* as "steered," but the word's connotations of divine guidance should not be missed.[20] Tyche, therefore, is presented in these opening verses as one who directs men's affairs in an orderly way and brings them to salvation.

Nisetich has demonstrated the strongly antithetical character of the passage which follows immediately: "But up, and then down, cutting through idle falsehoods, many and vain are they whirled—men's hopes."[21] The word order is significant here. After the opening stress on safety and order, we suddenly hear expressions of uncertainty (ἄνω, τὰ δ' αὖ κάτω), frustration (ψεύδη μεταμώνια), and aimlessness (κυλίνδοντ'); it is only at the very close of the sentence and the strophe that we are told the agent of so much disruption—men's hopes. Nisetich amply reviews the archaic (and especially Pindar's) notions of *elpis.* He notes that *elpis* is regularly contrasted with *telos,* and so easily takes on connotations of futility. The word is also found in contexts that suggest connections between men's tendency to hope and their mortality.[22] All of this illuminates the particular use of *elpis* in *Ol. 12,* where it appears as a disruptive force, antithetical to the order described in the opening prayer.

It is only now, after Pindar has juxtaposed order and disorder, salvation

9

and frustration, that the victor Ergoteles is introduced and his victory described. The introduction of the victor in the concluding verses of the poem has the effect of a synthesis, for in Ergoteles' success disappointment and vindication are inextricably mixed. "Son of Philanor, like a cock that fights in home matches only (*endomakhas*), the renown (*tima*) of your feet would have lost its leaves without glory (*akleēs*), by your native hearth, had not conflict which sets men at odds deprived you of your Cnossian fatherland. But now, crowned at Olympia, and twice at Pytho and Isthmus, Ergoteles, you exalt the warm baths of the Nymphs, accompanying them beside your own (*oikeiais*) fields" (13-19).

Ergoteles' present *kleos* combines his prowess at racing and his turbulent history, both of which are necessary conditions for his eminence. The two phases of the argument that went before are merged. The loss of his home on Crete corresponds to the turbulence associated with humanity and its hopes; his finding a new home and warm baths suggests Savior Tyche, who guides things aright and sets them in their proper place. The naming of the victory sets a capping stone to the poem, not only because it climaxes an orchestration of encomiastic motifs[23] but also because it subsumes the oppositions in the earlier parts of the poem. The "synthesis" has the effect of modifying materials in those earlier parts. For example, the opening description of Himera as the special darling of a benevolent goddess changes in the finale, where the victor's "own fields" (19) in Sicily contrast with his "native hearth" (12) on Crete. That is, Himera is now seen as a city among other cities; the fair fortune she enjoys is balanced by the ill fortune of others.

Pyth. 7 is another brief poem, which looks quite different from *Ol.* 12 so long as it is described purely in terms of the traditional parts. *Pyth.* 7 opens with praise for the victor's city Athens (1-12) and moves on to list Megacles' victories (13-18). The ode concludes with gnomes on jealousy and the uncertainty of human happiness (18-21). Despite the surface differences, however, we see in *Pyth.* 7 a contrast just as stark and sudden as that in *Ol.* 12 between order and turmoil. Having celebrated the athlete's city and his recent success, Pindar says:

νέᾳ δ᾽ εὐπραγίᾳ χαίρω τι· τὸ δ᾽ ἄχνυμαι . . .

In your new good fortune do I rejoice. But I am grieved . . .

The poet's contradictory emotions are responses to a contradiction in Megacles' situation. On the one hand, there is the secure preeminence of Athens among cities. Pindar uses an architectural metaphor to suggest the stability of its renown. "The great city Athens is the finest prelude for laying the foundation (*krēpid᾽*) to songs in honor of the mighty race of the Alcmaeonids and their horses" (1-3/4). This metaphor is later picked

10

up by the brief mention of the "wondrous house" that Athens built at Delphi (11-12).

In contrast to the grand solidity of the city's glory, however, is the jealousy (*phthonos*) that all worthy achievements must encounter (*phthonon ameibomenon ta kala erga,* 19).

The terms of the contrast in *Pyth.* 7 are similar to those found in *Ol.* 12, where the order guaranteed by the goddess Tyche is juxtaposed with men's unruly behavior. In *Pyth.* 7, we have the secure renown of the athlete's city offset by men's jealous reaction to the victories of others.

The closing sentence of the poem, like the climactic praise of Ergoteles in *Ol.* 12, merges this opposition into a single, comprehensive view. "And yet they say that a stable (*parmoniman*) flourishing happiness brings now this, now that (*ta kai ta*)" (19-21). Here stability and flux are subsumed in a single statement; Megacles' *eudaimonia* contains the security of Athens's renown as well as the disruptions and frustrations other men's jealousy can cause.

The surface structures of *Pyth.* 7 and *Ol.* 12 may be schematized as:

> *Pyth.* 7: city-praise &   gnome on happiness
> victor-praise /jealousy /& inconstancy
> *Ol.* 12: prayer /gnome /victor-praise

So described, the two odes appear to have little in common. I have argued, however, that the relationships between the parts are very similar in the two poems. Furthermore, the corresponding parts in the odes (e.g., city- and victor- praise in *Pyth.* 7; opening prayer in *Ol.* 12) perform a like function in developing the argument of the poem. It would seem, therefore, that the conventional parts of the epinician (e.g., praise, gnome, prayer) are not discrete and ultimate building blocks. Rather, they are means Pindar has for realizing the essential structure or argument of the ode.[24] Any of these parts can perform any of the functions (for example, they can serve as thesis, antithesis, or synthesis, in poems showing this pattern).

In both odes, Pindar turns from the "thesis" to the "antithesis" by means of a pivot. In *Pyth.* 7 the pivot is the poet's emotions: "I rejoice . . . but I grieve." In *Ol.* 12 the pivot seems to be the boat that figures in the nautical imagery. Tyche is described as "steering" ships; we view the ship, as it were, from inside. Pindar has only to turn to the ship as seen from outside, however, and describe it riding "up and down" on the waves, "cutting through phantoms," in order to portray human hopes. The most common "pivoting" device in the poems, however, is to move from the time after the athlete's success to the time before. Thus, a poem opens with a description of the victory festival and expresses a sense of triumph and security; when Pindar moves to the time before the victory was won, however, the necessary place of toil and uncertainty in *nikē* becomes clear. The finale then subsumes both the toil and the triumph in a single comprehensive description of victory. This movement in time can be done either with or without a mythic narrative. We will consider examples of each.

Pyth. 12, in honor of Midas's victory in the flute (*aulos*) contest, opens with a prayer to the local deity (Acragas), who is asked to receive Midas's crown (*stephanōma tod'*, 5). Since Athena was said to have invented the *aulos,* the victory easily suggests the account of Athena's protection of Perseus and her creation of the instrument to imitate the cries of the Gorgons when Perseus had beheaded Medusa (9–27). The ode concludes with a rather lengthy gnomic passage on the inextricability of *olbos* and *kamatos,* and the uncertainty in men's lives.

The ode begins with an expansive invocation of Acragas and a prayer that she will be gentle (*hilaos*). "I ask you, splendor-loving, most beautiful of mortal cities, seat of Persephone, who inhabit the sturdy hillock by the banks of Acragas that feeds the flocks, ruler: together with men and immortals, graciously receive this Pythian crown for the renowned Midas, and receive him as well, who surpassed Greece with his art, which Pallas Athena invented of old, weaving together the fierce Gorgons' murderous laments" (1–8).

Little comment is necessary on the opening prayer. The epithets suggest that Acragas is considered now as a goddess ("splendor-loving . . . [you] who inhabit . . . ruler"), now as a city ("most beautiful of . . . cities, seat of Persephone"), so that the opening verses function both as prayer and city praise. Pindar stresses the glorious effects of victory. Midas offers his victor's crown to Acragas, since he has surpassed Greece in his art (6). The following allusion to Athena as the inventor of the *aulos* (6–8) functions as a heightening of the victory and its significance.

In the second triad, however, Pindar describes what happened before Athena invented the *aulos.* In a terse, jagged style, he relates the beheading of Medusa, the wailing of the Gorgons, the vengeance that Perseus inflicted on Polydectes for the tyrant's outrages on Danae, Perseus's mother (9–18). Then:

> But once she had saved her friend (Perseus) from these toils, the maiden (Athena) invented the polyphonic music of the flutes, to imitate with the instrument the piercing cries forced from Euryale's greedy jaws. A god invented it. But having invented it for mortal men to have, she named it the 'song of many heads,' that woos the people to the contests with fair fame. The sound slips through thin bronze and reeds which dwell by the Graces' city with its choruses, in the holy place of Caphisus, the dancers' loyal wit-

12

ness. If there is any happiness among men, without toil it does not appear (18-29).

The myth performs a function like that played by the jealousy motif in *Pyth.* 7, or the gnomic sequence on men's hopes in *Ol.* 12; that is, it introduces motifs (in this case, bloodshed, terror, wickedness) that are the very opposite of those found in the opening part, which stresses beauty (*philaglae*), security (*Akragantos eudmāton kolōnan*), and serenity (*hilaos*). To include the myth in the logical development of the ode, Pindar first projects the victory festival onto a mythic plane by speaking of Athena's role in the history of the *aulos*, then turns to the time before the invention and to the incidents that prompted Athena to create the flute. When he returns, ring-fashion, to consider Athena's invention, the *aulos* is described as an intimate mingling of *olbos* and *ponos;* in this way, the *aulos* works the synthesis of the opposing elements in the earlier parts of the ode.

The flute joins together the Gorgons (whose cries are imitated) and the Graces (from whose land come the reeds that make the flute); it is a blissful instrument for terrible cries. The *aulos*, with which Midas won his victory, has been developed into a symbol of that contradiction which any victory contains within itself, between security and insecurity, glory and toil, permanence and flux. It thus functions in the same way as *eudaimonia* in *Pyth.* 7, or Ergoteles' own history in *Ol.* 12.[25]

Pyth. 12 differs from those poems, however, inasmuch as it does not end once it has achieved a comprehensive expression of the contradictory elements in victory. Instead, Pindar goes on to a gnomic passage about human subjection to the gods. "A daemon will accomplish this today—what is fated cannot be escaped—but there will be this time (*houtos chronos*) which, dashing our expectations, will grant us one thing we did not expect, but another, not yet" (29-32). The mortal's inability to extricate *olbos* from its necessary concomitant *ponos* (and so secure an unblemished happiness) suggests our subject state and the preeminence of the gods in human efforts. The gnomic passage defines the way men achieve their victories; they succeed when the daemon grants success, they are disappointed when the daemon withholds it.

This presents Midas's victory in a light different from that found in the opening verses, where Midas was said to "surpass Greece in his art" (6). There, Midas seemed responsible for his victory. The daemon at the conclusion of the poem, however, takes a much more extensive part in Midas's victory than did Acragas, invoked at the beginning. The goddess was asked simply to receive the fact of the victory; however, once Pindar has moved back to consider the time before the success and the *ponos* it entails, he expands the role of the gods so that it includes the granting of victory as well as the reception of it.

The development of the poem can be traced through the expanding role played by the several divinities alluded to in it. Acragas has the strictly circumscribed role of receiving the victor. Athena enters not only into the celebration of Perseus's victory, but also into the winning of it. The daemon generalizes Athena's extensive role to all human victories and states even more emphatically the preeminence of the gods. While the constant allusion to deities helps secure a formal coherence for the poem, it is the differences pointed out by the repeated material that contribute to the unfolding, thematic development.

In *Nem.* 11 we have a poem in which Pindar moves from the time after the victory to the time before, without using a mythic narrative.[26] The opening is again a prayer, addressed to Hestia. Like the prayer to Acragas in *Pyth.* 12, this one considers only the time after the success; it focuses on Aristagoras and asks that he have a successful tenure in office.

Hestia is asked to "receive" (*dexai*) Aristagoras, who has been elected to the prytany, and his companions, who are described as sacrificing to Hestia. The description of the sacrifice is continued by praise for the company's hospitality. "The *themis* of Zeus, protector of guests, is cultivated on the ever-flowing tables" (8-9). This tribute to the perennial excellence of the people is associated with a second prayer, for future blessings. "But may he cross the twelve-month goal with glory and unwounded heart" (9-10). This first triad concludes with praise for Aristagoras and his father, and a gnomic warning: "If anyone, enjoying happiness, surpasses others in beauty, and by being best in the games has shown his might, let him remember that he is wrapped in mortal limbs and will one day be dressed in earth, the end of us all" (13-16).

The first triad of *Nem.* 11 would be a perfectly coherent and complete poem in its own right. It resembles poems like *Ol.* 5 and 14, which also cast their praise in the form of a complex prayer on the victor's behalf. There seem to be no signals that the poem will continue, until the second triad actually begins. There would appear, then, to be an element of surprise in this second triad, which would complement its antithetical function of going back to earlier disappointments in Aristagoras's life.

The victor's father has discouraged him from entering the Olympic contests, and a faltering heart has deprived the hesitant man of his "fine heritage (*oikeiōn kalōn*)" (30-32). Pindar shows just how illustrious the athlete's heritage is in the next verses (33-37): he descends from Peisander, a companion of Orestes, and Melanippus, one of those who died defending Thebes against the Seven. This notice of Aristagoras's genealogy yields in 37 ff. to a consideration of the play of flux over the generations.

14

"The black fields do not unfailingly give their fruit, nor are trees willing to bear their fragrant bloom, gold's equal, each circling year, but (only) in turns, and so does Fate lead on the mortal tribe" (39-43).

Fate *(moira)* joins the joyful and the sorrowful, subsuming them like Ergoteles' victory in *Ol.* 12, or the *aulos* in *Pyth.* 12; it represents the synthesis of the antithetical elements in *Nem.* 11. Being a superhuman force, *moira* redefines the mode of victory and failure, just as did the closing gnomic observations in *Pyth.* 12. If Aristagoras has been disappointed in the past, this may be due in a contingent way to the father's diffidence, but it has its ultimate explanation in the very mode of human lives and our subjection to fate.[27]

Having shown the domination of our lives by *moira,* Pindar goes on in the last verses to discuss the consequences of that subjection for human activity. "The clear goal *(tekmar)* from Zeus does not follow men. But still, we embark on glorious projects *(megalanoriai)* yearning for many deeds. Our limbs are bound to shameless hope. The streams of foreknowledge lie far away. We must hunt for the (proper) measure of possessions. Sharp are the madnesses of forbidden loves *(erōtes)*" (43-48).

The language Pindar uses recalls the gnomic passage in the first triad. In both, he refers to a condition of the human body. "Let him remember that he is wrapped in mortal limbs *(melē)*, and will one day be dressed in earth," Pindar had said there (15-16), by way of urging restraint and moderation on the victor. He now says, "Our limbs *(guia)* are bound to shameless hope" (45-46). In this instance, too, the advice is to be moderate and "seek the measure," but the reasoning is quite different from that found in the first gnomic passage. For Pindar no longer approaches it from the victor's point of view as he did before; cf. "If anyone, enjoying happiness, *surpasses others* in beauty, and *by being best* in the games has shown his might, let him remember that he is wrapped in mortal limbs . . . " (13-15). He speaks now from the viewpoint of one who is subject to the gods and denied foreknowledge or guarantee of the outcome of his projects. The prospect is no longer that of the victor, but of the competitor, whose limbs are "bound to hope" and who must hunt down *(thēreuemen)* the *metron.* In *Nem.* 11, therefore, Pindar moves from the time after to the time before the victory, and he synthesizes the descriptions of happiness and disappointment by means of a single, divine force, *moira.* He then takes material from the first part of the ode and reformulates it in accordance with the expanded focus. (That is, the advice on moderation at the close is prompted by the thought of human ignorance and subjection to fate; in the earlier part, the advice was suggested by the theme of victory.)

The procedure is very close to what we found in *Ol.* 12 and *Pyth.* 12. It would seem misleading therefore to let the presence or absence of mythic narrative be the ultimate criterion for a classification of the odes. Despite the fact that it does not have a central myth, *Nem*. 11 shows much the same thematic development as does *Pyth*. 12. These two poems, in turn, resemble each other, as against *Ol*. 12, since both move from the time after the success to the time before; *Ol*. 12 moves from inside to outside the metaphorical boat. Nonetheless, the arguments of all three poems are very similar and all treat the same themes: the contradictory character of victory, which contains both joy and sorrow, and the consequences this contradiction has for men's own activity.

I have also tried to make it clear that the similarities among these poems, though numerous and fundamental, do not impose a rigid sameness on them—they are of varying complexity. *Ol*. 12 is the simplest of these. Having described the control and order of Savior Tyche and the disruptive character of human hopes, Pindar presents Ergoteles' victory as a synthesis of the benevolent and the turbulent, and then closes. *Pyth*. 12 moves toward a synthesis (the *aulos*, combining delight and grief) but draws conclusions from the contradiction about the subjection of mortals to the gods. *Moira*, in *Nem*. 11, synthesizes success and disappointment and, at the same time, suggests the domination of mortals by divine powers; Pindar then goes a step further to discuss human activity in the context of human subjection. It is worthwhile noting that thematic material (the blindness of our hopes), which in *Ol*. 12 functions as an antithesis, serves in *Nem*. 11 as a climax. This again shows the suppleness of Pindar's structures and the variety to be found even among poems having the same structure.

There is a movement in *Nem*. 11 and *Pyth*. 12 from relevance to the individual victor to a more embracing relevance. The gnomic observations at the close of *Pyth*. 12 are valid for the mortal race in general. So too in *Nem*. 11, the closing advice on restraint and moderation is offered not from the special point of view of the victor but the more general standpoint of the competitor, whether victorious or not. The tendency of these odes, therefore, is to move past the confines of the victory festival towards a comprehensive, generally valid prospect. This movement seems not unrelated to the persuasive function of the poems, as discussed by W. J. Slater.[28] That is, the poems are arguments by the poet on the victor's behalf, meant to persuade the audience of the praiseworthiness of athletic endeavor and, more specifically, of the current victory. One of the ways in which the ode "persuades" the audience is by showing that victory is not only a special, singular experience but a phenomenon of concern to everyone. In this way, the athlete's success becomes a paradigm for all human effort and, as such, illuminates the experience of others.

We turn now to a longer and correspondingly more complex poem, *Pyth*. 8. Up until now, I have tried to show the various ways in which Pindar constructs poems evincing a development of the thesis-antithesis-synthesis type. I have argued that it is necessary always to consider the relationships existing among the several parts of the ode. Formats such as myth, gnome, and praise are not the ultimate constituents of Pindar's odes but simply the several means the genre has to realize the essential argument or structure of the poem. The consequences of this for a reading of *Pyth.* 8 are several. For example, I will argue that the normal division of the ode into opening-myth-finale can be misleading, since in this poem the first part of the mythic narrative (Amphiaraus's reflections on *phua* or innate character) continue the opening discussion of the family's excellence, while its later part (Amphiaraus's prophecy about Adrastus) provides the antithesis to the opening.

Moreover, it would be insufficient to stress the conventionality of the practice of enumerating earlier victories in the finale, without considering also how the list of victories relates to the surrounding material. I will argue that, in *Pyth.* 8, we see that same movement from mortal activity (the victory as a sign of the athlete's excellence) to passivity (the victory, expressive of men's subjection to the gods) as was found in *Nem.* 11 and *Pyth.* 12. When Pindar lists Aristomenes' earlier victories in the latter part of the ode (78-80), this serves not only to satisfy a point in the epiniciast program but also to complement the presentation of victory as a sign of the gods' dominion over men.

The opening parts of *Pyth.* 8 are more complex than the others so far considered and again show the danger of laying undue emphasis on the distinction in formats. In particular, I will argue that the opening prayer to Hesychia joins with the praise of the victor's family and homeland (21 ff.)—and also with the first part of the myth—to give a single, coherent description of victory, which lays stress on human excellence, before the emphasis on human subjection in the later part of the ode.

The opening prayer is addressed to Hesychia, or Tranquility, and M. R. Lefkowitz[29] has shown the pertinence of this goddess to the concerns of a victory ode—*hēsukhia* is used elsewhere in the odes to describe the victor's state after his success.[30] The prayer to Hesychia therefore resembles that to Acragas in *Pyth.* 12, in that both focus on the gods' relevance to a time when the victory has already been won; each goddess is asked simply to receive it (*dekeu, Pyth.* 8.5; cf. *dexai, Pyth.* 12.5). Hesychia is called the daughter of Justice (Dikē) and resembles Savior Tyche in *Ol.* 12, since both goddesses are said to preside over counsels and wars (3-4; cf. *Ol.* 12.4-5). As the daughter of Justice, Hesychia's actions are of a retributive kind: she rewards gentleness (*to malthakon*, 6-7) and punishes the insolent (8-14).

The description of her activity is followed by a description of Apollo. Apollo defeated the king of the Giants (16-18); he has now given a kind reception to the victor Aristomenes (18-20). Apollo obviously parallels

17

Hesychia. Like her, he punishes the insolent, and he already has done (*edekto,* 19) what Hesychia is asked to do (*dekeu,* 5).

Throughout this opening, stress is laid on the retributive character of the gods' activity. That Tranquility is the daughter of Justice suggests that the serenity of victory is the consequence of the individual's just behavior. The implications of Hesychia's genealogy are worked out in her *aristeia,* in which she is shown to respond in a retributive way, rewarding the just and punishing the insolent. By drawing the parallel with Apollo, who rules over the game where Aristomenes has won his victory, Pindar makes clear that the athlete's success has been in accord with *dikē,* justice.

The following triad, given over to praise of Aegina and Aristomenes' ancestors, brings out yet more clearly the emphasis on the excellence and effectiveness of the mortal's innate worth. Aristomenes' victory is presented as a continuation of a family heritage. "Tracing your uncles' steps in wrestling you did not discredit (*katelengkheis*) Theognētos at Olympia, nor the bold-limbed victory of Kleitomakhos at Isthmus" (35-37). This passage leads directly into the description of Amphiaraus's spirit as he surveys the Epigoni's successful attack on Thebes and comments on the continuity of excellence over the generations. "Bringing increase to the family of the Meidulidai, you bear the word which the son of Oiklēs (Amphiaraus) once darkly spoke (*ainixato*), when he saw his sons by seven-gated Thebes, standing firm (*parmenontas*) by their spears, when the Epigoni came down the road a second time from Argos. Thus he spoke while they battled, 'By nature (*phuāi*) does a noble spirit shine out, from father to son. I gaze upon Alcmaeon plying a spotted snake upon his gleaming shield, the first by Cadmus's gates'" (38-47).

We have now seen three parts of the ode: the opening prayer, praise of the homeland and family, and the mythic narrative. What I have argued is that over and above the distinctions in format, all of these parts cooperate to present a single description of men's excellence. It is a sanguine view that offers a picture of an orderly, even predictable world. Excellence is a permanent, continuing thing; moreover, accomplishments are in accordance with one's worth. When Pindar describes the might of Hesychia and Apollo in overthrowing their enemies or rewarding their friends, it is significant that their actions are prompted solely by others' justice or injustice; essentially, they react to others' deeds.

It needs to be stressed that, although this description of the world as a moral, orderly place is never rejected in the ode, yet it is by no means the only or the ultimate description. It represents one view, to be set off against another, which lays greater stress on the unpredictability and seeming disorder of the world. Thus, after his speech on *phua,* Amphiaraus turns to Adrastus, the only one of the original Seven against

Thebes to return with the Epigoni. "Having suffered from an earlier grief, he is now borne up by the message of a better omen, the hero Adrastus. Far differently will he fare, though, on his own threshhold. For he alone of the Danaans' army shall collect the bones of his dead son, and by the grace of the gods (*tukhāi theōn*) arrive home with his army unscathed, to the streets of Abas, spacious for choruses" (45-55).

The effect of this notice of Adrastus's life is to disrupt the opening description, for it mentions facts that a moral, retributive view of the world's government cannot easily handle. Adrastus's son presumably has his father's *phua*, but that does not prevent his death in war. Adrastus's own situation is perplexing and contradictory. He returns to Argos a victorious general, but he alone has had to suffer the death of a son. If there is *hēsukhia* thanks to his victory, there is also grief.

In the course of a single speech, therefore, Pindar moves from one description of victory (as peaceful, predictable) to suggest a more complex one (victory as disruptive, an intermingling of sorrow and joy). We may speak of a "thematic enjambment": in the course of the myth there is a fundamental shift in the description of victory and the gods' government of the world. The similarity in the logical development of *Pyth.* 8 and the other poems we have considered is clear, as is the greater elaboration of *Pyth.* 8. While the openings in those odes simply present the victory as triumph or *olbos,* the opening of *Pyth.* 8 builds this into a coherent description of the world, where victory is *olbos* because it takes place in a world governed by gods who reward and punish in an accurate (cf. 7.*kairōi sun atrekhei*), predictable way. This will yield in later parts of the poem to a description of the flux and unpredictability of the world, owing to the preeminence of the gods.

The immortals represent different things. On the one hand, they maintain and support mortal notions of equity and morality; on the other hand, they dash human conceptions of the world and of what is right. The presence of these two descriptions together in a single ode indicates that they do not represent two phases in the evolution of Greek religion (from the gods as awesome powers to the gods as champions of morality).[31] Archaic notions of the relations between mortals and immortals show that same profound ambiguity that all mortal things show. The gods protect and uphold men's institutions; they also overthrow them. It will be the purpose of the second chapter to investigate this puzzling contradiction in divine offices; it may be worthwhile, however, to consider a few passages from the *Odyssey,* which show that in *Pyth.* 8 we are dealing with a common way of structuring discussions of the gods' government of the world, and the puzzles their government occasions.

The opening scene of the *Odyssey* has been called "programmatic," since Zeus's speech there lays remarkable stress on men's own responsibility for their destinies and this emphasis on moral responsibility is felt to be characteristic of the poem.[32] Zeus wonders why people blame the gods for their troubles, and he refers to Aegisthus by way of example. Aegisthus, though often warned by the gods, refused to give up his evil ways and is therefore himself responsible for his own destruction. Zeus describes here what I have called a "moral, retributive" world, where men's fortunes are proportionate to their actions.

Athena immediately answers Zeus, however, and her remarks indicate the insufficiency of this moral-retributive scheme. "Yes, father, he richly deserved what he got, but I grieve for Odysseus, who longs to return home and is prevented from doing so. Has he never pleased you with sacrifices? Why are you so angry with him?" (Od. 1.44–62). That is, Odysseus has not offended the gods, and yet he does suffer. To this, Zeus can only answer, "How could I forget Odysseus? . . . But Poseidon who holds the earth is fixed in his anger over Cyclops" (64–69). Zeus explains the causes of Odysseus's bad fortunes, but never claims that Odysseus is simply getting what he deserves. Odysseus does not cause his own sufferings (as Aegisthus is said to be the cause of his own death); instead, the cause is the angry Poseidon, who will have to give up his anger (77–79).

Odysseus has just the same effect on Zeus's remarks as Adrastus has on the opening passages of *Pyth.* 8. Odysseus's *ponoi* cannot be adequately interpreted within an ethic that insists on men's responsibility for their fortunes; similarly, Adrastus, whose victory is also a tragedy, necessitates a certain widening of perspective in the poem.

Again, Athena's question and the disturbance of the "moral-retributive" ethic described by Zeus seem deliberate, not the result of an unnoticed contradiction in the ethical attitudes of the society that produced the *Odyssey*. Athena does not deny the truth of what Zeus says (cf. 46–47); she does not deny the validity of a frame of reference that emphasizes human responsibility. But she introduces other facts that call for a different frame of reference.

Elsewhere in the *Odyssey*, there is a troubling disparity in Zeus's behavior. In book 14, for example, Eumaeus confidently predicts that the gods will punish the suitors for their outrages of hospitality. This is a view quite like that sketched by Zeus in book 1, inasmuch as both Zeus and Eumaeus claim that evil is assured of punishment. Yet elsewhere in the *Odyssey*, we see Zeus disregarding his office as the protector of hospitality. In book 13, just before the scenes with Eumaeus, Zeus cooperates with Poseidon in ruining the Phaeacians who escorted Odysseus home, although they did so out of regard for the laws of hospitality. Or, again, in book 9, Odysseus thinks he is executing Zeus's own *dikē* when

20

he blinds and punishes Polyphemus, who has outraged hospitality (479). As he tells the Phaeacians his story, however, it is clear to Odysseus that even then Zeus was devising the destruction of his ships and companions (9.554-55); Zeus, that is, would not reward the champion of hospitality.

These passages do not indicate that Eumaeus is simply deluded in his trust in Zeus Xenios. Their effect is not to deny that Zeus protects the rights of guests and strangers; rather, they show that despite the certainty of retribution, the world remains an uncertain and unpredictable place; when Zeus confounds human expectations, this shows the limited validity, not the delusiveness, of those expectations.

In *Pyth.* 8 we find a similar division in the descriptions of the gods. Hesychia, as I have said, is shown as one who reacts to others' initiatives, rewarding them or punishing them as they deserve. In the later part of the poem, however, Pindar stresses the gods' own activity and men's subjection to it. "If a man wins good things without a great struggle, to many he seems a man wise among fools, for crowning his life by his right-counselling schemes. But these things are not within men's power. The daemon provides them. Throwing one man now high up, and another below his hands, he proceeds in measure" (73-78).[33] *Metrōi katabainei* (78) suggests that the daemon does not confound what seems proper or just, but the emphasis in this passage is quite different from the opening presentation of the moral Hesychia. Men are exalted or abased as the god wishes; that a man's own excellence secures good things is simply illusion. Despite the greater elaboration of the poem, the similarity between this passage and the closing passages in *Ol.* 12, *Pyth.* 12, and *Nem.* 11 is clear. In all of these poems, Pindar offers expressions that join together the *ponos* and *olbos* of victory. In *Pyth.* 8, the daemon expresses this, since it is he who exalts and abases men; victory and defeat both have their ultimate source in him.

In doing justice to both sides of victory, *Pyth.* 8, like the other poems, describes a world actively dominated by the gods and not necessarily governed according to mortal ideas of justice. Their government can suggest order, but it also implies their power over mortals and men's consequent inability to shape the world to their own satisfaction. The gods' government comes to suggest a world ultimately unpredictable and inexplicable. We may describe this as a tragic vision of the world, to distinguish it from the moral-retributive vision described above.

At this point, Pindar lists Aristomenes' earlier victories at Megara, Marathon, and at Hera's games (78-80). As well as fulfilling an item in the program, this list gives Pindar the opportunity to describe once again how victory is won, in line with the new emphasis on men's subjection to the gods. He now emphasizes the combat itself. "On four bodies you fell from on high, planning evil [for them]" (81-82). Struggle has been offered as a sign of men's dependence on the gods and their inability to ordain whatever they like (cf. 73-76). Hence, this description of the actual contest complements the emphasis on the gods' power over us. Victory is no longer described as the result of a permanent *aretē* (cf. 21-45), but as a fleeting thing. "In a moment mortals' delight is increased. And so does it fall to the ground, shaken by a judgment which turns it away *(apotropōi gnōmāi)*" (92-94). The famous verses that follow— "Creatures of a day! What is anyone? What is anyone not? Man is the dream of a shadow" (95-96)—represent the fullest expression in the poem of the mortal's "nothingness" and the domination of the gods.[34] Men's glory is not illusory, but far from being the product of their own labors, it is given by the gods (96-97).

There remains to be considered the troubling mention of a vision of Alcmaeon, which Pindar had as he journeyed to Delphi (56-60). Pindar calls Alcmaeon "my neighbor and the guardian of my possessions" (58) and says that the spirit touched *(ephapsato)* him with his innate skills of prophecy (60). Lefkowitz has argued that the passage uses diction that connects it to the rest of the poem, and, in particular, she demonstrates the correspondences between this passage and the opening.[35] Just as Hesychia holds the keys to counsels and wars, so does Alcmaeon serve as the protector of Pindar's goods. As she argues, even if we cannot be sure of the historical connections between Pindar and Alcmaeon referred to here, we can still see how these connections are used within the poem.[36] This is true, certainly, but it is important to notice the differences between the opening and the present passage. Pindar seems in these verses and in 61 ff., to redescribe the victory in accordance with the implications of Adrastus's ambiguous success:

> Such things Amphiaraus spoke. But I, too, rejoice and encircle Alcmaeon with crowns. I sprinkle him with my chant, because he, my neighbor and the guardian of my goods, met me on the way to Pytho, the earth's melodious center, and practiced his innate skills in prophecy.
>
> But you, Apollo, who hurl and strike from afar, who inhabit the glorious temple where all men come, in the vales of Pytho: it was in that place you gave Aristomenes the greatest of his joys, while in his homeland you earlier brought him, in the time of your festival, the enviable *(harpaleon)* gift of the pentathlon. Lord, I pray you, with a willing mind look upon the propriety of my every step.[37] Justice assists at this celebration and its sweet songs.
>
> Xenarkes, I am asking that the gods not look jealously upon your fortunes (55-72).

22

Just as the spirit of Amphiaraus witnessed the Epigoni and predicted the outcome, so did Alcmaeon, the prophet's son, appear to Pindar on his way to the Pythian games (56-60). At Pytho, Apollo gave the victory to Aristomenes, and in local contests as well (61-66); Adrastus's victory, too, was won with the gods' help (53). That is, the gods have been involved with the victory from the very start. Hesychia had only presided over the victory's aftermath, but the myth has indicated a broader involvement of the gods in Aristomenes' life: they predicted his success, and then they granted it.

It is at this point that Pindar makes his second prayer, for the gods' unjealous (*aphthonon*) regard for the man's future fortunes as well (71-72).[38] It is significant that Pindar refers here to the man's *tukhai* (his fortunes) rather than his might and main.

In *Pyth.* 8, therefore, we find an extra step in the argument. To return to the terms I have used for the other poems, *Pyth.* 8 opens with an elaborate thesis, consisting of a prayer to Tranquility, a description of her moral-retributive office, praise for the family's excellence, and Amphiaraus's reflections on Alcmaeon. The antithesis is introduced suddenly, when Amphiaraus turns to Adrastus and comments on his ambiguous victory. At this point, Pindar offers another description of Aristomenes' victory, laying greater stress on the gods' part in the achievement. We do not find a comparable item in the briefer poems we have discussed, which move from the antithesis directly to the synthesis. This last synthesizing stage is found in *Pyth.* 8.73 ff., where the daemon is described as the ultimate source of men's joys and disappointments. As in *Pyth.* 12 and *Nem.* 11, Pindar draws conclusions from the synthesis, and elaborates on men's subjection to the daemon.

All of these poems are structured along much the same lines. Despite the variety of materials that Pindar uses in the beginning, central, and final parts of the poem, the relations between these parts show a stable pattern and the parts play characteristic functions in developing the argument. I have argued that the structure described here enabled Pindar to deal with contradiction and *nikē* as subsuming contradiction, in an orderly poetic scheme. The structure, therefore, is not only a formal device but thematically expressive as well, since it is only when we appreciate the relations existing among the parts that the poetic treatment of contradiction emerges clearly.

The last several poems have emphasized the disparity between man and god; the gods' participation in achievement disrupts the opening description of victory and introduces a new vision of men's subjection to the immortals. However, the relationship between god and man can also be presented as a complementary one, as for example in *Ol.* 8.

23

In this poem, we find much the same polarity as in the poems above, although the order in which the gods' role and men's role are presented is reversed. Rather than moving from the athlete's *aretē* to his mortal subjection to the gods, Pindar reverses the movement and begins with an emphasis on the gods' role in the attaining of victories. He then moves via his mythic narrative toward an emphasis on the mortal's excellence. In the last part, then, Pindar celebrates the death-defying powers of good works (67–73) and prays to Zeus for continued good fortune (84–88); he thus presents the mortal and divine components of human achievement in perfect equilibrium.

A consideration of the poem will serve to show once again that the structures I describe in this chapter are by no means iron-clad but capable of supple variations and greater or less elaboration. *Ol.* 8 may also serve to show the expressive powers of structuring, since the effect of the poem, more confident and less dark than *Pyth.* 8, depends to a certain extent on the order in which Pindar introduces the material. "O mother of the gold-crowned games, Olympia, mistress of truth, where prophets, judging from burnt sacrifices, make trial (to see) if Zeus of the bright lightning has any word about the men who yearn to win great excellence for their spirit and rest from their labors. It is accomplished for men's prayers in reward for their piety" (1–8).

The ode begins with a description of the prophets at Olympia, attempting to see "if Zeus has any word" for those who are about to compete. When Olympia is called "the mother of truth (*alatheia*)" in this context, the reference seems to be to the truth that is made known to the prophets by Zeus.[39] There is no guarantee in this *alatheia;* the prophets can only attempt (*parapeirōntai,* 3) to see if Zeus will speak.

When Pindar says that the results are in accordance with men's reverence toward the gods, this may remind us of the opening to *Pyth.* 8, where he also suggested that victory is awarded to the just. This reciprocity in the relations between gods and men serves, in the opening verses of *Pyth.* 8, as an expression of men's power over their lives—that is, they behave properly and then reap the rewards. In its present context, however, the reference to such parity does not indicate that one can be confident of the results of one's efforts. There may be several pious athletes competing; the priests cannot say for certain which of them will win the contest. The verse suggests, rather, the gods' powers over men, whose accomplishments are simply functions of how well they have treated the gods. Pindar says "It is accomplished *for*" the athletes.

Everywhere in the opening this power is stressed. In 13–14 Pindar says, "Many are the roads of good fortune with the gods' help (*sun theois*)," and the victories of Alkimedon and his brother Timosthenes are attributed to fate (*potmos*), which has allotted them to Zeus Genethlios

(15-16). The unusual deification of Olympia is part of a general tendency in the opening verses of this poem to stress the gods' supreme role in human affairs.[40] *Ol.* 8, significantly, opens by describing the time before the victory (when prophets try to foretell the results); this is just the reverse of the poems considered above, where Pindar moved toward a description of the struggle and uncertainty which go before any success.

In the latter part of the poem, when he turns to a lengthy praise of the trainer Melesias, Pindar uses language which recalls the scene of prophecy at the start. "To teach is easier for one who knows. Foolish is the failure to learn beforehand (*to mē promathein*). For the minds of the inexperienced are flightier. But that man (Melesias) beyond others could tell those deeds, saying which way will advance the man who intends to carry a most enviable glory from the games" (59-64).

A comparison of 62-64 and 2-6 shows the parallels between the opening and the praise of Melesias. In both passages we hear of one man giving information to another about success in the games (cf. 62 κεῖνα δὲ κεῖνος ἂν εἴποι ἔργα περαίτερον ἄλλων and 2-4 μάντιες ἄνδρες. . παραπειρῶνται Διός. .εἴ τιν' ἔχει λόγον). The men who seek the information are described similarly (cf. 63-64 τίς τρόπος ἄνδρα προβάσει. . μέλλοντα ποθεινοτάταν δόξαν φέρειν and 4-6 ἀνθρώπων πέρι μαιομένων μεγάλαν ἀρετὰν θυμῷ λαβεῖν). In 60, too, the use of προμαθεῖν seems intended to present athletic training as a form of prophecy inasmuch as it provides some foreknowledge of the outcome, enabling athletes to be confident of their skills and strength. (That the praise of Melesias is part of a continuous treatment of prophecy will be clear when the mythic portion of the ode is discussed below.)

The repetitions, however, serve also to highlight the significant differences between the two passages and thus point up the thematic development of the ode. For the knowledge provided by the trainer is based on his own works; it is now men's own training and skill which provide some foreknowledge of the games and their result. In a sense, the trainer is the superior prophet: he can say "beyond others" (*peraiteron allōn*) those works which will advance the athlete (62-63). This whole section illuminates another aspect of Olympia as "mistress of truth" (2), for it is at this site that mortals enter in competition and give proof of their strength.[41]

This later passage does not deny the importance of the gods' influence over our lives, certainly. After his tribute to Melesias, Pindar describes Alkimedon's achievement as a perfect merger of divine and human: ὃς τύχᾳ μὲν δαίμονος, ἀνορέας δ' οὐκ ἀμπλακών (67). This mingling of the two orders is also portrayed in the central myth, the narrative of Aeacus's partnership with Apollo and Poseidon in building the Trojan walls. It was fated (*peprōmenon*, 33) that the wall be destroyed, and the reference to fate recalls the emphasis placed on the gods and *potmos* (15) in the opening part. However, precisely because (*hoti,* 33) the destruction of the walls was fated, the gods required a mortal partner (*sunergon,* 32), for the gods' work is necessarily invulnerable, as the scholiast points out (Dr.1.248; 44b,c,d). Therefore, human effort is necessary, if fate is to be fulfilled.

Once the wall is complete, an omen occurs, which is then interpreted by Apollo. The whole poem, therefore, is constructed around a series of prophecies: the prophets', the god's, and the trainer's.

The omen consists of three snakes who attempt to leap over the wall; only one succeeds. Apollo interprets: "Pergamus is taken nearby (*amphi*) the work of your hands, o hero; thus speaks to me the vision sent from deep-roaring Zeus, son of Cronus" (42-44). The death of the two snakes evidently took place, therefore, in the parts of the wall built by the two gods, and it shows the invulnerability of their work. The one snake who does succeed, however, implies the vulnerability of the walls.[42]

The omen as a whole indicates that fate (the destruction of the walls, 34-36) will be accomplished, and it suggests the inferiority of the mortal Aeacus's handiwork to that of the gods. On the other hand, Apollo goes on to tell Aeacus that it is Aeacids who will overwhelm the Trojan defenses (45-46).[43] They would not have been able to do this had not Aeacus contributed to building the wall and so ensured that it would be vulnerable. What Apollo shows his mortal partner, then, is ambivalent: the vulnerability of the wall is at once a sign of mortal subjection and inferiority to the gods and a pledge of Aeacid glory. The ambivalence expressed in the omen is also expressed by the structure of the poem; the opening suggests human dependence on the gods, while the praise of Melesias stresses rather the importance of men's own works. The mythic narrative, coming between the two, suggests the divine-human partnership.

Ol. 8 is not an example of the thesis-antithesis-synthesis odes. The central myth synthesizes elements found before and after: the gods' part in granting victories, as presented in the opening verses, and the role of human effort, emphasized in the praise of Melesias after the myth. In terms of the polarities it sets forth and seeks to subsume, however, *Ol.* 8 bears a certain relation to the other poems considered above. Where it differs most from those poems is in its emphasis on the complementarity of god and man. In the poems considered above, the role played by the gods in human achievements does not imply partnership so much as the subjection of mortal to immortal.

It should be emphasized, then, that my argument does not seek to establish "laws" of structure, valid for all the odes. However, although the structure I have sketched for *Pyth.* 12, *Ol.* 12, *Nem.* 11, and *Pyth.* 8 cannot be generalized for the whole corpus, it cannot be confined to a single, neatly defined group of poems either. In the way they unfold themselves, evincing a certain conflict and resolution, these poems show something generally true of the victory ode—that is, the ode is an action, in which the poet undertakes to ratify and complete the athlete's victory. As an action, it mingles elements that exist in opposition to each other— activity and passivity, for example, or mortality and immortality. A description of victory as the result of a person's *aretē* is countered by a description of it as a *pathos,* something given by the gods. The "action" of these poems ends when a certain equilibrium is achieved; a description accommodating the different elements of victory provides a proper conclusion for the ode.

The ode as *praxis* emerges even more clearly in another group of poems, in which we are shown the poet at work composing the ode. In these odes, Pindar calls attention, by a number of means, to the process of creating the final work. At the beginning, for example, he calls on the Muse to help him, or states that the song is overdue and so now must be composed, or apologizes to others whose commissions must wait until Pindar completes the work at hand, or suggests that he composes the song in a time of grief.[44] He begins a mythic narrative, only to cut it off short, on the grounds that it is inappropriate or scandalous and he has been mistaken to relate it.[45] Each such passage will have its own particular function in the specific ode, but, in general, the poet's "intrusion" into his own poems must make the audience aware of the fact that the poem is the result of a person's making it, choosing this or that theme, weaving different themes together, expanding or cutting back as seems fitting.[46] He may conclude the ode by "sending off" the completed product to the victor, or by describing how poets go about their enco-miastic work.[47]

The ode, we have seen, is regularly described by Pindar with meta-phors stressing its mobility and liveliness. The poem is an action in several ways. It is effective, in the way deliberate action is. The song makes "even toil painless" (*Nem.* 8.49-50); it confounds Zeus's enemies (*Pyth.* 1.13-16); thanks to it, victory becomes an enduring thing and the vic-tor's success is perfected.[48] The song also resembles other great under-takings, too, in that it is dangerous. "Many things have been said in many ways; but to find something new and put it in the scale to weigh—there is every danger" (*Nem.* 8.20-21; cf. *Ol.* 5.15-16 and 6.9; *Pyth.* 4.71). The danger confronting song is the jealousy of others and the risk of *koros* (satiety). The poet has to mediate between giving too much praise (which would weary and annoy the audience) and too little praise (which would offend the victor). Both victor and audience must respond favorably to the song if it is to succeed in giving the athlete his due and persuading the community of his praiseworthiness.

In confronting danger and overcoming it, the poem is an action in which the polarities of activity and passivity, divinity and mortality can be seen. The poet is a skilled worker, one with a *tekhnē*. He also has an innate worth (*phua*), which enables him to succeed.[49] On the other hand, he is utterly dependent on the divine Muses if he is to succeed. In *Paean* 7b.15-20, for example, he says, "I pray to Heaven's daughter in her fine dress, to Memory and her daughters to give me resourcefulness. Blind are men's minds—whoever seeks the deep road of wisdom without the daughters of Helicon" (cf. *Paean* 6.51-61). The action of the poem's composition, therefore, shows both the poet's skill and the gods' benevolence to the poet.

The mingling of divine and human that the poem represents is shown in a striking way by *Ol.* 14, an ode that takes the form of a prayer to the Graces, thanks to whom "all things delightful and sweet come to mortals, if a man is wise, beautiful, shining" (5-7). The poem is itself made possible by the Graces, even as it asks for their help;[50] *Ol.* 14, then, is both request and answer to the request at once, as I will argue.

What Pindar asks of the Graces is to "hear," a request he makes twice (*klut'*, 5 and *epakooite*, 15). The word is a frequent one in prayers, where the supplicant, as it were, gets the god's attention by asking him or her to listen to the request. The request "hear" is preliminary to the request proper.[51] What is unusual in *Ol.* 14 is that Pindar asks for nothing from the Graces except that they hear. Rather than introduce the request, "to hear" is itself one. The strangeness of this serves to emphasize the request, as does the repetition.

"To hear" is a verb found in the vocabulary not only of prayer but of poetics as well. The Muse speaks to the poet what she knows, and the poet then speaks what he has "heard" from the goddess. For example, Homer addresses the Muses before beginning the catalog of ships. "Tell me now, Muses, who dwell in Olympian homes; for you are goddesses, are present and know everything, while we only hear (*akouomen*) their fame, and have not seen it" (*Il.* 2.483-86).[52] Pindar too speaks what the Muse tells him. "Begin the hymn of glory for the ruler of cloudy heaven, (you who are) his daughter; I will confide it to the voices (of the chorus) and the lyre" (*Nem.* 3.10-12). The Graces, too, oversee Pindar's efforts. "Graces, sing (*humneite*) of Argos, the city of Danaus and his fifty daughters with their shining thrones, a house fit for Hera" (*Nem.* 10.1-2). It is only with the Graces' help that Pindar succeeds in making an enduring song (*Nem.* 4.7-8; cf. *Ol.* 9.21-29).

However, in *Ol.* 14 the relationship between Pindar and the Graces is somewhat different from its description elsewhere. The Graces are closely associated with Orchomenus (cf. 4); they therefore are patrons of the athlete Asopikhos, in whose honor the victory ode is performed. When Pindar says that "all things delightful and sweet come to mortals" from the Graces, this pertains to the athlete's victory as much as to Pindar's song—that is, the victory has been won thanks to them (20). *Ol.* 14, then, is a celebration of the victor's divine patrons at the same time as it is a prayer for the goddesses' blessing. The phrase *"klut' epei eukhomai"* might therefore be deliberately ambiguous. It could mean, "Hear me when I pray [as a poet in need of your help]." But it could also mean, "Listen, when I make my vaunt [in celebration of you and your athlete]."

That there is a deliberate ambiguity here receives support from another ambiguity later on in the poem. Pindar hails one of the Graces, Thalia, as *erasimolpos,* "craving song" (16). The epithet represents a heightening of *philēsimolpos* ("song-loving"), used of Euphrosyne in 13.[53] *Eran,* however, is a verb closely associated in the odes with the athlete's drives (e.g., *Pyth.* 10.60; *Nem.* 3.30, 8.5, 11.48), and the athlete too may be said to crave song, or celebration. In *Nem.* 3.6-7, for example, Pindar speaks of the "thirst" and "love" that victory has for song (cf. *Nem.* 4.45, 9.48). *Erasimolpos* seems to suggest at once, then, Thalia's supernal, divine office as patronness of song and her likeness to the yearning, striving athlete whom she has favored in the contests.

The Graces, therefore, are the objects of Pindar's praise, a part of the theme he has come to sing "in Lydian mode, with all care (*en meletais,* 18)." They are also the ones who enable him to sing his celebration of them. The Graces, then, must both "hear" him when he prays and "listen" when he vaunts. *Ol.* 14 represents at once the poet's dependence on the gods (whose help he supplicates) and his excellence as a poet (who bids the Graces hear *him*). Moreover, the prayer (or invitation) "hear" stresses the character of *Ol.* 14 as an object that makes noise and is heard. Thus, the ode concludes with the prayer to Echo to bring the famous or "heard" (the Greek word is *kluta*)[54] report of victory to the underworld (20-24). *Ol.* 14 is brought to our attention as an object in its own right, one manifesting both mortal and immortal characteristics.

In odes where Pindar shows the work that goes into composing the final product, we are also afforded an insight into the polarities that qualify any human *praxis.* The completed poem, like victory, suggests the *olbos* of mortal accomplishments. The poet's labors, which have produced the final product, resemble the athlete's competition; they, too, involve *ponos* which is inseparable from that *olbos.* Such odes serve as excellent vehicles for the ideas of victory that Pindar wants to express. For the ode as *praxis* is present and immediately available to the audience.

It does not talk about events that have already taken place so much as it provides a sort of miniature of action which, unfolded before us, brilliantly illuminates that mingling of the joy and labor which shape human works.

At the beginning of *Nem.* 3, we must imagine that members of the chorus have come to Thebes and are waiting for Pindar to give them a song.[55] Pindar begins with a prayer. "O lady Muse, our mother, I beg you: come to the Dorian isle, Aegina of the many guests, in the sacred month of the Nemeans. For by the waters of the Asopus stand the young builders of sweet-singing festivals; they yearn for your voice."

The reason the choristers have come to Pindar's home in Thebes by the Asopus is that he is late. Pindar does not explicitly say this, however, until the last part, where the reference to the poet's tardiness serves as foil to the divine, time-defying powers of song. "Farewell, friend. I send this to you, honey mixed with white milk, its foam stirred up and brimming; a drink of music, to the breath of Aeolian flutes—although late. It is an eagle swift among the winged; it spots its tawny prey from afar, and, in an instant, snares it with its feet. Chattering daws fly low. But a light from Nemea, Epidaurus, and Megara shines upon you; such is the will of Cleo on high for your resolve that wins victories" (76-84).

The poem is a contracted job, subject to certain time limits and deadlines. It is rooted in a particular time and place, and the poet is a workman who, like other mortals, must meet his everyday obligations. On the other hand, the poem is a gift from the Muses, a divine thing, swift and untrammeled in its flight.[56]

One of the most notable features about *Nem.* 3 is that it presents itself as a work in progress, for Pindar describes himself in the act of composing the ode. This is the point of the stage setting in the opening verses, where Pindar describes the chorus members waiting for their song and prays to the Muse to give him help. What follows is praise for the victor's family and advice not to "transgress Heracles' pillars" after his success (cf. the warnings, similarly placed after praise, in *Ol.* 3.43-45 and *Nem.* 11.11-16). The following expansion on Heracles (22-26) is suddenly broken off. "Heart, toward what strange cape do you lead me? I tell you: bring the Muse to Aeacus and his family. The flower of justice follows the saying: 'Praise the good man.' Loves for what belongs to others are not good to bear. Seek from what is yours (*oikothen mateue*)" (26-31).

Such a passage serves not only as a transitional device but also portrays the poet at work on his poem, and making mistakes; he rebukes himself for his errors, and goes on. Richmond Lattimore has pointed to this feature of Pindar's odes as characteristic of archaic poetry: rather than strike out a passage, the poet simply corrects himself and proceeds.[57] Yet in all the odes where we have what has been called "broken

30

myth,"[58] Pindar seems to be portraying himself at work on the poem. If Pindar breaks off a myth and rebukes himself for his mistake, this is done partly to insist on the poem as a product of a fallible, mortal poet, and as a work in progress.

Having recalled himself to his proper theme, Pindar catalogs several Aeacids, and celebrates their innate excellence; he introduces the boy Achilles and his education by Chiron. After a prayer to Zeus on the victor's behalf, then praise and gnomic reflections, Pindar ends by sending off the poem to the victor (76 ff., quoted above).

There is described in the poem a simple but complete dramatic situation. A poem is overdue; Pindar asks the Muse to help him. He makes a mistake and reminds himself of the proper attitude when offering praise. Finally, he sends the poem off. Within this very elaborate frame is an epinician which demonstrates all the familiar generic items: praise (12-21); myth (32-63), final prayer (65-66), and praise (67-70); gnomic material (70-76).

By presenting *Nem.* 3 as a work in progress, Pindar emphasizes the nature of song as mortal product. It is precisely this "work" that is the song in Aristokleides' honor. In the finale, the song is characterized as the will of the Muse Cleo (Fame) and is described as a soaring eagle, which accomplishes its will immediately (*aipsa*, 81). The speed of the poem overcomes its tardiness (*opse*, 80) and suggests its godlike character. In *Nem.* 3, the connections between *olbos* and *ponos* are even closer, and the antitheses are even more inextricable than in the other group of poems. In the closing passage, Pindar says *en de peirāi telos diaphainetai* (70-71), "in struggle the accomplishment appears." Pindar is addressing the athlete and talking about the latter's excellences, but it is clear that the words are true as well of his song. The poem (*telos*) consists in the efforts to make it (*peira*).

By drawing attention to his song as an activity, Pindar can use it as a model and mirror for the athlete's success. Throughout the ode in fact, Pindar is at pains to demonstrate the analogies between poet and athlete. Aristagoras traces his descent from the noble line of the Aeacids, and the supreme worth of *phua* or innate character is one of the major themes of his success (cf. 40-42, 65). Pindar too comes from a noble lineage, for his mother is the Muse (1). On the other hand, excellence is also a matter of performance and as such profits from training. So the young Achilles is educated in "all things fitting" by Chiron (53-63); similarly, Pindar is one who works and makes mistakes.

The elaborate format of the poem, therefore, does not distract attention from the athlete. Because song and sport are such closely related activities, Pindar can use the one to illuminate the other. Moreover, when he uses this format, Pindar does not have to speak about toil in the third

31

person but can give a present demonstration of it. The song is self-evidently a *ponos;* yet it is also *olbos* and divine, and these qualities consist precisely in the *ponos.* When Pindar tells Aristagoras that the *telos* appears in *peira,* his meaning is all the clearer because the poem is itself a demonstration of this.

As in *Nem.* 11, Pindar warns the athlete of the importance of moderation, of "seeing what is beside one" (φρονεῖν . . . τὸ παρκείμενον, 75.)[59] This advice would seem to be the conclusion Pindar draws from the mingling of *olbos* and *ponos,* and, more generally, the role of contradiction in human lives. Like *Nem.* 11 and the other odes, *Nem.* 3 is a treatment of the peculiar, contradictory character of mortal achievement.

A number of odes use the same format of self-reference—e.g., *Nem.* 4 and 8; *Isth.* 1 and 8; *Ol.* 9. It would seem, therefore, that just as *Ol.* 12; *Pyth.* 8 and 12; and *Nem.* 11 form a group, *Nem.* 3 can be classed with several others. It is clear once again, however, that even between groups of songs, severely drawn distinctions are misleading. One set of poems treats victory by speaking about it; *Nem.* 3 and others deal with victory by offering themselves as demonstrations of human excellence, its strains and contradictions.

It would burden the reader's patience unduly to consider the second group of poems in detail, nor would it serve the purpose of this chapter. I have not set out to elaborate a full-scale classification of the odes, but only to suggest another way of approaching the question of structure in them. I have argued that a number of the poems show a structure that seems intended to bring out the ambivalent character of the victory being celebrated. In order to do justice to the opposition subsumed by victory, the poet makes poems that themselves evince the tension and ambiguity of human *praxis.* I have tried to detail one way (the thesis-antithesis-synthesis pattern) in which Pindar structures his odes to express this, and I have briefly sketched one other way (the ode as work-in-progress), simply to suggest something of the variety of the poet's methods. In what follows, however, I want to look beyond the formal-structural level of the odes, to consider the relationships between the antitheses patterning them. How, precisely, does victory as "passive" relate to victory as "active"? In this chapter, furthermore, I have stressed the disparity between doing and suffering; yet Pindar lays great stress throughout the odes on just retribution as well. What, then, is the connection between *pathos* and retribution (what Aristotle calls *to antipeponthos*)? A consideration of these relationships will shed light on a number of Pindar's odes in particular; it will also illuminate the nature and purpose of epinician song in general.

EXCURSUS

Victory, as a mixture of human effort and divine benevolence, offers a possible dilemma to those who would praise it. Praise is a suitable response to others' worthy actions, but to fare well, which is out of the mortal's hands, may be thought neither praiseworthy nor blameworthy. As Aristotle says in the *Nicomachean Ethics,* "Praise and blame are for voluntary acts and passions."[60] However, since no success is the result purely of human effort, the encomiast must ask what precisely it is he is praising. It is perhaps the ambivalence of victory that leads Pindar to pray that his tribute be neither too much nor too little. "Yearning to praise (Hieron), I hope not to throw the bronze-cheeked spear outside the grounds, whirling it with my craft, but to throw it far, and surpass my opponents" (*Pyth.* 1.42-45).

In the famous scolion composed for the Scopadae and preserved mainly by Plato in the *Protagoras* (339b-c, 344c-346e) Simonides deals with the nature of the praiseworthy. The poem is best known, perhaps, for the seeming contradiction that Plato has Protagoras point out. The sophist quotes first what appear to be the opening lines, where Simonides comments on the difficulty of being or becoming truly good:

> ἄνδρ᾽ ἀγαθὸν μὲν ἀλαθέως γενέσθαι
> χαλεπὸν χερσίν τε καὶ ποσὶ καὶ νόῳ
> τετράγωνον ἄνευ ψόγου τετυγμένον·

On the one hand, to become a truly good man—foursquare in hands and feet and mind, fashioned without blame—is difficult.

Later in the poem, however, Simonides disagrees with the aphorism of Pittacus, who seems to say just what Simonides said at the beginning—to be good (*esthlon*) is difficult:

> οὐδέ μοι ἐμμελέως τὸ Πιττάκειον
> νέμεται, καίτοι σοφοῦ παρὰ φωτὸς εἰ-
> ρημένον· χαλεπὸν φάτ᾽ ἐσθλὸν ἔμμεναι

Nor is that saying of Pittacus right, as far as I am concerned: although it was said by a wise man. He says it is difficult to be good.

Before considering the possible relation between these two statements, it is worth noting that the ode is couched in the normal vocabulary of praising and blaming. In describing the good man, for instance, Simonides notes that "It is difficult to be without blame (*aneu psogou*, 3)." When he considers the powerful role circumstance has in human life, he remarks that "No man is utterly blameless" (*panamōmon*, 24). The man who

33

does not "love blame" (*philopsogos*) therefore must renounce the search for the totally happy, *agathos*, praiseworthy man (cf. 21-25), and be content with a more modest ideal.[61]

If mortals were in total charge of their lives, the encomiast's work would be simple. He would simply praise those who manage to surmount the difficulties of being, or becoming, *agathos* in body and mind. Mortals' activity would earn them the praise of others; the activity would be a perfect gauge of the person's worth.

Since men are not wholly in charge of their lives, however, their being *agathos* or *kakos* is not a function entirely of their merit. This is why Simonides disagrees with Pittacus when the latter claims that it is difficult to be good. "It is impossible for a man not to be bad (*kakos*) when irresistible disaster (*amēkhanos sumphora*, 16) takes hold of him. A man is *agathos* when he fares well (*eu*), and *kakos* when he fares badly (*kakōs*)." Since all are subject to *sumphora* ("circumstances" or "disaster"), *kakia* is only partially the person's fault, and therefore will not be the object of Simonides' blame. It is only the gods, not subject to *sumphora*, who are unequivocally good and praiseworthy (*theos an monos tout' ekhoi geras*, 14).

The preeminence of the gods suggests not only the imperfection of mortal *aretē* or *eudaimonia*, however; it also indicates that, in a way, it is "easy" to be *agathos*, since this quality is given to us by our circumstances. "Every man is good when he fares well, and base when he fares badly" (17-18). If Simonides objects to the famous saying of Pittacus, that "it is difficult to be good (*esthlon emmenai*)," this is because *aretē* is not earned and therefore is not "difficult," to the extent that our qualities depend on our circumstances. As something received by human beings from the gods, *aretē* is either easy or impossible; as something actively sought it is difficult.[62]

Some support for this reading may be had from the *Works and Days*, where Hesiod discusses *aretē* and says it is both difficult and easy. Socrates cites this passage to support his defense of Simonides' poem (340d). "The immortal gods have placed sweat before *aretē*; long and steep is the road to it, and hard at first. But when it comes to the top, then it is easy, although difficult (*rhēidiē dē epeita pelei, khalepē per eousa*)" (289-92). The passage may be taken as a familiar piece of encouragement. "Strive for excellence. Though difficult at first, it will eventually become easy." However, *rhēidiē* ("easy") and its cognate forms are frequent in *Works and Days*, and its meaning in this passage seems to draw on the associations built up around the word in the poem.

The opening verses of *Works and Days* first draw our attention to the motif of ease, by an anaphoric sequence celebrating Zeus:

The Ode as *Praxis*

ῥέα μὲν γὰρ βριάει, ῥέα δὲ βριάοντα χαλέπτει,
ῥεῖα δ᾽ ἀρίζηλον μινύθει καὶ ἄδηλον ἀέξει,
ῥεῖα δέ τ᾽ ἰθύνει σκολιὸν καὶ ἀγήνορα κάρφει   5-7

Easily does (Zeus) exalt, and easily does he lay low the exalted;
easily he diminishes the eminent, and raises up the obscure, easily
he straightens the crooked and withers the proud. . . .

This facility of accomplishment is characteristic of the gods in general, and serves as the great distinguishing feature of their existence.
The fact that mortals can not live "easily" distances them from the
immortals. Before the gods sent scarcity and deprivation on men, mortal
life was "easy." "The gods keep hidden away men's sustenance. For
easily (*rheidiōs*) in a day would you work (and get) enough to support
you in idleness for a year" (43-44).

The attempt to live easily, therefore, is foolish, because it fails to
recognize the present state of the world, when men can make their way
only with difficulty. The only thing which can be gotten easily is *kakotēs*
(287), that is, "baseness" or "inferior standing in society."[63] On the
other hand, the gods are said to reward the prudent "easily" (379) and
to darken "easily" the luster of the shameless (325).

When Hesiod says that *aretē* is "easy, although difficult" the significance of his words is enhanced if we consider them in this context of
mortal and immortal existence. Insofar as *aretē* is easy, it suggests the
gods and their mode of being. Insofar as *aretē* is difficult, it remains
securely rooted in the burdensome conditions of mortality. Insofar as it
is both at once, *aretē* exemplifies the ambivalence of any mortal
accomplishment.

The "ease" of *aretē* seems to suggest the participation of the gods in
mortal efforts, rather more than the banal lesson that training brings
facility. I infer this from the fact that whenever Hesiod speaks of the
ease of men's accomplishment, he is in fact celebrating the gods' power
and benevolence, which make the accomplishments easy. Thus, the king
who can urge his case eloquently and "easily" bring order to a turbulent
society (*Th.* 88-90) is able to do so thanks to the blessing of the Muses.
Moreover, honor comes "easily" to the man whose prayers are heard by
Hekate (*Th.* 418-19); Hekate's aid to athletes enables them to carry off
the prize "easily" (438). We may conclude, then, that if *aretē* is "easy,"
this is a sign of the gods' benevolent participation in human striving, by
which the striving is brought to its goal. The difficulty and ease of
aretē have to do, then, with the perennial ambivalence of human things
(although this does not rule out the meaning that the practice of *aretē*
becomes easier with time).

At this point, we can return to the seemingly contradictory statements in Simonides' poem. Each of them points out something valid about the praiseworthy in mortals; it is difficult (i.e., actively sought and struggled for) and not difficult (i.e., a matter of faring well). If these statements are in tension with each other, this is because of the distinctive character of mortal excellence, which is both active and passive. Just as Pindar shows the opposed significations of victory (as sign of human strength and of human subjection), so perhaps Simonides wishes to present both sides of *aretē*. [64] It is impossible to be certain, since the verses between the contradictory passages are lost. However, in the first elegy of Solon we have a poem that seems to be complete, and in which the poet clearly contradicts himself. It may strengthen the interpretation offered above of Simonides' poem, then, if the contradictory passages in Solon's elegy can be shown to express a similar ambivalence.

In the opening part of the poem, the distinction between good wealth and evil wealth is firm. The good wealth endures; ill-gotten gold destroys its unjust owner. Zeus oversees the proper working of retribution:

> The wealth which gods give stays by a man/a lasting thing, from bottom to top. That wealth which men go after with insolence, not as it ought/does it come, but yielding to unjust works/it follows unwillingly; soon destruction is mixed in. As from a small fire, the beginning/is trivial at first, but ends destructively. Not long endure for men the works of insolence. No, Zeus oversees the end of all, and suddenly/as the wind quickly scatters the clouds/in spring—moving the depths of the sea,/wavy and barren, and across the fruitful earth/having plundered beautiful works, it reaches the gods' high seat/in heaven and makes the aether visible again; the sun's might shines on the fat earth/a beautiful thing, nor can any cloud be seen—such is the retribution of Zeus (9-25).

In the closing part of the poem, however, retribution is not "just" any more. "In all works there is danger, nor does one know/where it will end, when something is begun. But one man trying to act in the right way, not seeing ahead,/falls into great and difficult destruction. To the man acting badly god gives in everything/good fortune, a release from folly (*aphrosunē*)" (65-70).

There is no longer a distinction between "good" wealth given by the gods, and "bad" wealth, hubristically sought by men. Rather, all wealth comes from the gods, and this gift is ambiguous, inscrutable, for mortals have not been shown the proper term, or end, for the gaining of wealth: "Of wealth there lies no end visible to men. For those of us who have the most resources/yearn for double. Who could glut them all? The gods make gains attend mortals. There comes from them [65] destruction: when

36

Zeus/sends (ruin) to bring retribution, different men at different times have it" (71-76).

The destruction that stems from the yearning for more and more wealth is no longer an expression of a person's *hubris,* but of the uncertainty and bewilderment attending all projects in mortal life.[66] The contradiction in the elegy, therefore, is analogous to that found in Simonides' scolion. If the reading of the poem offered above is valid, excellence was first presented by Simonides as difficult but attainable; it was within human power, and, I infer, the distinction between *agathos* and *kakos* was the difference between those who had successfully made the attempt and those who had not. Solon, too, opens by distinguishing neatly two kinds of wealth and two kinds of people; there are those who seek no more than the wealth given them by the gods, and those who greedily seek more. In both openings, events are presented as responses purely to men's behavior; the just and valiant are rewarded, the unjust punished.

In Simonides' poem, however, excellence soon becomes something granted or withheld by the gods. The distinction between the "good" and the "bad" falls aside, since anyone can be either, depending on the gods' will. A "moral" distinction between one kind of person and another yields to a nonmoral distinction between the prerogatives of the gods and of mortals. The same thing happens in Solon's elegy: a distinction between a secure, god-given wealth and a sinister, ill-gotten one yields to a single *ploutos,* which is both god-given and insecure; the distinction is finally between the gods who give wealth and mortals who receive it and are beguiled by it.

The contradiction in Solon's elegy has been widely commented on, and the response has been to soften it, or to explain it away.[67] I would argue, on the other hand, that the elegy is a deliberate movement between opposite poles, mediated by a series of transitions from thought to thought. Thus, after the description of the punishment inevitably visited by Zeus on the unjust, Solon reflects on the impossibility of knowing when precisely Zeus will exact justice (25-29). The villain himself may escape and leave his innocent (*anaitioi*) children to satisfy Zeus (31-32). Uncertainty, therefore, is necessarily bound up with the certainty of moral retribution, for while the punishment itself is certain, yet its time and occasion must remain unknown to men until it actually happens.

From here the poet moves easily to consider mortals' optimism and vain hopes. "We mortals, both good and bad, think thus. Each one expects to flourish, before he suffers (*prin ti pathein*); then we grieve again. But until then, we take delight, gaping at light hopes" (33-36).

It is significant that no longer does Solon consider mankind as divided into good and bad; all alike are bound to live in a certain insecurity, though buoyed with fair hopes of success and prosperity. In the parts which follow, Solon describes the various ways of earning this wealth—by sea trade, agriculture, the crafts, poetry, prophecy, medicine (43 ff.). Again, this is a significant move away from the opening point of view, where wealth was distinguished into that given by the gods and the wealth hubristically sought by men; all men now are shown to work for wealth. Their attempts to prosper are no longer divided into good and bad but are all of them subject to disruption and surprise.

Solon's conclusion does not negate what he said earlier about the certainty of Zeus's retribution.[68] It does, however, stress the uncertainties that exist within the very broad guarantee of divine retribution. Solon switches from the world viewed from Zeus's vantage point, where the infallibility of his justice can be seen, to the mortal's view, which is necessarily blind to what lies ahead (34-35). Though Solon and his audience may rest assured of the god's defense of justice, this is scarcely any guarantee for the success or failure of their projects.

What appear as contradictions in the two poems by Simonides and Solon, I argue, are not due to the poets' inadvertence but are deliberate attempts to catch the ambiguity attending excellence or wealth, or, more generally, all mortal things. Solon's poem shows, by virtue of its step-by-step development, how one view of the world seeps into a quite different view of it. The elegy is perhaps not a discussion about wealth, which ought to have the coherence and consistency of an essay. It might better be thought of, like the several Pindaric odes considered above, as an action in its own right, a movement in which the distance between two poles is traced out. The structure of the poem is again a vital expressive device: not merely a formal way of ordering the material, but the means by which the audience is led from the certainties of just retribution to the more bewildering prospect of mortals' subjection to the gods.

Unlike Solon, Simonides goes on to draw a conclusion from the ambiguous nature of *aretē* after showing the two poles of its meaning. Since the praiseworthy is partly a matter of circumstance (and all are subject to hard circumstances), no one is completely praiseworthy so long as the encomiast bases his praise simply on results. To refuse praise to a man who is *kakos* because of uncontrollable circumstances (*amēkhanos sumphora*), Simonides says, leads the encomiastic poet into an impossible hope, for he will never find an "all-blameless" (*panamōmon*) man. If one is going to praise mortals, it is necessary to lower one's sights, as Simonides does in the following passage. He says, "I praise and love all who do nothing shameful willingly. Not even gods fight with necessity."

He will praise the man who is not "excessively resourceless (*agan apalamnos*) and knows city-helping justice, a healthy man."

The encomiast, like the judges in *Works and Days,* should know that the "half is greater than the whole" (*WD* 40). In demanding perfect blamelessness, the encomiast effectively puts himself out of business; he must rest contented, then, with a qualified ideal of the praiseworthy. The encomiast, as presented by Simonides, is an observer and judge of mortal things; to offer praise requires a sober appreciation of the curious and troubling ambiguity that informs everything human.

The scolion is often presented as marking a new phase in the evolution of the Greek consciousness. Simonides distinguishes deliberate, voluntary activity from circumstances, and he suggests that *agathos* (good) refers not to the complex of behavior and circumstance but only to willed behavior. The poem is thus seen as evidence of a new ideal of personal morality, as distinguished from the aristocratic ideal of social prestige. It is perhaps impossible to prove or refute such assertions; however, it should be remembered that, in distinguishing a modified human ideal of praiseworthiness from a perfect, divine ideal, Simonides is well within the province of stable encomiastic motifs. In the earliest Pindaric ode we have, for example, we find a similar distinction.[69] "One ungrieved at heart would be a god; but for the wise, happy and worthy of song (*humnētos*) is the man who, prevailing with his hands or the excellence of his feet, takes the best of prizes by daring and strength, and, still alive, sees his son duly win the Pythian crowns" (*Pyth.* 10.21-26).

The perfection of happiness is a strictly divine prerogative, Pindar says. Victory in contests of strength and speed is presented, therefore, as a modified ideal of the praiseworthy; as Pindar says, "The brazen heaven never can (the victor) mount" (27). Victory is the most one can hope for, since continuous happiness is impossible. It is the wise who appreciate this and are content therefore to celebrate the victor.

As in Simonides, the reason mortal happiness is imperfect is that it is not securely within our own power; it can be given or taken away without regard to the individual's deserving. Thus, just before the quoted passage, Pindar prays that the victor and his family not suffer reversals sent by the jealous gods (19-21); earlier, he stresses the powerful influence of the gods on men's affairs. "Sweet grows men's goal and beginning when a daemon speeds them on" (10).

In both *Pyth.* 10 and the Simonidean scolion, the poets use a discussion of *to ainēton,* the praiseworthy, as a way to comment on men's limited powers of securing excellence or happiness for themselves. Simonides' ideal may seem to be more personal and "moral" than Pindar's, yet, in each of their poems, we find the attempt to sort out what in human beings may be worthy of poetic celebration. From a description of the gods' power over mortals, both poets see the unattainability of one kind of happiness and so turn to a frankly lesser kind, which nonetheless suffices for the encomiast's theme.

2
Action and Retribution

There is a sense in which the person is less than his works. After the mortal man has died, the work remains. The person toils and endures the risk of failure; the work exists in stable tranquility. The poet is mortal, but his songs are godlike. So, for example, in *Nem.* 4, Pindar celebrates the power of song to restore and make permanent. "Festal joy is the best doctor for toils that have been judged (*kekrimenōn*). Songs, wise daughters of the Muses, touch and soothe him. Warm water does not soften the limbs so well as praise, comrade to the lyre. A longer time than deeds lives the word (*rhēma*) which the tongue, with the Graces' help (*sun Kharitōn tukhāi*), draws from the deep breast" (1-8).

Nonetheless, throughout this ode, Pindar stresses the mortal characteristics of its composition. The singer must struggle against plots; he has enemies to contend with (36-43). Pindar deliberately juxtaposes these two views of poetry—as a divine power and a mortal product—in the concluding verses. He emphasizes first the godlike powers of song to exalt. "Gold when it is boiled shows all its rays, and a hymn of good deeds makes a man of like destiny (*isodaimona*) to kings" (82-85). He then describes the poet making his song. "In praising Melesias, what a combat (*eris*) he would roll out, weaving phrases, unbeatable in words, of gentle will toward good men and waiting to compete harshly with enemies" (93-96). The poet is like a wrestler; his poem can make others like kings.

The same disparity may be found separating the athlete and his victory. Victory conquers death; news of it is heard in the underworld and cheers the dead kinsmen of the athlete. However, the athlete himself must undergo training, work, competition if he is to succeed.[1]

This opposition between the individual and his works is analogous to that opposition of "divinity" and "nothingness" existing within the individual, and it poses an interesting problem for mortals' activity. Men are bound to flux, uncertainty, a world of contradictions, and yet the products they fashion have clarity and stability as ideals. The order and predictability that mortals yearn for and seek to create are at odds with their own nature, the conditions of life imposed on them by the gods. The dilemma can be couched in the terms of the familiar nature-culture distinction.[2] Culture is men's attempt to construct a world of form and equity. It tries to secure just retribution in men's dealings with each other, and to avoid incursions of the violent or unpredictable. However, goods like equity and reciprocity are the antithesis of men's natural condition, which is necessarily rooted in flux and liable to *pathos*. Culture therefore presents a problem, since men are bound to fail should they attempt simply to ignore or deny their nature. How then can human cultures respect the contradictory, "strife" character of nature, and at the same time escape its conditions?

i

To consider this question requires a closer look at the nature of *praxis* and *pathos* and the connections between these. Having considered the disparity between the agent's *praxis* and its results, we may now turn to investigate ways in which the final product tallies with the action that has gone into producing it. In what circumstances is action likely to succeed, and when will it fail? Archaic moralists—for example, Hesiod—taught that "just" activity will be rewarded and "unjust" actions punished; every action will receive its proper recompense. What is the connection between such recompense and *pathos*? Can a "moral" description of the world (where justice and injustice get their appropriate rewards) be related to a "tragic" description of it (where *pathos* is disjunct from one's *praxis*)? I will argue, in this chapter, that victory stands both outside and within the province of morality.

People do not undertake actions in a vacuum. They confront a real and resisting world; they are of a particular nature that has its own limits and strengths. The origin of the current shape of mortal life makes a familiar tale. Hesiod, in both *Theogony* (535-616) and *Works and Days* (47-89) tells the story of Prometheus and the consequences of his trickery for mankind. In retaliation for the deception of Zeus and the theft of fire by Prometheus, Zeus sent Pandora to Epimetheus. Through Pandora plagues came into the world, as well as scarcity. Men no longer participated with the gods in the fellowship of the banquet (cf. Hes. fr. 1.6-7 *MW; Paus.* 8.2.4). Henceforth, mortal and immortal were distant.

In *Works and Days*, Hesiod deals with several aspects of the new dispensation that came about after the removal of Zeus's favor from men. One of the most important of these is strife, which the gods have sent down among men (*WD* 15-19), just as Zeus sent down Pandora. In a world of scarcity, mortals must not only toil for their sustenance but compete with each other. Strife "wakens even the unresourceful man to work. For one man, with no work, regards another, rich man, who speeds on to plough and sow and to set his household in order. Neighbor

42

envies neighbor, speeding to wealth. This strife is good for mortals. Potter is angry with potter, and builder with builder; beggar is jealous of beggar, and singer of singer" (*WD* 20-26). The good strife has been embedded by Zeus in "the roots of the earth" (18-19). *Praxis* is part of mortals' *pathos;* that is, it is part of our very condition—something we "undergo"—that we must act and compete with each other. "The sufferer does" is just as true as "the doer suffers."

To say that activity is part of the condition imposed on men by Zeus is not to say that human deeds are determined. The individual is free to compete honestly or not. Strife is simply the condition in which action occurs; it does not cancel the individual's responsibility for his action. Hesiod distinguishes a good and a bad strife and urges his brother Perses to avoid one and embrace the other. The good strife prompts one to compete in order to win a larger measure of prosperity. Evil strife, on the other hand, is associated with war and discord (14); it is connected, too, with legal disputes (29) and the laziness that leads Perses to waste his time skulking around the *agora* (28-29).

The exact circumstances that impelled Hesiod to compose *Works and Days* are unclear. It seems that Perses has been trying to replenish his squandered inheritance from his brother Hesiod's portion. Rather than work honestly for his wealth, Perses has sought an easy gain by manipulation of the court.[3] In avoiding work and the promptings of the good strife, Perses will land, Hesiod warns, with the evil strife—discord and fighting. Perses sought to avoid strife, but he has succeeded only in provoking a pernicious form of it.

There is a measure of ignorance in Perses' actions. He sought to avoid what cannot be avoided. In seeking an easy gain, he did not realize that mortals are not such that they get anything easily. Hesiod says of the "kings" who took the bribes: "Fools: they do not know how much greater is the half than the whole, nor what advantage there is in mallow and asphodel" (*WD* 40-41). By "half" Hesiod means a toilsome life in which a certain prosperity is achieved; the "whole" is an utterly untroubled life such as gods enjoy, but which is fraught with danger for mortals. The kings, in their ignorance, attempted to escape the inescapable conditions of mortality, and to live as gods in ease. In seeking to avoid toil (the good strife), they succeed only in courting their own destruction (the evil strife).

One never escapes hardship, then. The choice is between embracing it—thus directing it so that it yields a measure of prosperity—and suffering an unexpected and ruinous fall after a time of specious happiness. If mortals follow the bad strife due to their ignorance of the world, we may infer that they follow the good strife when prompted by a recognition of the world and its character. That is, a man sets himself to work

43

and competition because he recognizes the inescapability of these. It is in this way only that prosperity is possible for us. To ignore these conditions and to try amassing wealth without regard for them can only end by the utter frustration of the attempt. The free and deliberate activity of mortals is effective, then, only when it takes into account the nature imposed on them and the world by Zeus. Actions can be successful only to the extent that they respect contradiction. Thus, one who would be wealthy must lead the life of a laborer; one who wants ease must endure the rigors of work and rivalry.

Before considering the consequences of this for the connections of *praxis* and *pathos*, let us look at two more aspects of the mortal condition. Hesiod says in the *Theogony* that the creature fashioned by the gods to deceive men was the ancestor of the female sex (590). As such, she inaugurates a new era in which the union of the sexes, with its responsibility and griefs, replaces the old fellowship of mortals and immortals at the same table. As a condition of mortal life, sex has the same ambivalence for Hesiod as does *eris*. Woman is a bane on the male's existence; nonetheless, she is necessary, if the man is to escape a lonely old age and the dispersal of his goods among strangers after his death. The account of Pandora's origins in *Theogony* sets forth this paradox most clearly.

> From her comes the baneful race and tribe of women, a great sorrow dwelling among mortal men. . . . Thus high-roaring Zeus made women as an evil for mortal men, his partners in grievous works. And he sent another evil instead of good: whoever refuses to marry, flying from marriage and women's destructive works, comes to a dire old age, with no one to tend him. While he lives he is not short of sustenance, but when he is dead, strangers divide up his property (*Theog.* 591, 600-607).

Just as strife, imposed on men as a harsh condition, can be made to yield some good if duly acknowledged and properly used, so too is woman a symptom of the diminished mortal state, but she can be the source of good (provided one observes the advice on selecting a mate in *Works and Days*, 695-705).[4]

Characteristic of men's present condition, too, is the dearth of *bios* or sustenance. The individual can expect only a portion of the wealth available, and, therefore, boundaries distinguishing different men's portions become necessary. This is to say that *dikē*, in the sense of "legal decision" and the adjudication of disputes concerning boundaries, is a necessary consequence of scarcity.[5] The lack of *bios* imposes the necessity of the proper distribution of the available goods and so has

44

dikē as its necessary concomitant. Just as Zeus implants the Strife goddesses among men, therefore, he also sends Dikē. "The son of Cronus has ordered this usage (*nomos*): for fish and beasts and winged birds to eat each other, since *dikē* does not exist among them. But to men he gave *dikē*, which is by far the best" (*WD*,276-80). Dikē, like Strife, is a condition of our existence; our attempts at winning prosperity are bound to be in some relation to the goods and rights of others. Just as one is free to choose the good or the bad strife, however, the mortal can choose to execute *dikē* "straightly" or "crookedly" (e.g., 219, 225-26, 264; cf. 268-69). With *dikē* as with strife, men's *praxis* occurs under conditions established by the gods, although the man is responsible for his action.

Strife, sex, and *dikē* are thus three prominent aspects of mortal life, expressive of several ambivalences in that life. Their kinship to each other is suggested by the common narrative pattern that structures the brief scenes with Pandora, the Erides, and Dikē, all of whom are personified as females sent down by Zeus among mortals.[6] Their descents are not perhaps three distinct episodes, so much as a triad conveying the several facets of men's condition and their separation from the gods.

Insofar as these ladies have been sent by Zeus among mortals, they suggest the kind of life imposed on men by Zeus; they are connected with the "tragic" vision of the world that distinguishes the uncertain, turbulent conditions of mortal existence from the serene prospects of Mt. Olympus. On the other hand, strife (or competition), sex, and *dikē* are all means available to men for achieving and maintaining prosperity. The wise man will acknowledge their necessity and make them conducive to his well-being. The fool will ignore or abuse them and will pay the price for his folly. These features of mortal life thus have a moral aspect as well and distinguish the base from the noble, or the foolish from the wise. Thus, the same thing (e.g., strife) can be either the condition placed on men by the gods or the response by men to this condition; as response, it can be either good or bad (and so, Hesiod speaks of the "good" and "evil" strife).

This complexity finds expression in one of the most distinctive features of Hesiod's diction: the multiple meanings and values of a single word.[7] For example, *aidōs* (shame) is used both of proper and improper attitudes. It is bad when it is "timidity" and opposed to *tharsos* (319), or when it is "shame" at having to labor (311). As a reverential fear of the gods, however, it is a good thing. But *aidōs* is not simply a moral attitude (whether worthy or unworthy). She is also a goddess, whose departure from mankind leaves them defenseless against evils (199-201). As a goddess who leaves men, Aidos resembles Nemesis (200) and Dikē herself, who, having been dragged about by "gift-eating men" (220-21), reports to Zeus on those who have outraged her (256–62). (The journey of goddesses away from earth is a counterpart to the sending forth of goddesses by Zeus to dwell among men.)

The Strifes are similarly complex. As goddesses sent by Zeus, they represent an unavoidable condition; insofar as strife can be good or evil, however, it has a moral character—that is, can be either wisely embraced or foolishly abused. While one is good and the other evil (and, as such, moral) they are nonetheless both strife (and, as such, an imposed condition). Both are descended from a single mother (Night).

It does not seem fanciful to compare Hesiod and Perses themselves. They are brothers (just as the Strifes are sisters), yet one is wise and the other foolish (just as one Strife is good and the other bad). Thus, the concrete situation prompting Hesiod to address his brother is of a piece with the structure of the world. The *Works and Days* affords one of the most striking examples of the way archaic poets refer a present situation to the timeless pattern of mortal life.

The wise man recognizes the world for what it is; he appreciates the contradictions structured into it, and his own activity is in accordance with these. He is thus able to direct the world, to an extent, to his own purposes. The foolish man, on the other hand, is blind to the true character of the world and his own mortal status. The misfortune he suffers is simply the perennial strife and difficulty of the world making itself known to one who has ignored or denied it. All activity, then, is really a testing of one's knowledge of the world, and the results of one's activity show the adequacy or inadequacy of one's perception. Hesiod is a moralist, for he insists that the results of an action respond to the worth or worthlessness of the action. Just behavior brings a prosperous city and fertile land; unjust behavior the very opposite of these.

What is significant about the evils suffered by the unjust and the foolish is that they are the same in kind as those evils imposed on the world by Zeus, which characterize the mortal condition.[8] Men's folly leaves them defenseless before these *kaka*. In describing the departure of Aidos (Shame) and Nemesis (Retribution) from the men of the iron age, Hesiod says, "Harsh woes will be left for mortal men; there will be no defense (*alkē*) against evil" (200–201). Moreover, Hesiod uses the same language to describe both the evils brought by Pandora and those suffered by the unjust. Compare, for example:

223: ἠέρα ἑσσαμένη, κακὸν ἀνθρώποισι φέρουσα

and

103: αὐτόματοι φοιτῶσι κακὰ θνητοῖσι φέρουσαι

46

So, too, Zeus brings a "great woe" on the unjust city—hunger and plague (*limon kai loimon*, 243). These ills are the same as those which Zeus imposed on the mortal race after Prometheus's trick—viz., scarcity (42) and diseases (102). The unjust city, therefore, does not seem liable to punishments designed and sent by Zeus specifically to humble it; rather, the city is exposed to the most hostile aspects of the world Zeus has designed for all humans.

When injustice is punished, this does not cancel out that other world view, wherein men suffer unmerited evils, sent by the awesome gods to confound mortals.[9] Wise or just actions win prosperity, in Hesiod's view, because they recognize the world for the harsh, resisting place it is and wrest from its conditions (e.g., strife) a measure of prosperity. The foolish ignore the world and are taken by surprise when reality asserts itself. The world is not designed to respond to men's justice (by rewarding them with prosperity) or their injustice (by visiting plagues on them). Rather, the world is what it is; we discover its nature by acting upon it. The harsh conditions of the world can be made to yield a certain prosperity for the one who appreciates the "advantages of mallow and asphodel"; these same conditions overwhelm those who do not see that the half is greater than the whole.

We may now compare tragedy, victory, and just retribution in terms of *pathos* and *praxis*. The action of tragedy resembles the ruin of the foolish man, as described by Hesiod. The fool acts in ignorance and suffers something unexpected and contrary to his intentions. The same is true in tragedy. In dealing with plots containing a recognition (*anagnōrisis*), Aristotle describes how an action is undertaken in ignorance of the way things are—e.g., a mother is on the point of killing a young man, not knowing that this man is her son. The project is confounded when the true state of affairs manifests itself (*Poetics* 53b1-54a15).

The fool and the tragic hero both suffer an unexpected *pathos,* which disrupts their project. What distinguishes the two is the kind of action they contemplate, as well as the scope of their ignorance. Hesiod's fool simply wants to be rich yet is ignorant of the normal order of things. He does not even know how to maintain himself day to day. A person is culpable for ignorance of this sort; he "gets what he deserves." Tragedy, on the other hand, deals with extreme situations, in which the ultimate insufficiency of mortals to control the world is explored. The tragic hero attempts an extraordinary act like murder; he cannot be expected to know the true state of affairs that will confound the act. Tragedy deals with the disparity of the person's deeds and *pathos;* if it is to have its proper effect, the person must not deserve what he gets.

The tragedian and the moralist share the vision of the harshness of the mortal condition. But the moralist deals with activities of a limited scope, where the mortal can manipulate the world to his own benefit. In the last analysis, however, the world cannot be known by the individual, nor will it bend to his will; situations that expose the mortal's ultimate subjection to the gods provide the theme of tragedy. Tragedy and morality do not have incompatible visions of the mortal world. What distinguishes them is the kind of situations they deal with, which illuminate different aspects of that world.[10]

The connection between the tragic hero and the fool is shown in a striking way by the famous expression *pathei mathos,* from Aeschylus's *Agamemnon* (177). The chorus of old men says that Zeus has established, as a law for mortals, that "learning is through suffering." The phrase takes on a complex meaning in the *Oresteia;* in its immediate context, however, it seems to be a reflection on the intermingling of opposites that characterizes the human condition. The security and certainty of knowledge come only through the danger and uncertainty of *pathos.*[11] There is a passive element in wisdom, which can be forced on us without our looking for it or wanting it. Wisdom (*sōphronein,* 181) comes even to the unwilling, the chorus says; the grace (*kharis*) of the gods is violent (180–83). *Pathei mathos* suggests that there is no knowledge enabling the mortal to avoid catastrophe; people are necessarily ignorant and vulnerable. Only once their world has fallen in on them can they know it.

The expression can be traced back to a Homeric phrase: $\dot{\rho}\epsilon\chi\vartheta\grave{\epsilon}\nu$ $\delta\acute{\epsilon}$ $\tau\epsilon$ $\nu\acute{\eta}\pi\iota\sigma\varsigma$ $\check{\epsilon}\gamma\nu\omega$ (*Il.* 17.32; cf. also Hesiod *WD* 218 $\pi\alpha\vartheta\grave{\omega}\nu$ $\delta\acute{\epsilon}$ $\tau\epsilon$ $\nu\acute{\eta}\pi\iota\sigma\varsigma$ $\check{\epsilon}\gamma\nu\omega$, and *WD* 89, of Epimetheus, $\alpha\grave{\upsilon}\tau\grave{\alpha}\rho$ $\acute{o}$ $\delta\epsilon\xi\acute{\alpha}\mu\epsilon\nu\sigma\varsigma$, $\acute{o}\tau\epsilon$ $\delta\grave{\eta}$ $\kappa\alpha\kappa\grave{o}\nu$ $\epsilon\grave{\hat{\iota}}\chi$', $\grave{\epsilon}\nu\acute{o}\eta\sigma\epsilon$). In the *Iliad* passage, Menelaus warns Euphorbus to stand back from Patroclus's body before suffering some hurt (*prin ti kakon patheein*). He concludes, "The fool knows something only when it happens to him." The context is quite similar in *WD* 89; Prometheus's advice to Epimetheus not to accept gifts from the gods is ignored. Only when the evil is visited on him does Epimetheus understand what he has done. What Aeschylus does is to generalize the fool's plight to all mankind; men are all such as to be able to learn only by experience.

If the tragic hero and the fool bear a certain resemblance to each other, so too do the victor and the wise man. Both understand the rule of strife and undertake a life of competition; both are successful. Hesiod's wise man, spurred on by envy of others' prosperity, works hard to earn wealth for himself. The athlete, fearing anonymity and desiring renown, girds himself for the rigors of the contest. Yet, their different competitions divide them. In the competition Hesiod describes, there are "prizes" for all men of wisdom; one has only to enter the contest to win. Life lived along the straight and narrow path will bring prosperity.

In the athletic contests, on the other hand, only one of the competitors can win. Good men are pitted against each other and the victory of any one entails the defeat of all the others. The structure of the contest exposes the final insufficiency of any individual's wisdom or strength to assure a desired result. The distinction between victor and wise man, therefore, is the same as that between tragic hero and fool. Hesiod's wise man can look forward to receiving his just deserts because he is seeking only his sustenance and a certain security in the world. The advantage of mallow and asphodel lies in the fact that it can be secured by means readily described. The athlete, on the other hand, cannot predict his success or failure; if he is to win immortal renown, he must take his chances and hope for the gods' help.

What distinguishes victory and tragedy, on the one hand, from the wise man's prosperity and fool's loss on the other, is the scope of the *praxis*. If this scope is modest enough and concerns no more than getting on with one's life (the situation in *Works and Days*), the results of the activity can be predicted: justice will succeed, injustice will fail. If more than this is undertaken—for example, an attempt at immortal renown, or vengeance, or purification of the city (cf. *Oedipus Rex*)—we have a situation in which the individual's vulnerability is posed. Morality distinguishes between good and evil persons, because it is concerned with what is within human power. The thrust of both tragedy and victory, however, is to distinguish between men and gods, because the actions they describe aim at results ultimately not within the scope of men's unaided resources.

Several odes explore the more intricate connections between *praxis* and *pathos,* as these have been sketched in this chapter. They deal not only with the disparity of what men do and what they suffer but also with retribution and the parity of doing and suffering. Pindar urges a particular kind of behavior; he gives moral advice. In looking at these odes, I want to show how such advice, which inevitably stresses the significance of deportment, relates to the description of victory as caused, ultimately, by forces outside men's control. My concern is no longer primarily structural, as it was in the first chapter (although it will be evident that *Pyth.* 3 and *Ol.* 1, two of the odes to be treated here, have a number of similarities in this regard). Nonetheless, the discussion continues that of the previous chapter, by expanding on the themes of *praxis* and *pathos.*

Pyth. 3 is an anomalous ode, in that it was not composed on the occasion of a victory. It may be described as a "poetic epistle," which Pindar sent to Hieron, tyrant of Syracuse, when the latter was ill. Whatever the exact circumstances of the composition of the ode, however, the poem is clearly a treatment of evils (*kaka*) in human life, and the variety of their causes. The ode illuminates the manifold connections between folly and tragedy, tragedy and victory, and victory and wisdom.

49

The ode gives a first impression of falling into two parts. In its first part, Pindar asks what might be the most suitable prayer during Hieron's illness. Is it perhaps the crowd's prayer, that a new Chiron and Asclepius be born, so that Hieron may be cured? The mythic *exempla* of Coronis and her son Asclepius that follow show the folly and danger of wanting the impossible, and so Pindar refrains from the extravagant hopes which most people entertained. David Young has shown the neat ring structure of this first part (1-79),[12] where Pindar moves from doubts concerning the propriety of the "common prayer" (*koinon eukhos*, 2) that "one who has departed might live," through a series of negative *exempla*, to end with a rejection of the common prayer. After this neatly defined unit, Pindar turns in the latter part of the ode to Hieron, reminding him that the gods "dispense two sorrows for every one good thing" (81-82); Peleus and Cadmus are offered in proof of this (86-103), since both men experienced the greatest of joys (fellowship with the gods) and the keenest of sorrows (loss of their children). It is only the good (*agathoi*) who can bear with this truth (82-83).

Pindar seems to address first himself, and then Hieron. Yet each half of the poem is unmistakably concerned with the sufferings undergone by mortals. Moreover, there is a careful symmetry to the poem, so that in each half we hear of two characters—Coronis and Asclepius in the first part, Cadmus and Peleus in the second.[13] Each pair illustrates a particular aspect of human suffering. Thus, Coronis and Asclepius are both destroyed for their own folly. Coronis "loved what was absent (i.e., impossible or forbidden)" (20)[14] and accepted a mortal lover, while still carrying Apollo's child. When Asclepius tried to cure the ultimate disease, by raising a man from the dead, he was himself killed by Zeus (54-58). Both mother and son wanted the impossible (59-60, 19-23); their sad ends were provoked by their own blindness. It is necessary, Pindar concludes (59-60), for mortals to seek from the gods only that which is suitable (*ta eoikota*).

It is the work of the second part of the poem to show what precisely is suitable for men, and why. If certain things are beyond mortals' reach, this is because our powers have been strictly circumscribed by the gods. "No happiness comes to men's life a safe thing . . ." (105-6);[15] "the immortals dispense mortals two sorrows together for every one good thing" (81-82); "life was safe neither for the Aeacid Peleus nor godlike Cadmus" (86-88). Evils are part of our condition, and, as such, are not caused by men but rather imposed on them.

The similarities and differences existing between the fools and the innocent heroes are clear. Coronis, Asclepius, Peleus, and Cadmus all suffer evils, but the first two have richly merited theirs by their ignorance and greed, while Peleus and Cadmus are good men and yet suffer. But the evils the latter suffer illuminate the structure of the world rather than their own moral character.[16]

Before speaking of Peleus and Cadmus, Pindar says that the gods give two sorrows for every joy. Having concluded their story, he shows the opposite side of the coin. "If any mortal has in mind the road of truth, he must fare well when he chances on (good fortune) from the gods. The breaths of winds falling from on high are different at different times. Men's happiness does not come as a thing safe for a long time, when it attends us large and brimming" (103-6). Peleus and Cadmus are not precisely tragic characters; rather, they are both victorious and tragic. Pindar contemplates the rise and fall of men's fortunes, as meted out by the gods; victory and tragedy are simply phases in this continuing rise and fall. In both of them, the person's excellence falls short, whether of securing happiness or averting unhappiness.

The proper response to a world of chance is resignation. The good (*agathos*) man makes the best of what he has (cf. 83 *ta kala trepsantes exō*). Pindar says that he will be "small in small times, great in great times" (107). This resignation is essentially a recognition of the way the world is; hence, what Pindar urges on Hieron is similar to what Hesiod urges on Perses. Yet, there is a difference between the two, which is again largely a matter of the scope of the individual's ambitions. Perses, having recognized the harshness of the world, can make use of his knowledge by setting out to work with the expectation of success. Hieron and Pindar, on the other hand, can put their recognition to no such use, since what they recognize is the impossibility of securing their goals without the gods' favor. Having come to know the world, they can only resign themselves to it. The moral advice offered by Pindar to Hieron differs from that offered by Hesiod to Perses by its uselessness. There is no material advantage to be had from resignation; one simply avoids being foolish.

Pyth. 3 was suited for an unhappy occasion, one of the "small times" when fortune had turned away from Hieron. *Ol.* 1, on the other hand, celebrates Hieron's victory in the horse races at Olympia. The description of the human condition and the advice offered in the poem are not very different from what we find in *Pyth.* 3, but these take on a new light from the happiness of the occasion that prompts them.

The structure of *Ol.* 1 is similar to that of *Pyth.* 3. Just as in that poem Pindar compares two groups of people (Coronis and Asclepius, Peleus and Cadmus), in *Ol.* 1 we find an implicit comparison of Tantalus and Pelops. Their two lives are part of a discussion of "what is best" for mortal men. Tantalus's life of ease and fellowship with the gods might seem the best life for men. "If the guardians of Olympus ever honored a man, it was this Tantalus" (54-55). However, such happiness is "indigestible"

51

(cf. 55). It made Tantalus foolish, since he hoped to escape the gods' notice when he gave their food to his mortal friends (60-64). Tantalus was punished severely, but there is no suggestion that his sufferings were anything but deserved (57-60).

As another consequence of Tantalus's fall, his nephew Pelops, who had been brought to heaven as Poseidon's lover, was sent back to earth to live as a mortal.[17] Pelops differs from Tantalus, in much the way that the wise man differs from the fool. Bereft of his immortality, Pelops has a clear-eyed appreciation of his mortal estate and what is possible in it. At the ocean's side, Pelops invokes Poseidon's help in the contest to win Hippodameia for his wife. He explains why he is undertaking this. "Great danger does not threaten the weakling. But those for whom death is necessity—why would anyone sitting in the darkness nurse a nameless old age in vain, without a portion of all fair things? This contest I shall undertake; grant me dear accomplishment" (81-85).

Pelops's decision to enter the contests is explicitly a response to the inevitability of death. More than this, Pelops actually courts death by vying for Hippodameia, as Pindar makes clear by stressing the number of men who have already lost their lives in trying to win her for their wife. It is only by risking death that Pelops can win fame and a greater abundance of life.[18] The cessation of existence is a necessity laid down for men, yet at the same time it is the way in which mortals win a more bountiful life for themselves. The hero becomes heroic by taking on mortal risks and facing down death. Here again, the similarity between Pelops and the Hesiodic wise man is evident. Like strife in *Works and Days,* mortality is recognized as a condition imposed on men, and also the distinctive way in which men show their strength (viz., by courage and daring in the face of death). It is Pelops, not Tantalus, who has the "best" life, for he is able to make the best of his diminished circumstances.[19]

Pelops's wisdom is like that of Peleus and Cadmus. All of them know the reign of sorrow and frustration in men's lives. This is signified in *Pyth.* 3 by the expression "The gods give two sorrows for every joy," and in *Ol.* 1 by Pelops' speech about mortality. In times of misfortune, when the gods have turned from us, the awareness of the mortal condition suggests resignation; when the gods are benevolently disposed, however, (as Poseidon is to Pelops) this awareness prompts the individual to extraordinary effort. The close connection between the wisdom of resignation and of competitiveness is suggested by the fact that Pindar concludes *Ol.* 1, in which the will to compete is celebrated, by urging moderation and contentment with the "good which is always present, day by day" (99-100). "Seek no further," Pindar urges Hieron (114), even as he hopes that Hieron will go on to win a yet greater victory (108-11).

The strongest statement in the odes of the effectiveness of deeds and their power to secure goods is to be found in *Ol.* 2, composed for another of the Sicilian tyrants, Theron of Acragas. The poem could be read as a treatment of activity and the certainty of its effects. It will provide us with a last comparison of Pindar's and Hesiod's moral precepts. After naming Theron's several victories at Olympia, Delphi, and the Isthmian games, Pindar says:

τὸ δὲ τυχεῖν
πειρώμενον ἀγωνίας δυσφρονᾶν παραλύει.
ὁ μὰν πλοῦτος ἀρεταῖς δεδαιδαλμένος
φέρει τῶν τε καὶ τῶν
καιρὸν βαθεῖαν ὑπέχων μέριμναν †ἀγροτέραν,
ἀστὴρ ἀρίζηλος, ἐτυμώτατον
ἀνδρὶ φέγγος ·   51-56

Success in one's attempt at the contest frees a man from sorrow.[20]
The wealth that is decked out with excellences, and that prompts
a deep yearning for endeavors, brings various fortunes, but it is a
blazing star and the surest light for men.

A person's actions have an eternal worth, as the remarkable "Orphic" passage emphasizes. The underworld, unlike the world, responds perfectly to men's notions of equity.[21] The good—those "who have dared to keep their soul from injustice" (69-70)[22] and who have respected their oaths (65-67)—enjoy a blissful existence; sinners are punished (57-60, 67).

In the first triad of the poem, we find an expression of the stable effects of one's deeds, as well. The statement, however, comes across as an expression of men's impotence rather than as a reassurance of their ability to affect the future. Pindar prays that Zeus will bless the future (12-15) and then adds, "The completion of deeds done, whether justly or unjustly, not even Time, the father of all, could make undone" (15-17). The past seems merely intransigent. The stability of men's deeds is as much a sign of their weakness (since they can not undo what they regret) as it is of their strength.

The movement from the first passage to the later one is instructive. Since men cannot change the past, Pindar concludes, one can only hope to be able to forget it. There begins now a lengthy development on the theme of *moira* (fate) and its powers to uphold or bewilder men. The discussion is developed in an alternating series of gnomic reflections and mythic *exempla*. "Malignant sorrow dies, subdued by noble joys, when the god's fate sends up a towering joy," Pindar says in 19-22. The lives of Semele and Ino are briefly told in illustration of this, for both were divinized after their sad deaths (22-30). This story in turns gives on to another gnomic passage, similar to the first, but drawing a more pessimistic moral from the tale of the heroines. "Surely, the boundary line of mortals' death has not been marked out to see, nor when we shall complete a tranquil day, child of the Sun, with undiminished good. At different times, different streams with good cheer and toils come to men. So fate, which controls this family's fair destiny from of old, does bring, together with god-sent happiness, a sorrow contrary to another time" (30-37).

Moira, who gave happiness after sorrow in 21-22, is now seen to give sorrow after a happiness (cf. *moira pempei olbon*, 21-22, and *moira pēm' agei*, 35-37). The following story of Oedipus and his sons shows an instance of Moira's darker side. For them, there was no happy turn in fortune, as there was for the Theban princesses: Oedipus slew his father, and the Erinys slaughtered his sons (38-42).

At first, Pindar comforted Theron's past sorrow by suggesting that Fate can turn sorrow to joy. The comfort fails, however, because Fate can do the opposite as well, and men have no way of knowing when or how. If mortals were powerless to alter the past, it now seems that they are powerless to affect the future, as well. Moira is far too potent and ambiguous to be reassuring; any force outside of man and his control must fail to give comfort, since it is essentially his subject state, his vulnerability that most troubles man.

After the narrative of Oedipus's tragedy, Pindar turns to the athletic successes of his grandson Thersander, and, again, those of the latter's descendant, Theron (45-51). These suggest a new solution—that successful effort comforts men. There follows the celebration of human activity that we have already considered.

Ol. 2 is an elegant treatment of the ambiguities attending both *praxis* and *pathos*. The indelible permanence of men's deeds leads mortals to look to Moira for comfort; Moira may allow them to forget the sad past. On the other hand, Moira may confound them as well; men therefore have recourse once again to their deeds for comfort. In 18, Pindar says that "With a happy fate (*potmos*) we can forget (past sorrows)." In 51-52, he says, "When the competing man (*peirōmenon agōnias*) succeeds, it releases him from his sorrow." In the earlier passage, one is comforted by *pathos*, by forces external to man; the later passage deals instead with *praxis*, speaking of the effort the man himself expends in order to effect change.

The poem offers a fine statement of the complexities of retribution, as presented by Pindar. For him, nothing is unequivocal, even the assertion that men's deeds get their just rewards. Morality and retribution seek to make a clear order, in which different categories (good, evil) may be distinguished from each other. In showing the ambivalence of retribution—the way it both confounds and comforts men—Pindar offers a strong expression of the ambivalence of all mortal things. It should be noted, moreover, that even in celebrating men's efforts and *aretai,* Pindar does not deny the role of *potmos;* one puts forth an effort and then "happens" on (*tukhein,* 51) success.

Whatever the abilities of *praxis* to secure happiness for men, it is still linked indissolubly with *pathos.* To return to the terms used at the beginning of this chapter, culture never escapes nature. The world of forms, categories, and predictable retribution that men construct for themselves is subject ultimately to the conditions of flux and uncertainty set down for men by the gods. Culture and its rules work only within certain limits; within these, one can have a straightforward morality. But once these limits are surpassed, as they are in the kind of situations depicted in tragedy and the epinician, morality is subjected to stress, becoming uncertain and ambivalent.

ii

Victory is beyond the pale of morality in the sense that the athlete, in seeking to win a victory, cannot count on the success; his wisdom and justice, even his strength, are not sufficient to assure him of a first place and the honors attending it. However, having won the victory, the athlete looks for a just recompense of praise and acknowledgment by the community. Several times in the odes, Pindar stresses that victory puts others under the obligation of doing honor to it.[23] In this sense victory is closely associated with retribution and morality. It is just to give the victor praise; it is very wrong to deny it to him. There is a double movement, then, in victory—both away from and back to a cultural realm of equity and retribution. This double movement and its connection with themes of *nostos* will be explored in chapter 4. What I want to do now is to consider more closely the nature of human communities and the place of epinician song in the community. The basic question to be dealt with is: why does victory put others under an obligation to praise it? The question may be subdivided into two. First, what is there in victory that puts a claim on others? And then, what is it about the others—the victor's community—that enables them to satisfy the victor's needs?

It was one of the distinguishing features of the national Greek contests, at least in historical times, that athletes entered the competition not to win property but only honor. So in Herodotus 8.26, one of the Persians urges retreat from Greece when he learns that at Olympia the only prize for victors was a wreath. "Good heavens, Mardonius, what kind of men have you brought us to fight against—men who have contests for no material reward, but only for honor!" As Pelops' speech in *Ol.* 1 makes clear, an awareness of his mortality prompts the athlete to enter the lists. In lieu of an immortal life, he seeks an immortal renown (*kleos*). But for renown, the athlete needs a community in which to be renowned.

In a sense, community is based on the individual's depletion; because personal immortality is impossible, one must seek to live through others. In *Works and Days,* Hesiod clarifies the social consequences of men's fall from grace. Henceforth, men are necessarily involved in strife with others, and their attempts at prosperity involve boundaries and the adjustment of fair portions (*dikē*). Moreover, every male must take a female, or else suffer the knowledge that his wealth will be distributed among strangers after he dies. Strife, *dikē*, sex—all of these are of a social character. What Hesiod says, essentially, is that the individual, no longer self-sufficient, is inevitably cast into a relationship with other individuals. What is true of the Hesiodic man is true also for the Pindaric man. Anyone who seeks some form of immortality must have recourse to his fellows. Only within the community can one enjoy an undying *kleos.* The person's name can live so long as there are people to hear it. *Kleos* is the immortality which community makes possible.

Epinician song is a means of according the athlete public praise and of ensuring that his renown lives on among his fellows. More than this, the song of praise is the cultural product *par excellence* since it is partly by means of it that individuals form and maintain stable institutions of fellowship. (It should be understood in the following discussion that I am dealing with song as a response to the athlete's activity, rather than as a parallel to it. As an activity, the poet's work involves just the same ambiguities of *pathos* and *praxis* as does the athlete's. As a response to activity, however, it represents just recompense.)

A striking example of the importance of praise to the community can be found in the eighth book of the *Odyssey,* when Odysseus visits the court of the Phaeacians.[24] In the last scene of the book, the Phaeacians and Odysseus, who has yet to identify himself, have gathered for a banquet, after the contests in which Odysseus won the discus throw and Demodocus, the court poet, delighted the Phaeacians and their guest with the song of "Ares and Aphrodite." Demodocus sings at the banquet, too, and is praised by the stranger, who requests a song about Odysseus and the Trojan Horse (487-98). If the singer tells the tale *kata moiran* (correctly, appropriately), Odysseus promises to tell all men about the gods' gift to the singer (496-98). While Demodocus's song belongs to the same genre as Homer's (epic), it is very close to epinician poetry, in that it celebrates the victory of a man still living and present (albeit unrecognized) among this company of people. Demodocus's song redounds to the glory of the hero (Odysseus) as much as it does to the singer's; it therefore expresses the reciprocity of praise existing between host and guest, *laudator* and *laudandus*.

This happened in the evening of Odysseus's second day at Alcinous's court. Up until the afternoon of that day, Odysseus had not only refused to speak his name, but made it clear that he wished to have as little to do with the Phaeacians as possible; he wanted only to be escorted home, so that he might look upon his native land and die (7.208-25). In book 8, the story is told of how Odysseus eventually outgrew his alienation and self-induced loneliness and entered into a warm friendship with his hosts. The crucial scene comes when Alcinous, king of the Phaeacians, brings his mysterious guest to watch the young people compete in athletic contests.

Laodamas, the king's son, invites the stranger to join in the games; Odysseus refuses, explaining, "There are griefs in my heart greater than games (*aethloi*)." Hearing this, another of the Phaeacian youths, Euryalus, insults Odysseus, calling him no athlete and guessing him to be nothing more than a merchant.[25] At this point, Odysseus undertakes to vindicate himself by entering the contest and hurling the discus, of a type much thicker than that normally used by the Phaeacians. When the discus lands, the disguised Athena marks its place and says, "Even a blind man, stranger, could distinguish this sign by touch. Since it is not mixed in with the rest, but is the first by far. Take heart in this game. No Phaeacian will reach or supersede this" (*Od.* 8.195-98).

The Greek text which follows runs:

> Ὣς φάτο, γήθησεν δὲ πολύτλας δῖος Ὀδυσσεύς,
> χαίρων οὕνεχ' ἑταῖρον ἐνηέα λεῦσσ' ἐν ἀγῶνι.
> καὶ τότε κουφότερον μετεφώνεε Φαιήκεσσι   199-201

Thus she spoke, and much-enduring godlike Odysseus rejoiced,
Delighting to see a kind companion in the company,
And then more lightly he addressed the Phaeacians. . .

Odysseus's rejoicing represents a remarkable change in demeanor, for up until this moment he has insisted on remembering and nursing his griefs (cf. *Od.* 7.208-25, 8.153-57).

Significantly, it is acknowledgment of his merit that turns Odysseus's sorrow into joy. This motif of acknowledgment, so essential to the epinician, is also central to the theme of *nostos,* as developed in the *Odyssey.* Athena tells Telemachus in book 3, "As for me, I would want to suffer many sorrows, come home and look upon the day of return, rather than come and be slain by the hearth, as Agamemnon was slain by the deceits of Aegisthus and his own wife" (3.232-35). *Nostos* depends not only on the hero's return to his home but also on his being welcomed when he arrives. Penelope therefore plays a crucial role in the story of Odysseus's return. In the Second Nekyia (Bk. 24) the shade of Agamemnon, having heard the dead suitor's account of Odysseus's return and revenge, says, "Happy son of Laertes, wily Odysseus! With great excellence (*aretē*) you took a wife. For good was the mind of blameless Penelope, daughter of Icarius. She remembered well Odysseus, her wedded husband. So the fame (*kleos*) of his excellence will never perish for him, and the immortals will make a delightful song for wise Penelope" (24.192-98).[26] Like an epinician poet's acknowledgment, Penelope's reception helps to secure the hero's renown. Her reception is itself praiseworthy, and so the gods will fashion a charming song in her honor.

In book 8, the effects of acknowledgment by the disguised Athena are immediate. Odysseus is delighted to find a "gentle companion," who announces his success. He is now able to speak "more lightly" (*koupho-teron*) to his hosts. Alcinous in his turn praises Odysseus and invites him to watch a demonstration of those skills in which the Phaeacians are preeminent. "For we are not excellent boxers or wrestlers, but swiftly we run on foot, and we are unsurpassed in ships; always we have our dinner, the lyre and choruses, changes of clothing, warm baths, and bed." He wants Odysseus to see these things so that he might tell others of the Phaeacians (241-45). Demodocus is brought on to sing the song about Ares and Aphrodite; Odysseus delights in the song just as the Phaeacians do (367-69) and offers his praise to the dancers (382-84). Thus, the acknowledgment is reciprocal; guest and host alike pay tribute to each other. The *laudator* is also the *laudandus,* and vice versa. By virtue of this mutual praise, they form a close, affective bond of friendship.

In *Od.* 8, then, we find a poetic treatment of the way praise and mutual regard for one another's *aretē* is a constituent element of community. Dumézil, interestingly, has argued the importance of praise and blame in Rome and India, and the function played by praise in maintaining a society.[27] Pindar's odes, too, serve to strengthen community by acting as a kind of intermediary between the community and the returning victor. The athlete, through the poet, urges the community to accord him the renown that is his due. The community, in the person of the epiniciast, assures the victor that it will ratify his victory by its acknowledgment.[28] *Nem.* 4 provides an interesting example of the way in which praise is at the heart of the community. In this ode, we find a movement from the bonds of kinship, which are necessarily exclusive, to those of social institutions—more open than kinship, and based on praise.

The ode begins and closes, as was shown earlier in this chapter, with a discussion of song and its divine and mortal characteristics.[29] The passages could be understood as praise of the victor's family, since the athlete Timasarkhos had several epinician poets in his clan. Pindar stresses, again at the beginning and end of the poem, the family's poetic talents. "If your father Timokritos were still warmed by the powerful sun, often he would sing a varied hymn of fair victory, plucking the *kithara,* bending over this strain" (13-16); "Euphanes, your aged grandfather, once celebrated (*Kallikles*). . ." (89-90). *Nem.* 4 is, in consequence, one of the few poems where Pindar has a kind word for his fellow epinician poets. Rather than distinguish himself from deceivers or "chattering daws," Pindar speaks rather of the *common practice* of epinician poets in accomplishing the task of praise. Thus, in the closing verses, he describes the struggles that *any* epinician poet would wage and says that every poet desires to make outstanding poetry of his subject; "whatever any one happens upon, each one hopes to say something surpassing" (91-92).

The presence of poets in Timasarkhos's family, however, has another consequence as well. Under other circumstances, Timokritos, the victor's father, would have composed the victory song. The occasion thus presents Pindar with the opportunity to state the reasons why he, though not a member of the family, offers praise. Pindar seems first to mark himself as an outsider. There is a sea between him and Aegina (36-37).[30] He asks that his song be received hospitably by the Aeginetans (11-13), an unusual request in Pindar's odes, where it is rather the office of the poet and his song to secure a hospitable reception for the athlete.

Because Pindar is not kin to the athlete, he points to other ties that bind him to Timasarkhos. If Pindar asks hospitality for his song, he can also remind Timasarkhos of the hospitality that he—the victor—has enjoyed among Pindar's townspeople, the Thebans. "The Cadmaeans by the splendid mount of Amphitryon willingly mingled (*meignuon*) him with flowers for Aegina's sake" (19-22);[31] Timasarkhos is a "friend coming to friends" (22).

The poet and victor, therefore, are bound by double ties; each one is guest and host alike for the other. This reciprocity is then projected onto the heroic plane (25-32) where Theban and Aeginetan appear as Heracles and Telamon, who fought together at Troy.[32] The host-guest relationship yields to that existing between comrades-in-arms.

In the stanzas following, Pindar makes it clear in what sense he is a "warrior." He speaks of plots against which he must struggle. These are not necessarily (or even probably) plots laid against Pindar. Rather, the poet fights those jealous men who would denigrate the victory. He does this precisely by giving praise.[33] The jealous man rolls his vain thoughts in the darkness, but the *aretē* that Fate (*potmos*) has given Pindar will come to its fulfillment with time (41-43).

The description of Pindar as a warrior, struggling against plots laid by the jealous, gives on to a catalog of Aeacid heroes and, in particular, Peleus, whose struggle against lies and eventual vindication suggests comparison with the poet. When Peleus was slandered by Hippolyta for rejecting her advances, her husband Acastus plotted against him. Peleus got the better of his opponent, and "what was fated came to pass" (56–61). The situation of this story clearly matches that of the victory, as this has been described in the poem. Peleus, who wrestled with Thetis (62–65), is an obvious predecessor of the boy wrestler Timasarkhos (10); however, he is relevant to the poet as well, since both must "struggle" and both are vindicated by fate. The narrative of Peleus indicates, once again, the close ties binding poet and athlete. They are bound not only by guest ties, but by virtue of being involved in "struggle"—whether literal or metaphorical.[34]

In both *Od.* 8 and *Nem.* 4, the praise is offered within a community and asserts or strengthens the ties binding members of the community. In *Od.* 8, although Odysseus and Alcinous are already bound by guest-host ties, it is not until Odysseus is praised that there is a mutual warmth and friendliness between the two men. In *Nem.* 4, in order to offer tribute, Pindar must first establish that he and the athlete are fellow members of a community. He reminds Timasarkhos that he and the poet are bound by ties of hospitality. The poet's struggle, moreover, allies him with the athlete he praises. The similarity of Pindar's and Timasarkhos's *ponoi* implies a community of interest and ambition for them. In *Nem.* 4, the parallels between the poet and athlete do more than indicate the relevance of song to the athlete's interests; they suggest that the poet, even though not a blood relative, is right to offer praise, and that his praise is an expression of the fellowship or community of which he and the athlete are part. In the course of the poem, Pindar disengages praise from the kinship relation (which is necessarily exclusive) and bases his praise on a more inclusive, open-ended community, in which *xenoi* might participate.[35] When he closes the poem with a description of the struggle all epinician poets wage in trying to subdue detractors and offer praise, he is suggesting that there exists a common fellowship to which poets of good will belong.

There is an outward thrust to the poem, complementing this move from kinship to a more open community. For example, Pindar names several Aeacid settlements scattered throughout the Greek world, in 46–54; the extent of the colonies suggests that Aegina, the Aeacids' native land, opens onto the wider reaches of the world. Moreover, Pindar includes a series of water images, with successively larger bodies of water. The song of praise is at first compared to "warm water" (4). In 36, Pindar refers to the sea separating him from Aegina. The passage is controversial,[36] but if we suppose that Pindar presents himself composing the ode at his home in Thebes, the sea he refers to is the Saronic Gulf. Finally in 69-72, Pindar suggests that the Aeacids' praises are a vast ocean, which cannot be traversed; therefore, the encomiast must "return to Europe" and not continue on beyond Gadeira to the west.[37]

Praise therefore seems to be one of the constituent elements of community; it takes place within a community, either creating or maintaining the bonds between individuals. The public show of mutual regard enables individual competitors (in the Hesiodic sense that all are competitors) to band together. Without praise and the just acknowledgment of merit, the community has a difficult time maintaining itself. As Hesiod says, "May I not be just among men—neither myself nor my son— since it is a base (kakon) thing to be a just man, if the more unjust man will have the greater settlement (dikē)" (WD 270-72). Since the merits of his case have not been duly recognized, Hesiod sees that the distinctions, vital to the life of the community, between noble and base, just and unjust, have been badly obscured. The community exists because it helps the individual obtain what he wants; if it does not do so (for example, if it does not give the proper acknowledgment and honor to one who has deserved it), it seriously compromises its reason for existing.

In the great speech in Il. 9, when Achilles refuses to be reconciled with Agamemnon, he says:

ἴση μοῖρα μένοντι, καὶ εἰ μάλα τις πολεμίζοι·
ἐν δὲ ἰῇ τιμῇ ἠμὲν κακὸς ἠδὲ καὶ ἐσθλός·
κάτθαν' ὁμῶς ὅ τ' ἀεργὸς ἀνὴρ ὅ τε πολλὰ ἐοργώς

Il. 9.318-20

There is an equal portion for the man who remains behind, and the one who battles; in one honor (are held) the base and the noble. Equally they die: the man who does nothing, and he who does many things.

Achilles juxtaposes a biological fact (all men die) with a social protest (the good and the base are honored equally). He means that since all men die, whether good or evil, there should at least be some distinction made between them during their lives. It is the office of culture, and more specifically of those who distribute honors, to maintain the distinctions between good and bad. If a society fails to do this, there exists in effect a state of nature, confounding good and base, and condemning them to a single fate. Activity becomes pointless, because it will be rubbed out by time; hence, Achilles refuses to rejoin the Achaean army and fight.

Achilles' speech is very close to the argument in the opening passage of Nem. 7, which has been well explicated by David Young.[38] Pindar, too, reflects on the indiscriminate character of death: "rich and poor man alike go to death's tomb" (19-20). The universality of death is matched by that of birth; Pindar begins the poem by invoking Eleithyia, the goddess of birth, who is responsible for the origins of all alike. "Eleithyia, who sit by the Fates of deep counsel, daughter of mighty Hera, mother of children, hear me! Without you, neither day nor black night do we see; we do not obtain Youth, your sister with the shining limbs" (1-4).

Against the sameness that prevails at the beginning and end of human lives is set the distinctiveness of the individual, which obtains during the person's life. "All of us live, but not for the same destiny; different things yoked by Fate constrain different men. With your help, goddess, Thearion's son Sogenes as well is set apart (*kritheis*) by his excellence" (5-7). In order to preserve this distinctiveness against death, public acknowledgment in song is necessary; otherwise, the deeds fall into obscurity and eventually pass away with the person's own demise. "If one's actions succeed, he casts a honey-minded theme into the streams of the Muses. For great deeds of strength have much darkness should they go without song. We have a mirror for fine works in just one way: if for the sake of Memory with her gleaming fillet a recompense for the labors be found in glorious songs of words" (11-16).

Praise, duly given to those who have deserved it, and distinguishing them from those who have not, makes activity worthwhile, because it assures individuals that their deeds will live on after them. Without just praise, the community cannot fulfill its office of assuring individual *kleos*. It then ceases to be of any use, as far as Achilles is concerned; it offers nothing to distinguish itself from the state of nature. The ability to establish differences among people, then, is vital to a culture. "Order, peace, and fecundity depend on cultural distinctions," René Girard writes. "It is not these distinctions but the loss of them that gives birth to fierce rivalries and sets members of the same family or social group at one another's throats."[39]

iii

Summing up the argument so far, we can say that the qualifications a cultural product must fulfill if it is to be successful are as follows:

1. It must find some means of incorporating nature. Failure to acknowledge and respect the particular conditions imposed on mortals by the gods assures that the product will be ruined when these conditions assert themselves, as they eventually must.

2. It must secure some good, suggestive of divinity (e.g., prosperity, certainty, immortality), which is otherwise unavailable. This feature explains why the gods are often portrayed as bestowing culture or its institutions on people. Similarly, Athena, rather than Alcinous or any

of the other Phaeacians, praises Odysseus, and so makes possible the fellowship between Odysseus and his hosts.

3. It must distinguish between good and bad.

4. It seems necessarily to involve a number of people and to be a structured means whereby the individual confronts the other members of that community.

We can test and clarify these criteria by comparing song to the poetic treatment of another cultural institution, no less vital to the well-being of society: the jury and its dispensation of *dikē*. I will consider the *Oresteia* as a treatment of the dilemmas inherent in mortal life and of the way in which the jury represents a resolution of these dilemmas and enables the establishment of a stable society. I select the *Oresteia* partly because its greater length makes possible a clearer picture of the cultural product than can be gleaned from the Pindaric odes. It will be seen, however, that Aeschylus's presentation of the dilemmas and the means of solving them is very similar to Pindar's discussion of mortality and the desire to have one's deeds immortalized. Moreover, Aeschylus uses the themes of epinician poetry throughout the *Oresteia,* and the trilogy as a whole evinces a structure remarkably like that found in several of Pindar's odes. I shall argue that the structuring is as vital to Aeschylus's meaning as it is in the epinicians.

The difficulty presented by *dikē* in the *Oresteia* is the same as was sketched briefly at the beginning of this chapter: mortals, subject to conditions of strife and uncertainty, nevertheless require, if any kind of communal life is to be possible, a stable and univocal justice, one that will command universal assent. Men have only purely mortal means at their disposal to achieve something that is in some way beyond the pale of mortal conditions. In *Agamemnon* and *Choephoroe* (hereafter *A* and *C*) the characters search unsuccessfully for a means of working justice.[40] Agamemnon's attempt to do so at Troy is hailed by the chorus, but those celebrations inevitably turn to brooding, sinister hints of destruction for the Atreids.[41] If Agamemnon has worked justice at Troy, this justice is nonetheless inseparable from the pollution he incurs. Clytaemnestra claims to have worked justice by murdering her husband, but her assertion wins no one's assent.[42] The great *kommos* in *C* is given over in large part to urgent requests that the retributive acts of justice be looked upon with favor by the gods, and Orestes, while certain of the justice and necessity of what he does, yet is in no way confident about the consequences of his act (*C* 269–305, 434–38, 973–1006, 1010–17, 1021–33.)

When the characters in the *Oresteia* do see the contradiction between what they seek to accomplish and what they must do to accomplish it, they have no way to reconcile the two; they must therefore simply deny one or the other. This emerges most clearly in the second episode of *A,* where a soldier just returned from Troy announces Agamemnon's impending arrival. In his first speech, the soldier greets the gods who have, contrary to all his expectations, brought him back to Greece (503–17); he insists on the justice of Troy's fall (518–37). In his second speech, however, the messenger goes on to speak of the many hardships attending the victory at Troy: the discomforts of camplife, the cold at night, the wet dew in the morning, the verminous clothing. The messenger then effectively denies the significance of the army's toils by insisting that they are over and done with (τί ταῦτα πενθεῖν δεῖ; παροίχεται πόνος, 567). It is not necessary, he tells the chorus, to take the dead into account,[43] or to grieve over hostile fortune (573–74). He tries to dissever the success from what preceded it, because he has no means with which to contain the labor and the success together; he must deny the one to save the other. The citizens are to confine their attention to the victorious completion of the army's mission and thus to offer their praise (580–82).

Comparison with the Pindaric ode is irresistible.[44] There Pindar is interested in the same antithesis of success and toil, but, unlike the messenger in *A,* he insists on the continuing significance of the *ponos,* and he concludes with a description of victory in which both the joy and the sorrow are comprehended. The audience's praise is invited for a career in which these opposites are inextricable; the messenger, on the other hand, claims Agamemnon's success deserves praise precisely because there is no need to pay attention to the cost. His attempt to deny the significance of the toils and sufferings involved in Troy's capture is decisively overthrown by the chorus's request for news of Menelaus, for no longer can the messenger deny that the success simultaneously involves a very possible loss (615 ff.).

The odes sung by the chorus of old men in *A* make for a no less interesting comparison with Pindar. As has been frequently pointed out, the movement of these stasima is regularly from a confident assertion of justice and its triumphant vindication to a darker, more troubled attitude, with dark hints of repercussions affecting Agamemnon himself.[45] The first stasimon certainly shows this pattern. Thus in 355–402, the chorus reflects on the appropriateness of Troy's fall. It is Zeus and Night who have punished the city (355–58), because of Paris's sin against Zeus Xenios (362). The punishment has been suited exactly to the crime (*epraxen hōs ekranen,* 369).

In the third strophe, however, when this image of exact retribution appears again, it is in the ironic guise of Ares, "gold-exchanger of corpses." Ares's office as *talantoukhos* (the one who holds the scales) is ironic because of the disparity between what he receives (the flower of Greek youth) and what he returns (ashes).[46] Moreover, the events at Troy are no longer described as the punishment wrought by Zeus, but as the bloody work of mortals. "The gods do not fail to heed those who kill many," the chorus says (461-62), and while the reference is deliberately left vague, yet the statement is clearly pertinent for Agamemnon and Menelaus.[47] The reaction to the military success at Troy is no longer jubilation at the vindication of justice but mourning for the dead (445-49). The chorus remarks on the bitter irony of the victors being buried in the land they conquered (452-55).

Victory and its ambiguities is one of the most important motifs of the latter part of the stasimon. The chorus speaks of the sinister character of excessive acclamation (*to d' huperkopōs kluein eu baru*, 468-69). It speaks of the man who is *tukhēros* (464); we have seen, especially in *Ol.* 12 and *Pyth.* 8, the importance of *tukhē* in describing the relationship between the victor and his victory. The encomiastic motifs of jealousy (450) and ill-speaking (456) are also present in the latter part of the stasimon.

The whole lyric might be described, then, as moving between justice (the punishment of the guilty by one who executes the will of the gods) to victory (the triumph of one party over another, as the outcome of a battle or competition). It is a movement from clarity and security to one of doubt, for if justice is said to be the execution of the gods' will, victory suggests, rather, the result of a combat between two mortals. The outcome of a crusade against those who have offended Zeus is guaranteed; the outcome of a battle between armies not at all so. To describe the events at Troy, therefore, as a "victory" tends to subvert the description of them as "justice."[48] The one-sided interpretation of *dikē* as godlike and secure is counterbalanced by an equally limited interpretation of *nikē* as disruptive and almost sinister.

The first stasimon resembles an ode like *Pyth.* 8 in its movement from a simple, retributive notion of justice to a view that is rather less sanguine, and more sensitive to the frustrations and upsets visited on mortals by the gods. The great difference between the stasimon and the epinician, however, is that the latter comprehends both human activity and human subjection and assimilates joy and sorrow alike in its description of victory; in the stasimon, we are left with a flat contradiction. There is a movement simply from divine activity (the punishment visited on Troy by the gods) to human activity (the war and bloodshed over which Agamemnon presides). The closing observations on the sacker of cities (*ptoliporthēs*, 472) and on those who have killed many (461)—clearly relevant to Agamemnon—do not offer a synthesis of Agamemnon's personal activity and the cosmic justice realized through him; rather, they set Agamemnon against justice and indicate that he too may fall victim to *dikē* (cf. 461 ff.).

SONG AND ACTION

The intransigence of the contradiction (between what Agamemnon sets out to accomplish and the means he must use to accomplish it) is expressed by the inability even of song to overcome it. Song, in fact, is regularly frustrated in *A* and *C*. The *humenaion* becomes a *thrēnos* (cf. *A* 706-11). The old men of the chorus, in seeking to praise Agamemnon when he finally returns, find themselves in some embarrassment as to the proper response;[49] the contradictions involved in Agamemnon's campaign against Troy bewilder them.

It is a contradiction expressed several times and in various ways throughout *A*. In the parodos, for example, the chorus relates the story of the omen visited on the Greek armies assembled at Aulis (104-59). The attack by the vultures foretells the Atreids' victory over Priam and his city; yet the same omen is susceptible to a contradictory interpretation, which stresses rather the plight of the helpless, who are brutally attacked by the vulture. The omens are at once propitious and sinister (*dexia men katamompha de phasmata,* 145). The reason a single omen can contradict itself is that the very means of effecting justice—the attack upon and physical destruction of an opponent—compromises the interpretation of the event as a "just punishment." Such an event can with equal, or even greater, validity be portrayed as a struggle in which one or the other agonist has the advantage; this is precisely how Artemis does define it and insists that the portent, interpreted in this way, be fulfilled.[50] In the omen, therefore, as in the first stasimon, the tension between *dikē* and *nikē* as rival descriptions of the same event is clear.

The powers of *nikē* to subvert claims to justice indicates one of the most fascinating aspects of the so-called "hymn to Zeus" (*A* 160-83), which is, in fact, closer to an epinician. This at least is the name the chorus gives its song (*Zēna de tis prophronōs epinikia klazōn,* 174), and Zeus is portrayed as the great victor.

οὐδ' ὅστις πάροιϑεν ἦν μέγας,
 παμμάχῳ ϑράσει βρύων,
οὐδὲ λέξεται πρὶν ὤν·
ὃς δ' ἔπειτ' ἔφυ, τρια-
 κτῆρος οἴχεται τυχών·
Ζῆνα δέ τις προφρόνως ἐπινίκια κλάζων
τεύξεται φρενῶν τὸ πᾶν·   167-75

The one who once was great, brimming with all-battling courage, will be spoken of as if he had not existed. The one who came after met his master and is gone. But the one who earnestly sings victory odes to Zeus will obtain wisdom in everything.

Zeus is described as a wrestler who has overcome all his opponents; his victory is so great that the chorus denies significance and power to the gods who preceded him. This suggests that Zeus, however much he may be the guardian of *dikē*, nevertheless does not effect an unequivocal kind of justice. Victory in the *Oresteia* is equivocal, since it is the outcome of a combat between two parties, each seeking a successful conclusion; neither has a prior right to success. Attempts to make victory something other than equivocal are bound to fail.

It is suggestive to compare the chorus's claim that Zeus is the undisputed victor (171-72) with the messenger's insistence that Agamemnon's success ought not to be disputed (*ti tauta penthein dei; paroikhetai ponos*, 567). The messenger gives himself the lie, when he recounts the disappearance of Menelaus (*A* 636-80); it is clear that the *ponos* has not "gone away" at all. The same holds true for Zeus' victory. Here, too, it is claimed that those defeated by Zeus have gone away (*triaktēros oikhetai tukhōn*). But the old gods have not gone away, as is made most clear in *Eumenides*. There the Furies distinguish themselves from the new gods; they are the old gods, and not only are they present, they are powers to be reckoned with (*E* 162, 778 ff., 837 ff.). Moreover, in *E* 644-51, Apollo saves Zeus's credibility as an upholder of the father's rights only by pointing out that Zeus did not kill Cronus and that the imprisonment of the older god can yet be undone (*E* 644-51). Cronus, therefore, has not completely "gone away" either.

Immediately after describing Zeus's opponents as "happening upon" (*tukhōn*, 173) the wrestler god, the chorus speaks of the man who "will happen upon" (*teuxetai*, 175) wisdom in everything, by singing epinicians with good will (*prophronōs*) to Zeus. Wisdom seems to be described here as a victory and, certainly, the development of the passage is quite like what is found in epinicians. That is, we find a movement from activity (one obtains wisdom by singing victory odes with good will) to passivity (180-81: "Wisdom comes even to the unwilling"). Wisdom is developed in much the way that victory is in Pindar's odes; like victory, it emerges as something actively sought and, at the same time, received. Wisdom, too, is subject to the mortal conditions whereby even activity is to a large extent a passivity, an ambiguity neatly summed up in the famous phrase *pathein ton erxanta*, "the one who does, suffers" (*A* 1564).

Activity is a putting on of the yoke of necessity, as the chorus says of Agamemnon and his decision at Aulis to sacrifice his daughter Iphigeneia (*A* 218-27). The passage has caused some controversy. *Anagka* has been variously seen as a reference to the family curse that impels Agamemnon to become his daughter's murderer,[51] and to the necessary consequences that follow upon the freely willed act of killing Iphigeneia.[52] We might do better, however, to refer this necessity to the mode of contradiction and of violence that Zeus has imposed on men.

Comparison with *WD* is suggestive. In sending Pandora to Epimetheus, Zeus imposes a world where opposites are inseparable from each other; this is the unavoidable and necessary condition of mortal life. Thus, in embracing the beautiful Pandora, Epimetheus also embraces his own sorrows (*kaka*). Such contradiction, however, is not confined to foolish or evil actions; even the man who would be excellent must embrace difficulties, in order to attain the delights of *aretē* (*WD* 289-92).[53] In short, any human action, whether good or evil, is a "putting on of necessity," since, through his activity, the mortal enters into and grapples with the world, which has been structured in a particular, unavoidable way by the gods.

Agamemnon, then, "puts on the yoke of necessity" by undertaking to act. He decides that he must respect the *summakhia* of the Greek hosts and their anxiety to depart for Troy (cf. 211-17). In deciding to satisfy the army, however—a goal which is certainly proper (*themis*, 217)—Agamemnon undertakes the murder of his own daughter, an action that is "blasphemous, impure, unholy" (cf. 219-20). However, he would have put on the "yoke of necessity," too, by deciding not to sacrifice Iphigeneia, thus trifling with his obligations to the assembled armies.

It is because of this necessary, contradictory character of human action that justice—univocal and universally acknowledged—proves so elusive for the characters in the *Oresteia*. Agamemnon's sack of Troy is both justice and pollution. If people are to hail it as the work of justice, they must ignore one important aspect of it; this is precisely what the messenger urges in his second speech. However, people refuse to blind themselves to the polluted aspects of Agamemnon's crusade. The Greeks mourn their dead and murmur against the Atreids who are responsible for so many deaths. Clytaemnestra refuses to forget Iphigeneia and so plots to avenge her daughter's death.

The first part of *A*, therefore, is given over to an analysis of one attempt to work justice and the contradictory character of this attempt. However, the *Oresteia* as a whole is less concerned with the Trojan War than with the unending chain of reprisals within the Atreid house itself. If the attempt to effect justice is unstable (since it is comprised of both justice and injustice), this instability is also played out over the course of time. For the criminal aspects of Agamemnon's act invite punishment by Clytaemnestra, who in turn claims that she has done a just deed (*A* 1431-36, 1497-1504, 1525-29). This act of justice, however, is itself an act of injustice, as the chorus points out (1407-11, 1505-12), and as Orestes, Electra, and the libation bearers make clear in *C*. Clytaemnestra's

68

act, compounded of opposites, thus invites another act (Orestes'), again inevitably self-contradictory. The movement of justice through time is as troubling as the instability of the single act of justice, for the movement can with equal validity be described as going from crime to punishment (e.g., *C*319-20, 330-31, 383-84, 398, 471-73) or from violence to violence (e.g., *C*309-14, 400-402, 555-57; cf. *A*758-70).

There is, however, another description of events that is one of the greatest importance for the reconciliation finally achieved between the contradictions of justice. Toward the end of the kommos in *C*, Orestes cries that "Ares will clash (*xumbalei*) with Ares, Dikē with Dikē" (461).

It is noteworthy that Orestes describes the proposed revenge both as war and as justice, since the two were contradictory in *A*, and since characters regularly insisted on one or the other description of the success at Troy, but never both. This is in line with that aspect of Orestes, pointed out especially by Peradotto,[54] by which he sees and admits both the justice and the horror of the proposed matricide. In this he is distinguished from the messenger, Agamemnon, and Clytaemnestra, all of whom ignore or attempt to ignore the full complexity of events.

Also significant is the reference to a combat between opposing *dikai*. In *A*, *dikē* was kept distinct from struggle and its uncertainties; Orestes now suggests, however, that justice itself participates in such struggle. The whole situation depicted in *C*, in fact, suggests the same thing, for Aeschylus has set most of the action in the time immediately before the act of vengeance, while the outcome is still uncertain; the expectations and fears of the perpetrators provide the material for the drama. Such a setting inevitably emphasizes the agonistic character of the vengeance. The chorus calls Orestes' encounter with Aegisthus a "wrestling-match," and hopes for his victory (*C*866-68). The motif of rival claims to justice is given a stunning dramatic realization, when Clytaemnestra calls for an axe (889) to battle with the son who is trying to murder her. In *E*, the dispute between the Furies (on Clytaemnestra's behalf) and Apollo (on Orestes' behalf) presents even more emphatically this contest between different claims to justice, and the jury's split vote underlines the validity of the different claims.

Neither of the opposing claims to justice is invalid; no more is either of them absolutely, decisively valid. The limited validity of the rival *dikai* is made clear in *E*, where the strengths and weaknesses of both disputing parties are manifest. The Furies are presented at first as sadistic and disgusting; they rejoice in bloodshed and the torments they bring (e.g., *E*349-96, 179-97). On the other hand, the fear they provoke is a salutary one, since without it men cannot be expected to live justly. Not only do the Furies claim this, but they are seconded by Athena as well (e.g., *E*490-565, 690-706). And yet, the Furies confine themselves

69

to situations where kindred blood has been shed; for this reason, they did not punish Clytaemnestra (E 208–12, 604–608). While clearly having a claim to justice, therefore, the Furies cannot be its sole representatives.

Apollo, on the other hand, is more sensitive to violations of marriage. He cites Zeus's decision to marry a female already his sister as proof that the marriage tie is more important than blood kinship (E 213–18). Later on, however, arguments based on Zeus prove an embarrassment to Apollo, when the Furies point out the contradictions in Apollo's claim that Zeus himself ordered vengeance for Agamemnon's death (E 613–18; cf. 622–24). Zeus bound and tied his own father (640–43), the Furies argue, and so it is a contradiction to claim that he respects the rights of fathers rather than mothers. Apollo defends Zeus by pointing out that Zeus did not do an irreparable deed; in arguing thus, he plays into the Furies' hands, for Orestes is guilty of just such an irreparable crime (E 644–56).

The dispute between the Furies and Apollo, therefore, is not a dispute between univocal right and univocal wrong but between rival claims, each one with a measure of justice, and each one somehow compromised. It is, in short, a struggle between equals.

It is only now that justice becomes possible as a constructive, stabilizing force in human society. As long as men are under the illusion that *dikē* can be kept distinct from the inescapable mode of strife, their attempts to effect justice are confounded, and *dikē* remains murderous and inexorable. But once *dikē* is presented as something that results from the dispute and *agōn* of competing claimants, it can take its place in a society of mortals, for it itself participates in the mortal mode of strife.

The similarity between the *Oresteia* and several of the victory odes we have considered is unmistakable. Pindar begins those odes with a description of victory as something already accomplished. There is no mention, at this point, of the sweat and toil that went into the accomplishment of the victory. This has an analogy in *A*, where the messenger and the king insist that justice has been executed and try to deny any importance to what preceded the final destruction of Troy.

In the subsequent parts of the odes, however, Pindar returns to the time before the victory and shows the roots of the current success in the athlete's combat and uncertainty. This is also what Aeschylus does in moving from *A* to *C*. In *A*, the victory over Troy is past and done with. Neither do we see Clytaemnestra plotting her husband's death; she does not speak about it in an outright way until it has been accomplished. In *C*, however, Aeschylus sets the action, for the most part, before the act of vengeance, to show the uncertainty and anxiety attending *dikē*. Orestes, Electra, and the chorus must pray that their attempt will have success.

70

It is the victory's rootedness in mortal modes of strife that makes of it not an individual's special privilege but a universally valid phenomenon; it is by insisting on these roots that the poet is able to recommend the victor to the attention and admiration of all mortals. Again, a similar development in the *Oresteia* is evident. The uncertainty attending the attempt at revenge in *C* points out the agonistic or competitive character of what Orestes does and suggests the description of events as *"dikē against dikē."* In *E,* the debate between the Furies and Apollo makes even more explicit the strife between different *dikai,* and it is precisely this new presentation of *dikē* and strife that makes possible a valid, universally approved justice.

This new method of executing justice is established by Athena and consists not in one person doing violence to another, but a body of men listening to a debate between the opposing parties and making its decision by majority vote. The reason this is a successful means to justice is that it respects the necessary conditions of strife and uncertainty that have been imposed on mortals. The jury does this, first by calling for a debate between the disputants before any decision is made (*E* 428–42). Furthermore, the plurality of claims to justice is mirrored in the use not of a single judge, but several jurors. The decision handed down makes no pretense of being univocal; the jury's vote in *E* is as divided as it can be, as Athena announces. [55]

The most striking accomplishment of the jury, however, is that it brings the long history of bloodshed in the Atreid household to an end. Whatever the anger shown by the Furies when Orestes' acquittal is announced, they never threaten to violate the decision handed down by Athena and her jury. Thus, the jury manages a stable form of *dikē,* which now becomes a constructive force in society, a means of ending violence. This stability is a godlike thing, since the predominant mode of mortal life is flux and uncertainty. Thus, the jury's effectiveness parallels that of encomiastic song, which achieves a stable, "immortal" *kleos* for the individual. Moreover, the features of the jury system that enable it to effect this authoritative, final *dikē* are just those by virtue of which song can immortalize.

First, the jury format mirrors the necessarily agonistic character of *dikē,* and it formalizes the strife first into a debate between the disputing parties and then into a vote where the majority count wins. In designing an elaborate procedure after the model of strife, Athena not only acknowledges, but reveals, the nature of *dikē* as strife. The preestablished pattern of the trial casts its participants into certain roles. Those who appear before the jury are cast not as "just" and "unjust" but as agonists.

Song, too, can provide a miniature or formalization of strife, as we have seen in chapter 1. I argued there that song is, for Pindar, a *praxis,*

71

in which the poet struggles (cf. *Nem.* 4.93-96) to make something god-like. Throughout the odes, Pindar emphasizes the fact that song is work and *ponos*, which secures an undying renown for the victor. While the poem is itself a *praxis*, however, it also observes poetic decorum or *tethmos;* that is, it represents a structuring of labor and accomplishment so that these conform to canons of artistic order.[56] By imposing an order on the athlete's and poet's struggle and success, the ode makes of these a paradigm, a knowable object; it reveals the essential pattern of all mortal activity.

Another notable feature of the jury is that it is designed as an artificial federation of several individuals and thus overcomes the necessary limitations of the single person.[57] Individuals are necessarily set in opposition by their specifying characteristics (old-young; male-female); a new entity, however, comprised of many persons, subsumes and reconciles the opposites. We may refer to the "totalization" of qualities that the jury effects. That is, as presented by Aeschylus, the jury takes qualities that are contradictory in the natural world and includes them all in a new, artificial body, which is thus characterized by various qualities simultaneously. (This is not to say, of course, that the historical Athenian jury consisted of males and females alike, for it did not. However, it did represent a communal mode of arriving at authoritative legal decisions. To express this, and to suggest the way in which the jury format resolves certain problems inherent in human communities, Aeschylus uses the systems of sexual imagery he has developed over the course of the trilogy.)

The jury as "totalizer" finds its most striking expression in the character of Athena, who designs it; she subsumes and reconciles in herself the features separating the disputants. She is female (like the Furies) and yet honors the male in all things (737). Even so, Athena rejects the male in marriage (737) and therefore, although she supports Apollo's argument that the father is the true parent (736, cf. 657-66), yet she is like the Furies who neglect the marriage bond and, in Apollo's words, "dishonor Aphrodite" (*E* 213-16). Even in deciding for one disputant over another, therefore, Athena remains an ambivalent and reconciling figure.

Athena belongs to the younger generation of gods, and yet she respects and supplicates the older gods (the Furies, cf. 881-84). The jury, like its designer, also combines features of the younger and older gods. Characteristic of the younger gods is the contractual or consensual aspect of the jury. Both Apollo and the Furies agree to let Athena adjudicate the dispute, and they trust in her to make the proper decision; it is only because both parties do consent that the artifical jury format is able to have any effect. This feature suggests a certain kinship with Apollo, who emphasizes the importance of the contractual bond of marriage over the Furies' insistence on the blood ties between mother and child (*E* 210-21).

However, if the jury is a consensual, artificial system, it is also overseen and protected by the primal powers of the Furies. The jurymen are strictly bound to observe and execute justice; dread of the consequences of injustice provides the surety. The rival claims of Apollo and the Furies are in this way incorporated into the jury, and it is this combination (of what had been rival claims) that gives the jury its ability to execute a final, universally recognized justice.

By virtue of its corporate or communal character, then, the jury succeeds in achieving a stable *dikē*. The individual cannot work a final, universally approved justice on his own behalf. Similarly, the individual is incapable of winning immortality for himself. Just as Clytaemnestra's attempt to work justice results in a despicable crime, so does the attempt of Ixion, for example, to possess Hera end in his own destruction (cf. *Pyth.* 2). The athlete must be accorded his *kleos* by those who witness and understand his success, and especially by the poet. (A comparison of the victory ode and the jury suggests why the epinician is appropriately a choral performance. That a number of people offer tribute, rather than a single poet, indicates the social character of praise, by which the victor is welcomed back to his community.[58]) Both *dikē* and *kleos* are forms of acknowledgment by others of one's deeds. In working justice or securing *kleos,* therefore, structures or institutions are necessary, in which the individual and the community confront each other. Thus, the jury system establishes a means by which the disputants can gain a public hearing, and encomiastic song provides a means by which the returning victor and the community can address each other.

As for the distinctions between "good" and "bad" that a cultural institution must make, these are of a confessedly limited validity. Throughout the *Oresteia,* Aeschylus insists on the inextricability of opposites. Agamemnon is both a criminal and a divine avenger. Moreover, the jury is set up in such a way as to make clear that each of the disputants may very well have a measure of justice in this case. The encomiast faces the same dilemma, as may be seen most clearly in the scolion by Simonides considered in the excursus to chapter 1. There too, Simonides would distinguish *agathos* from *kakos,* but he sees that one easily becomes the other when circumstances dictate.

Throughout archaic poetry, in fact, there is an awareness that, in one way, people are not distinguished from each other; they form a single race of mortals, whose differences melt away before the far more staggering gap dividing gods from mortals. There is a natural condition, imposed by the gods, which cannot be legislated away by men. This is not to deny the validity of distinctions: Simonides goes on to define the type of man he will praise, and Athena and the jury of Athenians acquit Orestes. These distinctions, however, are always made with the awareness that they are not ultimate and exist in relationship to a certain intransigent sameness. To ensure that the distinctions between "guilty" and "innocent" have the validity that is possible for them, the jurors swear oaths and are answerable to the Furies. Similarly, Pindar insists throughout the odes on his good faith; he seeks to "praise the praiseworthy, sowing blame for sinners (*alitroi*)" (*Nem.* 8.39).

The several connections between epinician song and the jury indicate something more than the general coherence of the archaic outlook on nature and culture. Athletic games and justice seem to be connected historically as well as structurally. Karl Meuli has suggested that the origins of the national games may have been duels wherein the group ascertained the party responsible for a third person's death. The violent combat was a means of precluding further violence, brought on by the thirst for revenge. Less speculatively, Louis Gernet has pointed out the numerous similarities between legal procedures and games, as these are described in Homer. The connections between the *Oresteia* and Pindar's odes have predecessors in the similarities between the trial scene on Achilles' shield and the funeral games of Patroclus.[59]

This historical background alerts us, however, to a distinguishing feature of the games Pindar celebrated—viz., the athlete did not necessarily enter them in order to win property. In Homer, on the other hand, contestants expect prizes of real, market value. The prizes are not free "gifts" given by Achilles, the sponsor of the games. When a prize comes into the competitor's possession, the expressions used stress the fact that the athlete takes it on his own account, not as a gift (e.g., *aeirein, lambanein, haptesthai*). Gernet describes this taking as "self-help" and shows that a similar idea is involved in legal disputes, where the person who wins the decision "takes" the property that had caused the dispute.

The connections between Pindar and the victor are different from those between Achilles and the competitors. Although the poem resembles the prizes in the Homeric games, in that both serve as a public sign of the athlete's performance and success, yet the ode is closer to being a gift—that is, an exchange which creates or maintains a bond of *philotēs* between the two.

Pindar is allied with the athlete not only because he accords him praise, but also because he is a fellow contender. In the next chapter, I will consider in greater detail the bonds joining poet and athlete. Pindar uses the fellowship of the symposium and even erotic motifs to throw light on his friendship with the athlete, and so it will be necessary to consider Pindar's use of motifs from symposiastic and erotic

74

lyric poetry in his epinicians. The discussion should serve incidentally to throw light on the connections between epinician and other kinds of lyric poetry.

3

Victory, Symposium, and Eros

At the close of *Isth.2*, Pindar tells the victor Xenokrates that victory songs depend as much on the athlete's excellence as on the poet's. "Never silence your ancestral excellence, nor these hymns, since I have not worked on them that they may be idle" (44-46). The song grows from the athlete's, as well as the poet's, *aretē*. The friendship (*philotēs*) that binds the two men together is analogous to the jury, instituted by Athena as a means of banding members of the *polis* together. The song of praise derives from the partnership of poet and athlete, just as the legal settlement is a corporate decision by the jury. The similarity between song and jury is perhaps strengthened by the fact that the *philotēs* of poet and athlete is less a matter of emotional ties than an objective state associated with the institution of hospitality.[1] *Philotēs* is a pact concluded between the stranger and the head of a local house, whereby the two become *philoi* ("friends") and exist henceforth in a reciprocal relation of services and good will.

The institution makes possible a kind of portable community, so that the stranger is not unprotected. This relation can be inherited, as is clear, for example, from the encounter of Diomedes and Glaucus in *Il.6*. 119-236. When Glaucus identified himself, Diomedes rejoiced (*gēthēsen*, 212) and hailed him as a *xeinos patrōios palaios* ("an ancestral guest of our fathers," 215), since his grandfather Oeneus had once been host to Bellerophon, an ancestor of Glaucus.

Pindar stresses the fact that he and his patron are *philoi* and that his songs are a part of their bond of *philotēs*. He has received hospitality at his patron's table,[2] or he has ancestral ties with him, whether of kinship or guest rites.[3]

The bond of *philotēs* is a reciprocal one. So, in *Pyth.10* the patron Thorax is described as "yoking up the chariot" of the Muses of Pindar, and as "loving one who loves him, leading one who leads him" (*phileōn phileont', agōn agonta,* 64-66). Their common goals, their similarity in virtue and outlook are indicated by the fact that in some passages it is unclear whether Pindar is talking about himself or his patron; in such cases, the ambiguity would appear to be deliberate.[4] In *Nem.* 1.19 ff., for example, Pindar describes Khromios's hospitality, and goes on to discuss excellence more generally.

I stood at the court-gates of that guest-loving man, singing fine songs; there a proper dinner was arranged for me; that house is no stranger to men of other lands. He has won good men to bring water upon slanderers' smoke.[5] Men all have different skills. Walking on straight paths, by means of our inborn worth (*phua*) we must contend. For those who innately see what will be, might accomplishes by deed, mind by counsels. Because of your ways, son of Hagesidamos, you enjoy both this one and that. I do not love to hide and have great wealth in my halls, but to fare well and be esteemed in doing good to my friends. For common are the hopes of much-toiling men (19-33).

Throughout the passage, Pindar stresses the similarity of the two men. Khromios is generous (20-24); Pindar approves of this and conducts his life in the same way (31-32).[6] Khromios has won a victory with strength and intelligence (27), and Pindar too uses his native skills in silencing detractors (24-25). Both are men who labor (*poluponoi andres*) and their hopes, therefore, are alike (32-33).[7]

In *Nem.* 10, Pindar devotes the final part of the ode to the story of Castor and Polydeuces, and the brothers' loyalty to each other may have suggestions of the relationship between the poet and the athlete. Pindar describes the brothers' fight with Idas and Lynceus. Polydeuces managed to overwhelm both of them, but not before Castor had been fatally wounded. While Castor breathes his last, Polydeuces weeps and says:

Πάτερ Κρονίων, τίς δὴ λύσις
ἔσσεται πενθέων; καὶ ἐμοὶ θάνατον σὺν
τῷδ᾽ ἐπίτειλον, ἄναξ.
οἴχεται τιμὰ φίλων τατωμένῳ
φωτί · παῦροι δ᾽ ἐν πόνῳ πιστοὶ βροτῶν
καμάτου μεταλαμβάνειν

Father, son of Cronus, what release will there be from my griefs? Send death for me with this man, lord! Gone is honor when a man is deprived of his friends. Few among mortals are trustworthy in hard times, to take a share in the toil! (*Nem.* 10.76-79).

The language here would be appropriate in the political poems of Alcaeus, for example, where the poet celebrates the ties binding members of the *hetairia,* or political fellowship. In an epinician, however, the language suggests that the bond between Castor and Polydeuces is like the one between the athlete and the poet. Thus "release" (*lusis*) and related words (*lutērios, luō*) are commonly used in the epinicians of the time after victory, and, more particularly, of the release from anxiety afforded by acknowledgment and song.[8] "Trustworthy" (*pistos*) is regularly used to describe the poet in his disposition toward the victor,[9] and "friends" or *philoi*, as we have seen, refers to ties of hospitality, such as join the poet and athlete. Moreover, Polydeuces' wish to die, rather than live bereft of *timā*, is comparable to Pindar's accounts of Ajax's refusal to live after he had been denied the just acknowledgment of his worth (*Nem.* 7.24-31 and 8.27; *Isth.* 4.35-36b).

Thus, the *philotēs* of poet and athlete seems to resemble the loyalty of Polydeuces to his brother. That is, the kind of loyalty which finds expression on the mythic plane in Polydeuces' faithfulness to Castor can be seen, in contemporary situations, in the friendship of poet and athlete.[10] Polydeuces refuses life as a god for himself and chooses instead to alternate between life in heaven and an existence under the earth, so that Castor may have the same privilege and not die completely. The two Dioscuri are both chthonic and uranian; they embrace two different realms. Here too they perhaps provide a model for the partnership of the poet and athlete, who, as wise men and victors, mingle a godlike glory with a mortal condition.

In the *Nicomachean Ethics,* Aristotle devotes two books to the subject of *philia* ("friendship") and distinguishes three kinds, which correspond to the three objects of love—the good, the pleasant, and the useful (*EN* 8.1156a6-b32). There exists, that is, the friendship of good men (who esteem the goodness in each other), the friendship based on pleasure, and that based on utility. Each kind involves some kind of mutual regard and benevolence in respect to that which prompts the *philia*. For example, one member of a *philia* based on utility truly wishes well to the other, insofar as the other's well-being is useful to himself. Such a *philia* does not regard the person for his own sake, but only to the extent that he serves a purpose. The same is true of the *philia* based on pleasure; in such a bond, the members seek only the pleasure to be had from the other.

These two kinds of *philia*, then, are incidental (*kata sumbebēkos*) to the person. To translate them as "friendship" may be misleading, insofar as the English word inevitably suggests personal affection. As Aristotle stresses, however, the *philia* of utility does not necessarily entail friendly feelings; such "friends" may not even find each other's company pleasant and need not seek to spend time with each other. Business agreements and contracts for the exchange of services come under this heading.

The friendship of *agathoi,* men of similar excellence (*aretē*), is the perfect (*teleia*) friendship. It regards the person in his own right, and therefore is not "incidental" (*kata sumbebēkos*) to the person. It is en-

78

during, because it is not based on shifting interests but on the more stable ground of excellent character; that is, the *philoi* wish well to each other *qua* good. Such a friendship includes the other two kinds. For, as Aristotle says, the good that *agathoi* esteem is also pleasant to them. Moreover, the useful is useful in virtue of its being conducive to the good or the pleasant (1155b19-21), so that the friendship of good men seems to subsume the useful friendship as well.

The *philotēs* of poet and victor evinces characteristics of all three kinds of the Aristotelian *philiai*. Poet and athlete are both *agathoi*, distinguished for their excellence, and both desire good things for each other. The permanence of the friendship, emphasized by Aristotle as characteristic of this best kind, is stressed by Pindar, too, when he hopes for future victories for the athlete, which he will celebrate. On the other hand, Aristotle says that the guest-host relation—upon which Pindar most often bases his friendship with the victor—is considered a friendship of advantage or utility (1156a30).[11] Features associated with friendship of this second kind are also to be found in the odes. Money is requested, for example, or the ode is presented as a "contract job," with the poet apologizing for failing to meet the stipulated deadline. The poet-athlete relationship appears in such odes as a business friendship, compacted on set terms, with the promise that goods will be delivered by a certain date (cf. *EN* 1162b25-29).

Pindar's use of erotic language throughout the odes to describe the bonds between him and the victor suggests the third kind of friendship recognized by Aristotle: friendships of pleasure. Thus, Pindar presents his friendship with the victor in a number of ways, and the relationship of these various descriptions to each other has proved troublesome. In particular, the mercantile aspects of *philotēs* sit uneasily with the description of it as the mutual benevolence of good men.[12] I will consider, then, the connections among these three kinds of friendship.

If the friendship Pindar describes seems to embrace the different kinds of *philia* distinguished by Aristotle, the means he uses to describe his friendship are similarly embracing, for he makes use of motifs from symposiastic and erotic poetry as well to offer tribute to his victorious athletes. One reason Pindar can adapt these other kinds of song to his own purposes is that they too grow from the association or *koinōnia* of the poet and his or her fellows. The poet and his fellow banqueters are joined by the friendship of the table; this fellowship, moreover, often has close political ties, as in the sympotic poetry of Alcaeus and Theognis, and in several of the Attic scolia, or drinking songs.

Members of the *hetairia* are animated by a single political purpose that finds expression in these poems. So when Alcaeus's political enemy Myrsilus dies, it is time to get drunk. "Now we must be drunk and drink with all our might, since Myrsilus has died" (Alc. 332P). Alcaeus calls wine the window into a man (*anthropō dioptron,* 333 P), and he seems to mean by this that at the table one comes to know the true character of one's fellows. Xenophanes too presents the symposium as a way of discovering the praiseworthy man. "Praise (*ainein*) that one among men who, when he drinks, reveals noble thoughts as his memory and striving for excellence enable him" (1.19-20;[13] cf. also Theognis 499-502).

The precise nature of the circle of young girls who attended Sappho is controversial.[14] Sappho speaks of her *moisopolōn oikia* ("household of those who tend the Muse," 150 LP) and refers to her "companions" for whom the odes seem to have been performed. "These delights now for my companions will I sing," she says in fr. 160. The companions in the *thiasos* were not all from the vicinity,[15] and a number of the poems deal with the departure of girls from the circle for home or husband.[16] A cult of Aphrodite may have been a part of the life of the circle. In 2 LP, Sappho calls upon Aphrodite to come from Crete "to this pure temple, where there is a pleasing grove of quinces, and altars with burning frankincense; cold water echoes through the quince branches; the entire place is shadowed with roses, and sleep drifts down from the quivering leaves. . . "[17]

Certainly, the cultivation of song and dance was a part of their life. Not only have we Sappho's reference to the "household of those who tend the Muse," but the odes seem to have served as a way of communication between Sappho and the girls, the addressees of several of her poems. Moreover, a poem from the Greek Anthology (9.189) provides an interesting description of a chorus of women led by Sappho. "Come to the gleaming sanctuary of Hera with her eyes of a bull, you women of Lesbos, moving your feet in light steps. There you will make a fair chorus for the goddess. Sappho, with a golden lyre in her hands, will lead you. Happy in the joyous dance, you will seem to hear the sweet song of Calliope herself!" The circle seems to have provided an education; Sappho's companions are also called her *mathētriai* ("students").[18]

Whatever the exact nature of this company, there seem to have been others like it on Lesbos—young girls who attended and were instructed by a woman. We hear of Gorgo and Andromeda, who had "schools" of young female companions.[19] It has been argued that the ode to Aphrodite may give some evidence for the institutional character of such circles. In speaking of the girl she loves, Sappho uses words like *adikia* ("injustice") and *philotēs,* perhaps suggesting some quasi-legal bond of fealty among members of the *thiasos.*[20] In any case, the expression of erotic sentiment should be understood within this context of the ties binding young women and their teacher. Homosexuality, if in fact there was overt expression of it, must be understood as a part of the entire life of the circle. The girls were Sappho's companions and students and may have been her lovers occasionally as well.[21]

Sappho's erotic odes, therefore, emerged from the circle of the poet and her companions. In the odes are mingled two aspects—the erotic and the musical—of their life together.

Merkelbach writes that all poetry of the archaic period was composed for a society and was firmly rooted in the situation here and now.[22] So, for example, the military poems of Tyrtaeus are meant to heighten the communal spirit of the fighters, and in his elegies Solon urges the Athenians not to harm the *polis* (yet another form of *koinōnia*) by their injustice.[23] The drinking song, or scolion, sometimes urges concord and intimacy among the members of the party:

> σύν μοι πῖνε συνήβα συνέρα συστεφανηφόρει,
> σύν μοι μαινομένῳ μαίνεο, σύν σώφρονι σωφρόνει

Drink with me, be young with me, love with me, wear crowns with me; rage when I rage, be temperate when I am temperate (902 P).

In all these cases, the song not only is performed for members of the *koinōnia* but is itself an expression of the ties that bind together the members of the community.

What is distinctive about all these kinds of song is that the situation of the poet and his audience itself becomes the theme of the song. The singer speaks in the first person; he addresses someone by name and explains why he is speaking. In this, lyric is distinguishable from epic. The epic poet sings about a world distant from his audience and the occasion which has brought poet and audience together; the lyric poet makes his song out of that very occasion.

The lyric poem is not "about" a subject, in the way that epic is "about" Odysseus or Achilles. The symposiastic poem is not "about" the symposium; rather, it is a part of the celebration. No more is erotic poetry "about" love; it is itself a part of the lovers' relationship, a move in the lover's strategy to win the beloved. Similarly, the epinician is not a disinterested account of victory, nor is it a narrative concerning the victorious athlete; the poem—addressed to the victor—is itself the recognition and acknowledgment that is vital to the completion of the victory.

The epic song informs about a distant time or place, and the epic poet therfore prays to the Muses as a source of information. It is their control over the true and the false that is important. So the goddesses, when they inaugurate Hesiod as a poet, tell him, "We know how to speak many lies like the truth; when we wish, we know how to proclaim true things" (*Th.* 27–28). The other poets considered in this chapter do not need information, since their song deals with what is present. Rather than inform, they seek to charm, and so they pray to the Muses to make their words beautiful (e.g., Alcman 27 P).[24] The charm has a persuasive function; it is meant to effect in some way an ongoing situation. The epinician poet, for example, attempts to make the victor "memorable," someone whom people will talk about; in this he differs from the epic poet, who receives and transmits the memorable stories of old.

Hesiod offers a description of this persuasive power of song, in the passage on the Muse Calliope and the kings:

> She is preeminent among all the Muses. For she accompanies kings, who compel reverence. Whomever the daughters of great Zeus honor and look upon, as born from god-nourished kings, on this man's tongue they pour sweet dew; the words from his mouth flow sweet. The people regard him according judgments with staight decisions (*dikai*). He addresses them with no stumbling (*asphaleōs*); quickly and skillfully he stops a great wrangling (*neikos*). Kings are (called) wise, because when the people do injury to each other, they accomplish in the agora deeds which turn the situation around, and this they do easily, persuading with gentle words. . . . Such is the Muses' holy gift to men" (*Th.* 79–93).

The king's ability, thanks to the Muses, to influence events is comparable to the lyric poet's skills. Both address themselves to a current situation; for both, beauty and sweetness of language are all important.

We can distinguish the gift Hesiod describes here from the other gift, described earlier in the poem, when the Muses inaugurate the shepherd Hesiod as a poet. In that passage, the Muses describe themselves as knowledgeable, informative goddesses, with power over truth and falsehood (27-28). The poetic gift they give Hesiod is like the talent of the epic poet, in that this is poetry which informs about things not present. In the *Theogony* Hesiod celebrates both future and past (31); he is to sing of the gods who exist always (33). The subjects of Hesiod's song are separated either by time (the past, the future) or by space (the gods). The *Theogony* as a whole is within this tradition of poetry as knowledge of things not immediate.

On the other hand, the *Works and Days*, prompted by a specific situation and directed toward correcting the situation, is closer to the tradition represented by the Muses' gift to the king; that is, song as a potent force for effecting change within a community. We may see here an archaic classification of song, according to whether the song deals with things present or not present, whether it is "persuasive" or "informative."[25] The classification seems to be valid beyond the Hesiodic corpus. Much lyric poetry—including epinicians—is "present" and "persuasive" and, to that extent, may be classified along with Hesiod's *Works and Days.*

Pindar's frequent stress, in the epinicians, on the novelty of his verse[26] may have less to do, therefore, with the poet's independent stand toward tradition than with the genre of his song. That is, rather than receiving information about a memorable past, he seeks, as a "messenger" of victory, to give new information and to make it memorable.[27] He not only perpetuates a tradition, he seeks to add something new and contemporary to it, by his celebration of athletes.

Pindar's use of symposiastic and erotic poetry for his epinician songs, then, is facilitated by the kinship of these different kinds of poetry. This kinship is due to the fact that all grow from a *koinōnia* and in various ways reflect on it. A concrete instance of this kinship is the *kōmos*, an institution associated with both the epinician and the symposium. Pindar refers to the *kōmos*, or "revel," several times in the odes (e.g., *Ol.* 4.9, 6.98, and 9.4; *Pyth.* 4.1-2; *Nem.* 3.5, and 9.1; *Isth.* 8.4), and it is a staple of sympotic poetry as well (e.g., Theognis 886, 940, 1045-46; Alc. 374P). Wine and love making, in their turn, are intimately associated, as is most clear in the convivial odes of Anacreon (e.g., 14, 38 Gentili; cf. Attic scolion 902P, Theognis 877). Some of Alcaeus's symposiastic songs, too, seem to have been of an erotic character (Alc. 430P=Hor. *O.* 1.32.3ff.)

The symposiastic connections of the victory ode are suggested by Pindar's habit of comparing his own songs to drinks in a festal surrounding. Thus, the ode is a "musical drink" (*Nem.* 3.79), and in offering his song, the poet is like one who toasts the groom in the company of his *philoi* (*Ol.* 7.1-10). The ode as libation pervades *Isth.* 6, where the ode is compared to a drink offering to Zeus at a symposium (1-9) and Pindar speaks of "giving a drink from the pure water of Dirce" to the victor and his family (74); the mythic narrative too deals with a toast raised by Heracles, while Telamon and his company dined (35-56). Moreover, a number of motifs recurrent in symposiastic poetry are to be found in the victory odes as well. Victory and the symposium are both offered as "ultimate" happiness—the *eudaimonia* beyond which it is forbidden for men to seek.

Throughout his epinicians, Pindar defines the ultimate. In *Nem.* 9, for instance, he says, "If one wins renowned glory with many possessions, there is no further goal that mortal man may touch with his feet" (46-47); cf. also *Ol.* 1.99-100, 113-14; 3.42-44, 6.4-7. As for the symposium, Odysseus tells the assembled Phaeacians, "Surely it is a good thing to hear a singer such as [Demodocus], like in voice to the gods. For I say there is no consummation (*telos*) more pleasing than when festal cheer (*euphrosunē*) holds all the people, and the banqueters, seated in order, hear the singer throughout the house; the tables brim beside them with food and meats, and drawing wine from the mixing bowl, the steward brings and pours it into cups. This seems to my heart to be most beautiful" (*Od.* 9.3-10).

SONG AND ACTION

As "ultimates," victory and wine are ambiguous. Throughout the victory odes, Pindar warns against the insolence that good fortune may cause. Victory is undeniably a good, but it is also dangerous. The happiness of Tantalus, to cite just one instance, shows the peril of excessive good fortune (*Ol.* 1.37 ff.). Ambivalence toward wine is a common feature in sympotic poetry as well. So in Theognis we read, "Wine, I praise you, but also blame you. I cannot totally love or hate you. Good and evil you are. Who would blame you, who would praise you, if one has a measure of wisdom?" (873-76). It is perhaps significant that the poet uses the encomiastic language of praise and blame in a symposiastic context; conversely, in his victory ode, Pindar deals with Tantalus in terms of the banquets he shared with the gods (*Ol.* 1.36-39) and with mortals (*Ol.* 1.60-64). The victory ode and sympotic poetry, then, can each borrow the other's motifs. Moreover, the response to the ambiguity is the same in the victory ode and the symposiastic song, both of which stress the need for moderation.[28]

Wine and victory are alike in that each gives proof of the person's qualities. "Wine, lad, and true things," Alcaeus says (366P), and "Wine is the window of man" (333P). In Theognis, we read, "In fire, skilled men recognize gold and silver, but wine shows the mind of man" (499-500). The way a person handles his drinks offers a guage of his worth. Similarly, Pindar says that the trial (in athletic competition) shows the good man (cf. *Ol.* 4.18; *Nem.* 3.70-71; *Pyth.* 3.80-83) and, of course, response to victory separates the good from the jealous and unjust. Moreover, victory and wine enable one to forget the past. For Alcaeus, wine is *lathikadeos* ("forgetful of care," 346.3), and in *Ol.* 2, Pindar says that we can forget the sorrows of the past when we enjoy a happy *potmos* (18); cf. *Nem.* 10.24.

The praise of youth, a common motif in symposiastic poetry, can sound much like certain passages in the victory odes. Hence, in Theognis, we read: "I play, delighting in my youth. Like a voiceless rock I will lie below the earth for a long time once I've lost my life. I will leave the lovely light of the Sun, and though I am noble (*esthlos*), I will see nothing more" (567-70). Pelops in *Ol.* 1 is prompted to compete by similar considerations. "Those for whom death is necessity—why would anyone sit in the darkness and nurse a nameless old age in vain, without a share in all beautiful things?" (82-84).

I want now to investigate the symposiastic song for what it has to say about the connections between the victor and epinician poetry. It will be shown that human *koinōniai* are based ultimately on the distinction between mortal and immortal, and the consequent "kinship" of all mortals. At the same time, however, the distance between men and gods brings scarcity and therefore the need for the individual to look out for himself. There is a certain necessary distance between individuals, and hence a constant need to maintain equity and due proportion in their dealings with each other. Pindar's use of erotic motifs, as I will also try to show, is important for all aspects of victory, but, more particularly, illuminates the combination of intimacy and distance that characterizes the *philotēs* of poet and athlete. By referring his relationship with the victor to the basic conditions of the mortal race, Pindar shows the aspects of his *philotēs* that are characteristic of all human *koinōniai*.

The symposium looms large in *Nem.* 9, a poem composed in honor of the Sicilian Khromios, on the occasion of his chariot victory in the games at Sicyon. The ode presents the return voyage to Aetna of the victor and his retinue. In the first lines of the poem, we are in Sicyon, and the company is just preparing to leave. "We will revel from (the sanctuary of) Apollo at Sicyon, o Muses, to newly founded Aetna, to the prospering house of Khromios, where the open doors are overcome with guests (*xeinōn*)" (1-3). By the end of the poem, we have arrived in Aetna, and the symposium is about to begin. "Someone, stir it up, the sweet prophet of the *kōmos*. Pour out the violent child of the vine in the silver cups which once his horses won and sent to Khromios from Sicyon, with the crowns of Apollo, plaited in justice (*themiplektois*)" (50-53).

These verses show a number of motifs common in sympotic poetry—for example, the command to prepare the wine and the promise of exhilaration. In Anacreon 38 G, for example, we read:

φέρ᾽ ὕδωρ, φέρ᾽ οἶνον, ὦ παῖ,
φέρε ⟨δ᾽⟩ ἀνθεμεῦντας ἡμὶν
στεφάνους, ἔνεικον, ὡς δὴ
πρὸς Ἔρωτα πυκταλίζω

Bring water, Bring wine, slave! Bring us crowns of flowers; bring them so I may box with Eros.

The command to the servant to prepare the cup which we find here is seen in *Nem.* 9 as well. The "hortatory tone" is one of the traditional features of symposiastic poetry.[29]

Another common device in these poems is to name the occasion that prompts the symposium. So, in the Alcaeus fragment cited above, Myrsilus's death is named as the occasion of the drinking party. In other passages, too, Alcaeus takes care to say why a symposium is called for—e.g., 347 (hot weather), 338 (cold weather), 346 LP (twilight). Anacreon calls for drinks upon being freed from the snares of Eros (65 G). The symposium, moreover, is also appropriate in times of sorrow:

οὐ χρῆ κάκοισι θῦμον ἐπιτρέπην,
προκόψομεν γὰρ οὐδὲν ἀσάμενοι,

85

SONG AND ACTION

ὦ Βύκχι, ϕαρμάκων δ᾽ ἄριστον
οἶνον ἐνεικαμένοις μεθύσθην   Alcaeus 335P

We must not give our hearts over to evils; we will get nowhere by vexing ourselves; Bukkhis, the best cure is to fetch wine and be drunk.

Alcaeus begins his brief poem by identifying what one must not do (*ou khrē*); just as in the opening verses of 332P, the audience is told what it is necessary to do (*nun khrē*). In both 332 and 335P, Alcaeus identifies the drinking party as the proper response to a given situation. This suggests the question: Why is the symposium a proper response to hardship, and how does this relate to the symposium as a response to happy occasions (e.g., victory)?

In Alcaeus 38a, the poet draws some connections between grief and the drinking party. Alcaeus begins by proposing to his friend Melanippus a drinking session, and he follows this with a reminder of the inescapability of death. "Having crossed Acheron's whirling stream, never will you see again the pure light of the sun. Come! Do not aim at great things!" He alludes next to Sisyphus, who boasted that he would defeat death; the story continues:

ἀλλὰ καὶ πολύιδρις ἔων ὐπὰ κᾶρι [δὶς
διννάεντ᾽ Ἀχέροντ᾽ ἐπέραισε, μ[
α]ὖτῳ μόχθον ἔχην Κρονίδαις βα[σίλευς κάτω
μελαίνας χθόνος   7-10

But, though he was clever, he crossed whirling Acheron under the sway of doom two times; and the son of Kronos, king below the dark earth, planned hard labor for him. . . .

The lesson is the familiar one of the vanity of overweening human ambitions. If we trust the supplement *dis*, the verses may be more pointed: in attempting something as hubristic as the defeat of death, Sisyphus in effect dies twice, for he "defeats" death by crossing the river Acheron and entering Hades' kingdom. Alcaeus suggests the paradox of Sisyphus's "achievement"—viz., that it consists in doing twice what he wants most to avoid.

The remaining fragments of the poem give no clear meaning. They are translated by Page. "But come, do not . . . now, if ever . . . to suffer whatsoever of them . . . the wind Boreas. . . ." Despite the broken sense, it is clear that Alcaeus returns to address Melanippus, and urges a particular course of action. It is likely that moderation ("do not [aim at great things?]") and patience ("to suffer whatsoever of these") are urged. Thus, both before and after the Sisyphus passage, Melanippus

86

is urged to behave in a certain way. He is invited first to join a drinking party; he is soon urged to resign himself patiently. I want to argue that these two admonitions amount to much the same thing—that is, that drinking together is a sign of not wanting impossible things and of a willingness to shoulder the burdens sent to men by the gods. To support my argument, I will consider some passages in the *Iliad,* where the motifs of resignation and the shared banquet are joined. I argue that the relation between the symposium and patience in the Alcaeus poem is the same as that between the shared dinner and patience in the epic.

In book 19 of the *Iliad,* Odysseus urges Achilles to eat before returning to battle. It is the scene where Achilles abjures his wrath and is reconciled to Agamemnon and the Achaeans. Agamemnon had proposed a ceremony in which gifts would be given to Achilles as a pledge of their reconciliation (19.185-97), the son of Peleus, however, is all for returning immediately to the battle, to take vengeance on Hector. Until Hector is dead, he will take neither food nor drink (199-214); refreshment and grief seem to be mutually exclusive. In 216-37, however, Odysseus urges a different attitude on Achilles:

> There is no way for the Achaeans to grieve with their stomachs.
> For everyday too many fall, in throngs. When could we relax from
> the work (of grieving)? No, instead we must bury the man who dies
> and have an unpitying heart, grieving (only) for a day. And those
> who are spared by hateful war must remember food and drink, so
> that we may fight without ceasing against our enemies.

Odysseus's arguments to persuade Achilles to take some nourishment parallel the development in Alcaeus's invitation to Melanippus to drink. It is impossible to grieve for all the Achaeans who have died, and to remember them with fasts and protracted displays. We may compare Alcaeus's advice to Melanippus. "Do not aim at great (i.e., impossible) things." The theme of mortality is common to both warnings. Melanippus should not aim too high because he is bound to die; Achilles should not attempt an enduring grief, because the constant deaths of the Achaeans will overwhelm him.

Odysseus, like Achilles, suggests that eating and grieving are in a sense irreconcilable. The Achaeans cannot grieve with their stomachs. Odysseus, however, makes the opposition less stark; he offers a *modus vivendi,* enabling the warriors to attend to the dead and to their own needs as well. He urges that the dead be mourned for a decent period—one day—and that then the survivors look to themselves. Just as Alcaeus uses *khrē* to introduce the proper response to a situation, so too does Odysseus:

ἀλλὰ χρὴ τὸν μὲν καταθάπτειν ὅς κε θάνῃσι,
νηλέα θυμὸν ἔχοντας, ἐπ᾽ ἤματι δακρύσαντας   228-29

But it is necessary to bury the one who dies, with an unpitying heart, grieving for a day.

Odysseus and Achilles disagree over what should be remembered and what forgotten. Verbs of memory are prominent in both their speeches. Thus, when Achilles rejects the ceremony of reconciliation the first time, he urges:

νῦν δὲ μνησώμεθα χάρμης

Now, let us remember battle" (148; cf. 153).

More specifically, Achilles "remembers" Patroclus and his obligation to avenge his friend's death; cf. 19.314ff., 22.386-90, 24.509-12. Odysseus urges just the opposite course; having commemorated the fallen, it is necessary to forget them and to "remember" food and drink (19.231).

All these motifs are found again in *Il.* 24, when Achilles in his turn urges Priam to eat. "Now, let us remember our meal" (νῦν δὲ μνησώμεθα δόρπου, 24.601). Achilles reminds the old king of the story of Niobe, who grieved for her slain children ten days, and then "remembered" food (613). To eat is to turn from grief; the meal which Priam shares with Achilles signals that Priam will not indulge in an unabating grief. Having mourned Hector a proper time, he will turn from his sorrow and "remember" the present situation and its demands. As in book 19, eating seems to be a recognition of men's limited ability to control or improve the world.

In an earlier speech, Achilles tells Priam, "But since the Ouranians have brought this woe on you, always around your city there is battle and the slaying of men. Bear with it, and do not grieve stubbornly in your heart. You will accomplish nothing (*ou gar ti prēxeis*) sorrowing for your son, nor will you raise him up before you suffer yet another evil" (24. 547-51). Grief is presented here as an attempt to accomplish something, to bring the dead back. To the extent that mourning seeks to resurrect the dead, it resembles Sisyphus, in Alcaeus's poem, who boasted that he would defeat death. Obdurate sorrow, then, is to be avoided, for the same reason that hubristic ambitions must be avoided: both are attempts at the impossible. Because the death of Hector, and, more generally, evils sent by the gods are not subject to our control, we must "forget" them; to forget is to acknowledge one's inability to control them.

Achilles himself, in "remembering" to eat renounces his unending grief for Patroclus, since he too is unable to do anything to help his dead companion. In "remembering" Patroclus, Achilles was ultimately reduced to the repetitious and increasingly meaningless act of insulting Hector's corpse (24.1-18). The gods' preservation of Hector's body expresses the frustration of Achilles' attempt at a never-ending grief. In eating together,

Priam and Achilles recognize their common mortal condition of liability to the gods and the need, imposed by this condition, to turn from one's sorrow and "remember" the present time and its urgencies.

Why it is precisely a banquet or symposium that expresses this resignation is clarified by a consideration of Hesiod's accounts of primordial times. One of the great characteristic features of that time was that gods and men had banquets (*daites*) in common (cf. Hesiod fr. 1.6-7 MW). Moreover, it was at one of these *daites* that the split between the gods and mortals had its origin. "For when gods and mortal men were having a settlement at Mykone, [Prometheus] apportioned a large bull with kindly spirit, deceiving the mind of Zeus" (*Th.* 535-37).[30] There follows a description of Prometheus's famous trick. He wrapped the animal's bones in succulent fat, but the edible parts—the flesh and innards—he placed on the hide, and wrapped in the animal's stomach. Asked to select what he wanted, Zeus put his hands on the fat and found the inedible bones wrapped inside. Henceforth, in sacrifices, men get the edible parts and leave the bones to the gods.

In retaliation for Prometheus's deceit, Zeus sent evils on the human race. Sacrifice, therefore, in which the gods are given the bones, while the human participants enjoy the meat at a common banquet, suggests the origins of men's separation from the immortals and the beginning of those conditions that now shape human existence.[31] It should be remembered that, for the most part, meat eaten by the Greeks had come from a sacrificial victim; hence, the banquet is closely associated with the sacrifice and the relations between gods and men that are affirmed in the sacrifice. The symposium perhaps takes on connotations of mortal subjection from its natural association with banquets.

In Pindar, too, the banquet can serve as an appropriate setting for discussions of mortal life and its expectations. The honored state of immortality that Tantalus enjoys is expressed by his being a guest at the gods' table and a host for them in his turn (*Ol.* 1.36-39). Such fellowship, as Pindar makes clear in that ode, is dangerous in the present dispensation, where men and gods are distant from each other. Tantalus could not "digest" his good fortune (55-56); he attempted to make other mortals—his fellows at a symposium—partakers of divine food (60-64).

By partaking of such food, Tantalus had himself been made immortal (63) and he sought to confer this same honor on others. That is, he attempted to do away with the barriers separating gods and men, which Zeus had imposed. Tantalus's crime was to merge the fellowship of the symposium (61) with the fellowship of the gods' table. Once again, the symposium and the common celebration around the table are distinguished from joy and prerogatives not permitted to mortals; the symposium suggests the limits of mortal life, which cannot be fused with the life enjoyed by the immortals.

We may now return to *Nem.* 9, which resembles other invitations to eat or drink, in that it sets the symposium off against the hubristic attempts at the impossible; the drinking party becomes an expression of moderation and the wise recognition of the curbs placed on human ambition. In *Nem.* 9 Pindar tells the story of the expedition against Thebes; his purpose in doing so is the same as that of Alcaeus when he alludes to Sisyphus in the ode considered above; both passages present examples of hubris ultimately punished.

In the third stanza, Pindar begins with the time before the expedition, and he narrates the occasion for Admetus's inauguration of the games at Sicyon. Admetus had been forced into exile by Amphiaraus and deprived of his rightful kingship. "A stronger man puts an end to the former justice," Pindar says (13-15). Admetus had won his way back into town by offering to Amphiaraus "man-taming Eriphyle, as a trusty pledge." Eriphyle's epithet (*androdamanta*) is almost certainly sinister here, since it was the traditional story, clearly relevant to Pindar's narrative, that Eriphyle forced Amphiaraus to march with the army against Thebes, although he had foreseen the disastrous conclusion of the campaign.

Pindar then stresses the disasters and the omens presaging them. The expedition was not well omened (*ou kat' ornikhōn hodon,* 19); Zeus did not urge them to go, but rather to renounce the campaign (19-20). The army hurried to its own destruction (21). Amphiaraus was absconded by Zeus so that he might not show his back to the enemy (24-27). The story highlights themes of injustice, treachery, and folly.[32] In describing the soldiers' deaths, Pindar puts the vocabulary of banqueting to perverse use. "They fattened (*pianan*)[33] the white flowering smoke with their bodies, for seven pyres feasted (*daisanto*) on the young-limbed men" (23-24).

The point of Alcaeus's poem and the speeches of Odysseus and Achilles was to dissuade their addressees from hubris. The narrative in *Nem.* 9 may have such a purpose incidentally, but more importantly, it serves as foil to the following praise of Khromios, in which the scandals of the mythic past are opposed almost point for point.

Pindar turns from the myth quite suddenly and prays that the Aetnaeans be spared the Carthaginians' attacks: "If it is possible, son of Cronus, I defer as far as I can that proud trial for life and death against Punic spears" (28-29). This suggests one reason why the Seven's campaign was shown in a bad light; they were attackers, and Pindar is writing for a city on the defensive.

Moreover, Aetna has not been racked by the power hungry as was Argos (13-15); its citizens have their minds on things more important than possessions (32-34). Khromios, unlike Amphiaraus, has been courageous in battle, and he is described, significantly, not as attacking but as repulsing the enemy. He has been given "a warrior's heart to ward off (*amunein*) Enualios's havoc." Pindar says that "With their strength and spirit, few men can devise the repulse of the cloud of approaching slaughter into the enemy ranks" (37-39). In his prowess and counsel, Khromios resembles no one so much as Hector, the defender *par excellence* (39-42).

The next verses turn to the rewards for these excellences. "From the toils done in youth and in justice comes a lifetime peaceful into old age" (44). Again, we are meant to think of the Seven's unjust campaign, which was responsible for their death while still young men (cf. 24).

Having completed his praises and the prediction of a long and peaceful life for Khromios, Pindar turns to general reflections. "He must know that he has obtained a wondrous prosperity from the *daimones*. For if one wins renowned glory and many possessions, no other, more distant goal is there for the mortal's feet to touch. Tranquility (*hēsukhia*) loves a symposium; the new-thriving victory grows with gentle song" (45-49).

The excellences Khromios has shown, and the peaceful life they may obtain for him are the most that can be hoped for in a mortal life. The dark tale of Amphiaraus and Admetus suggests the dangers of attempting more. Khromios's successes therefore should prompt not a greed for more and more but a drinking party with his companions and a poet. The symposium, once again, appears to represent an acknowledgment of the necessarily limited scope of mortal ambitions and successes.

In all the passages considered above we can see the connection between resignation and membership in human society. In Alcaeus 38, Melanippus is urged to signify his recognition of mortality and its limits by joining with the poet in a drinking party. Odysseus urges Achilles to give up his grief and to join in the banquet so that his reconciliation with the Achaean hosts may be reaffirmed. One reason Achilles is unwilling to eat is that he does not wish to be reunited with Agamemnon and the army except on the most utilitarian level—that is, by joining once again with the others, he can avenge Patroclus.[34] Were he to eat with them, this would signify his voluntary membership in the Achaean society.[35]

The connection between resignation and community emerges most clearly, perhaps, in *Il*. 24, in the interview of Achilles and Priam. The two men are divided by everything except their sorrow and their common subjection to the gods, and it is on the basis of this that Achilles invites Priam to a meal in common. Again, in *Nem*. 9, the return voyage of Khromios from Sicyon to his native city and the symposium seems to suggest resignation, contrasting as it does with the hubristic voyage outward of Admetus and the Seven. In welcoming Khromios home to a *kōmos* and celebration in song, Pindar simultaneously invites the victor to recognize the limits on human ambition.

(The poet, too, is prompted to offer tribute by his awareness of his own and the athlete's mortality. As I have argued elsewhere, Pindar sees the jealous refusal to praise as the refusal to acknowledge the gods' will in awarding the victory.[36] The jealous are confounded, therefore, because their jealousy is a form of revolt against the gods. When one recognizes the gods' role in the victor's achievements, as well as his own obligation to submit to the gods, he will accord the victor his due.)

While the *philotēs* of athlete and poet is based on *aretē* and the wise recognition of the world's limits, it is also an eminently useful relationship. The poet performs a crucial service by acknowledging the victor's excellence. "Excellence darts up, like a tree with fresh dew, raised up among the wise and just of men, to the moist heavens," Pindar says. "Various are the uses of *philoi*. Their use in toils is greatest, but delight (*terpsis*) too seeks to offer a visible pledge" (*Nem.* 8.40-44). By *terpsis*, Pindar refers to the occasion of victory, when the *philos* offers a pledge by praising the victory. That this is, in fact, a service is stressed by the closing passage of *Nem.* 8. By means of his song, Pindar makes "even toil painless" (50). The epinician has a crucial effect on the athlete's effort; it is by virtue of it that the athlete's *ponos* becomes *olbos*. Pindar stresses the effectiveness of his songs when he calls them *epaoidai* (49), or "enchantments" such as Asclepius used to cure illness (cf. *Pyth.* 3.51).

Conversely, the failure to acknowledge achievement has a destructive effect, as the brief and quite bitter account of Ajax's suicide makes clear. The Greek army, in a secret vote (*Nem.* 8.26), voted to award the armor of Achilles, now dead, to Odysseus, rather than to the more deserving Ajax:

> Jealousy devoured Telamon's son, bending him around a sword. In the dire contest, [men's] forgetfulness held him down—a tongueless man, but brave of heart. The highest prize was awarded to glittering falsehood. For in the secret votes, the Danaans served Odysseus while Ajax, bereft of the golden armor, wrestled with death. Surely, no similar wounds had the two inflicted on the enemy's warm flesh with their menacing spears, when they fought over Achilles newly slain, or on the destructive days of other combat. Even of old was deceit an enemy, a companion of flattering words—scheming, malicious slander. It does violence to what is brilliant, and raises up a rotten glory for the obscure (23-34).

Acknowledgment makes the difference between a victory that is an achievement and a victory that frustrates the athlete. Because the song, which is that acknowledgment, is so important, Pindar hesitates before speaking. "I stand on light feet, taking a breath before I say anything. Many things are said, and in many ways, but when you search out new things and put them in the scale to test, there is every danger. Words are food for the jealous, and jealousy always attacks the good; it does not struggle with the inferior" (19-22).

Not only does Pindar stress the importance of his song, he emphasizes its character as a present deed, by presenting himself hesitating "before saying anything." When he does speak, his words must confound the jealous and change Deinis's *kamatos,* or hard work, into something delightful and painless. It is clear that *Nem.* 8 is not so much a discussion of the poet's duties to the athlete as it it an execution of those duties; *Nem.* 8 is itself the useful service the poet performs for the victor.

The beneficial act of *philotēs* that *Nem.* 8 represents is enhanced by the erotic motifs suffusing the poem. Pindar begins the ode with a prayer to Hora ("Season" or "Youth"), who is presented not only as an erotic deity but a goddess of fate:

> Ὥρα πότνια, κάρυξ Ἀφροδίτας
>   ἀμβροσιᾶν φιλοτάτων,
> ἅ τε παρθενηΐοις παίδων τ' ἐφίζοισα γλεφάροις,
> τὸν μὲν ἡμέροις ἀνάγκας χερσὶ βαστά-
>   ζεις, ἕτερον δ' ἑτέραις.
> ἀγαπατὰ δὲ καιροῦ μὴ πλαναθέντα πρὸς ἔργον ἕκαστον
> τῶν ἀρειόνων ἐρώτων ἐπικρατεῖν δύνασθαι

Lady Hora, messenger of Aphrodite's ambrosial loves, who rest on the eyelids of maidens and boys, one man you deliver to necessity's gentle hands, another man to ungentle hands. Contentment (*agapata*) is the ability to attain our better loves (*erōtes*) in every work without straying from due measure" (1-5).

Pindar refers to two kinds of love: *erōtes* and *agapata.* I have translated *agapata* as "contentment" in order to suggest the two meanings "that which is loved" and "that with which one must be satisfied." As "that which is loved," *agapata* is distinct from *erōtes,* as passive ("loved") is distinct from active ("yearning"). As "that with which one must be content," *agapata* is distinguished from the discontent of *erōs,* which drives the athlete to undertake more challenges. In general, the blessed life of Aeacus, as described by Pindar (6-10) corresponds to *agapata;* Aeacus attains to everything possible in a mortal life. Ajax—bereft, yearning, angry—corresponds to the *erōtes,* which may or may not be able to attain their goals.[37] *Nem.* 8 is Pindar's response to the athlete's *erōs*—that is, the athlete's yearning for renown.[38] By means of his song, Pindar enables Deinis to "achieve his better loves"; he turns the *erōtes* into things *agapata*.

Pindar's use of erotic motifs, like his use of symposiastic motifs, suggests comparison of his epinicians with other examples of lyric poetry. The ambition that prompts an athlete to enter the contests is described in terms reminiscent of the desire for love. Thus, in *Pyth.* 10.60, Pindar says:

$$\text{ἑτέροις ἑτέρων ἔρωτες ἔκνιξαν φρένας}$$

Yearning for different things scratches different hearts.

The presentation here of *erōs* as an external force, causing physical and emotional unrest, is common in lyric poetry.[39] From several possible examples, we may select Sappho 47 LP:

$$\text{Ἔρος δ' ἐτίναξέ μοι}$$
$$\text{φρένας, ὡς ἄνεμος κὰτ ὄρος δρύσιν ἐμπέτων}$$

Yearning shook my heart, like the wind down a mountain, falling upon the oaks.

In erotic poetry, madness is also stressed, as a corollary to the concept of *erōs* as an overpowering external force. So, Anacreon 111G says:

$$\text{ἀστραγάλαι δ' Ἔρωτός εἰσιν}$$
$$\text{μανίαι τε καὶ κυδοιμοί}$$

The dice of Erōs are madness and battle-noise.

Pindar, too, refers to the "madness" of love in urging moderation on one of his athletes:

$$\text{ἀπροσίκτων δ' ἐρώτων ὀξύτεραι μανίαι} \qquad \textit{Nem.} 11.48$$

Very sharp are the frenzies of loves not-to-be-touched.

Pindar also uses erotic language to present the gods' benevolence to the struggling athlete. Thus, in *Ol.* 1, Pelops is the beloved of Poseidon, who once had taken the boy to serve him on Olympus, when he was "tamed by desire" for Pelops (*Ol.* 1.40–45). Restored later to his mortality, Pelops requests Poseidon's help in the chariot contest with Oenomaus and reminds him of the passion once felt by the god for him when Pelops was a boy. "If the friendly gifts of the Cyprian goddess ever charmed you, Poseidon, restrain Oenomaus's brazen spear, and bring me on the swiftest chariot to Elis; bring strength near" (75–78). The prayer is successful; Poseidon "gave him a golden chariot and untiring winged horses" (86b).[40]

Pelops wants to enter the contest in order to win Hippodameia, who will be rewarded to the suitor able to beat her father Oenomaus in a race; Pelops enters the contest, prompted by the desire or *erōs* for a wife. His victory therefore is the effect of two loves: his own yearning for a wife and the god's (former) love for him. The story relates in erotic terms what happens in every victory: the athlete, spurred by ambition, enters the contest and is aided by benevolent gods.

Pyth. 9 also includes both the gods' love for a mortal and the mortal's love for a prize. The opening part of *Pyth.* 9 is given over to the story of Apollo's first look at Cyrene and his immediate love for her. He consults Chiron about her identity, and the centaur prophesies that Apollo will take the young woman to Libya, where she will give birth to a son.[41]

This story is relevant to the praise of Telesikrates that follows. Not only are both heroine and victor associated with the city Cyrene in Libya, but both are notable for their physical prowess (cf. 18-28 and 71-72). Just as Cyrene is looked upon with love (27-37), so do the women fawn over Telesikrates (97-100); both Cyrene and Telesikrates are said to be "received" by their homeland (cf. 55-56 *Libya dexetai* and 73 [*Kurana*] *dexetai*). More interestingly, Pindar uses much the same vocabulary to describe Telesikrates' victory and the consummation of love. So, in announcing the athlete's success, Pindar says he was mingled (*sunemeixe*) with chance (*tukhāi*) (71-72). "To mingle" had been used for Apollo's and Kyrene's union in verse 13 (*gamon mikhthenta*) and verse 68 (*migen*). *Tukha* appeared before in Chiron's speech. "Gods and men are equally ashamed to happen on (*tukhein*) the sweet bed for the first time so as to be seen" (40-41). The parallels between Cyrene's story and Telesikrates' victory illuminate the place of divine benevolence in winning a victory.

The poem concludes with another story about love; this one concerns Alexidamus's competition in a footrace in order to win Antaeus's daughter as his wife; this story, too, is pertinent to his descendant Telesikrates, whose victory was won in the *hoplitodromos* (a footrace run while clad in full armor). But the connections between this final love story and the victory are different from those we saw between the victory and the story of Cyrene and Apollo. Telesikrates is no longer comparable to the beloved so much as to the lover, who enters the race in order to achieve his desires. Victory is presented here no longer as a consummation but a hope, urging the competitor on.

In *Pyth.* 9 Pindar uses an array of erotic tales to give different descriptions of victory. At the start, we see victory as consummation, the splendid mingling of god and man, and Pindar shows how this pertains to Telesikrates. But the athlete also resembles Alexidamus, whose love suggests the nature of victory as a goad, spurring men on in constant hope.[42]

95

The story of the gods' love and the mortal's love is a recurrent one in Pindar's myths. He can shape it differently to suggest various aspects of victory. We are told in *Pyth.* 3, for example, that Apollo loved Coronis, who conceived Asclepius; Coronis, however, loved a mortal man while she was still pregnant with Apollo's son. Pindar presents this as an example of "loving what is absent" and illicit (*Pyth.* 3.19-23). It is a cautionary tale about excessive ambitions and *hubris*. In *Pyth.* 2, Pindar relates Ixion's attempted rape of Hera, a story that inverts the proper erotic relations of gods and mortals by making the mortal the initiator. As I have argued elsewhere,[43] the inversion is suggestive of jealousy, which is presented as a denial of the gods, or an attempt to subdue them.

Thus, Pindar uses erotic motifs to present the gods' role in the victory, as well as the athlete's desire to win *kleos* by competing in the games. Moreover, the poet's tribute of praise calls up a number of erotic motifs. For example, Pindar sometimes praises the athletes for their charm or beauty. He compares Hagesidamos to Ganymede in *Ol.* 10.99-105 and describes the boy Pytheas as "not yet showing on his cheek the season of harvest, mother of the tender vine plant" (*Nem.* 5.6). The archaic erotic song lends itself easily to encomiastic purposes, since a recurrent motif in the love poetry is the beauty of the beloved's ways or character (*ēthos*). So, for example, Anacreon (23G) sings:

$$\text{ἔραμαι } \langle δέ \rangle \text{ τοι συνηβᾶν· χαρίεν γὰρ ἦθος ἴσχεις}$$

I yearn to spend my youth with you; delightful is your character.

Compare Sappho 50 LP:

$$\text{ὁ μὲν γὰρ κάλος ὄσσον ἴδην πέλεται } \langle κάλος, \rangle$$
$$\text{ὁ δὲ κἄγαθος αὔτικα καὶ κάλος ἔσσεται}$$

The beautiful man is beautiful, so far as can be seen, but the man who is also good will be beautiful straightaway.

A just character, commonly singled out for praise by Pindar, is also a theme of erotic verses. For example, Anacreon 120G:

$$\text{καλὸν εἶναι τῷ ἔρωτι τὰ δίκαια}$$

A beautiful thing for *erōs* is justice.

Theognis (255) calls justice (*to dikaiotaton*) "most beautiful" (*kalliston*). The interest in the moral character of the boy grows from the ethical, educational function served by the friendship of an adult male and a young boy.[44] The erotic aspects of the friendship were but a part, ideally, of a more spiritual relationship, meant to educate the youth in the ways of *aretē*. Conversely, the inability to delight in a boy's charms indicates a greedy or unmanly character in the adult. In an encomium to Theoxenos, Pindar says, "Whoever fails to swell with yearning, from a glance at the sparkling beams of Theoxenos's eyes, has a black heart forged of steel or iron in a cold flame; dishonored by Aphrodite-of-the-curling-lashes, he labors in violence for wealth, or with womanly spirit is carried along every path to serve" (fr. 123SM). That a man's character is shown by his response to a handsome boy is comparable to the way in which men's responses to victory distinguish the just and the jealous. More generally, the concern in love odes with moral characteristics and qualities beyond the specifically erotic makes the use of motifs in epinician verse less forced than might at first seem the case.

In *Isth.* 2 Pindar discusses the relationship between erotic and epinician songs. He begins by distinguishing a former time when poets composed love songs for their favorites, and the present time when a man is identified with his money:

> Men of old, Thrasuboulos, who rode on the chariot of the gold-crowned Muses and plied the famous lyre nimbly (*rhimpha*) aimed their honey-voiced hymns at beautiful boys with the sweet down on their cheek to coax enthroned Aphrodite. For in those days, the Muse was not yet greedy, nor did she work for hire. The sweet, gentle-voiced songs of honey-throated Terpsichore did not have their faces silvered over nor were they for sale. But now she bids us heed the words of the Argive man, which come closest to the truth. "Wealth, wealth is the man," he said, deprived alike of goods and friends.

The scholiast tells us that the "men of old" (*hoi palai*) are Alcaeus, Ibycus, Anacreon, who all composed erotic verse.[45] They composed their songs "nimbly" (*rhimpha*), and this as been taken as a reference to one distinctive feature of monodic lyric. That is, the old poets were able to give praise spontaneously, and this spontaneity distinguishes them from the epinician poet, who depends on money and cannot compose without being given money. As Leonard Woodbury writes, "[The earlier poets] were free, as their successors are not, to give immediate expression in song to their wishes."[46] Epinician verse, of the kind composed by Pindar, Bacchylides, and Simonides, was written on commission, and it seems to have involved lavish expenditures. Thus, Woodbury concludes that Pindar draws a distinction between different modes of publication.[47]

While Pindar undoubtedly is referring to erotic lyric, and the conditions that once attended the composing of verse, I think the above interpretation gives too specific a meaning to Pindar's very general language. He does not balk at naming specific poets elsewhere;[48] why, then, does he refer to Anacreon, Ibycus, and Alcaeus so vaguely as "men of old," if in fact he means those men specifically? Moreover, there is one peculiarity about this passage that has gone, as far as I know, unrecognized: Pindar does not normally make a distinction between the past and present.[49] In general, he is interested in showing rather the persistence through time of patterns in mortal life, the better to connect his athletes to the heroic past. More particularly, when he discusses poetry, it is the continuity of traditions that he stresses. Thus, Homer is regularly presented as an encomiast, whose praise or failure to praise saves or destroys heroes. Pindar concludes *Nem.* 8 by assuring Deinis that "encomiastic song was from of old, even before the strife of Adrastus and the Cadmeans" (*Nem.* 8.50–51). It is remarkable, then, that in *Isth.* 2 he emphatically distinguishes the present from the past.

The bygone era was one in which poets composed "lightly" or "nimbly." It is this quality that seems to distinguish the earlier from the present era. Woodbury interprets it thus: "The old poets were able to give praise without delay or constraint."[50] That phrase again seems too specific. There is little doubt that Pindar is referring to something like freedom from delay or constraint, but the language he uses is more open-ended, more suggestive than that. In literalizing the metaphor, we risk a distortion of the poet's meaning.

The scholiast (Dr.3.213; 1a) explains *rhimpha* as meaning "easily" (*rhēidiōs*). The word "easily"—which figures prominently, as we have seen, in *Works and Days*—suggests that Hesiod might provide a useful parallel to the opening verses of *Isth.* 2. In *Works and Days,* Hesiod distinguishes an earlier era, when life was "easy," from the present time, when Zeus has imposed evils on mortals and life is "difficult." An attractive feature of this suggestion is that it helps explain why Pindar, contrary to his practice elsewhere, emphasizes the difference between past and present: he may be adapting a myth of the golden past to a discussion of song. There was a time when song making was easy, but now, Terpsichore urges poets to recall that "Money, money is the man."

It is significant that this was the saying of a man "bereft of possessions and friends" (*kteanōn . . . leiphtheis kai philōn,* 11). The condition of scarcity was one result of Zeus's revenge on Prometheus and mankind (*WD* 42) and is a main characteristic of men's present condition. The similarity between mortals in Hesiod and the Argive man in *Isth.* 2 suggests that when Pindar discusses wealth, he refers to something more than the ode's market price. That is, wealth and the need for it may be presented here as aspects of men's present condition.

The ode appears in *Isth.* 2 not as the product of a *philotēs* based on excellence, but as a business deal, whereby the poet increases his wealth. In *Ol.* 10.1–15 as well, Pindar makes clear that the poem is part of a business transaction and must answer to the terms stipulated in the agreement. To speak of the poem in this way does not deny or ignore the *philotēs* of poet and athlete, but it does throw a new light on it. If men are thrown together by virtue of their common mortal status they are in a way divided by it as well, in that each one must see to it that he at least has enough to subsist on. If food makes a community of men (the fellowship of the table), the need for food also turns them into competitors, who regard each other with jealousy and anger.[51] Men join together, but in order to ensure that individual needs are satisfied. It is by means of exchange and the just requital of goods that individuals can associate with each other.

Aristotle considers business deals under the heading of friendships of advantage and speaks, more particularly, of a legal (*nomikē*) *philia* that is on fixed terms. He writes, "Its purely commerical variety is on the basis of immediate payment, while the more liberal variety allows time but stipulates for a definite *quid pro quo*. In this variety the debt is clear and not ambiguous, but in the postponement it contains an element of friendliness (*philikon*)" (1162b26-29, Ross translation).

In friendships of advantage, the reciprocity (*to antipeponthos*) that comes so easily to those whose *philia* is based on excellence must be diligently safeguarded. Means have been developed to ensure that the value of goods can be measured exactly, so that just requital can be assured. This is Aristotle's analysis of money and its use in stabilizing a society. "It is not two doctors that associate for exchange, but a doctor and a farmer, or in general people who are different and unequal; but these must be equated. This is why all things that are exchanged must be somehow comparable. It is for this end that money has been introduced, and it becomes in a sense an intermediate; for it measures all things, and therefore the excess and the defect—how many shoes are equal to a house or to a given amount of food" (1133a16-22, Ross translation).

While Aristotle is discussing coinage specifically, his treatment is suggestive for an understanding of the relations betwen poet and athlete. As members of a *koinōnia allaktikē* (an association for purposes of exchange), poet and victor are incommensurate and no longer presented as men similar in *aretē*. It was a question debated by philosophers whether people who were alike or those who were not alike became friends.[52] In the victory odes, both the similarity and difference of poet and athlete are shown. As men of similar excellence, their friendship is a perfect one of generosity, mutual regard, and loyalty. As men with different skills, in need of each other, the two enter into a pact of mutual benefit, involving an exchange of goods.

We should understand Pindar's reference to wealth in *Isth.* 2 in a wider context than the price of the ode. The business transaction of poet and athlete is but an instance of the way people deal with each other, the associations or *koinōniai* they make. The mercantile character of the "friendship" illuminates the nature of the participants and the conditions that have brought about this kind of friendship. These are the conditions of scarcity that Zeus imposed after being tricked by Prometheus, those that force the individual to struggle for his subsistence. Persons who enter into friendships are needy, and they can associate only so long as equity and reciprocity in the exchange of goods can be maintained.

When Pindar speaks of the mercenary Muse, then, this is more than a reference to the payments made to the singer by the athlete; it is an attempt to situate epinician song (which has a price, unlike erotic poetry) in the context of men's present condition.

The distinction of different eras, characterized respectively by "ease" and "scarcity," implies that Pindar has patterned the connections of erotic and epinician along lines suggested by myths of an earlier golden age. This is not to say that Pindar locates the poets Ibycus, Anacreon, and Alcaeus in an unimaginably distant golden age, but merely to argue that a pattern of golden age and dissolution has shaped Pindar's discussion of song. If the use of mythic patterns for presenting historical characters seems unlikely, we should recall that it is dubious whether Pindar recognized a distinction between what we would call "myth" and "history."

In the opening verses of *Isth.* 7, for instance, Pindar enumerates several episodes from the Theban past, proceeding from "mythic" events like the birth of Dionysus (5) down in time to "historical" events like the Aegeid takeover of Amyclae (12-15).[53] Pindar indicates no qualitative distinction between these events; all are instances of a past in need of celebration. Similarly, in *Isth.* 2, when Pindar refers to singers whom we consider "historical," there is no reason to conclude that he must be dealing with them in a "historical" manner. I have argued that his language indicates that he presents his relation to the past in a way we would call "mythic."

How, then, does Pindar conceive the relationship of erotic and epinician verse? The epinician is a kind of song appropriate to the present mortal conditions of deprivation and work, such as Hesiod describes in *WD*. It is significant that the Muse who presides over epinician poetry is *ergatis*, a worker. Moreover, Pindar works at his songs (*ergasaman*, 46), and the songs themselves are not intended to rest idly (*ouk elinusontas*, 46; cf. *Nem.* 5.1).

What results from the work is a product of culture, which evinces both mortality (in its mode of production) and divinity (in the permanence of the product). In the formulation of Hesiod, it is "easy, although difficult" (*WD* 292). The song composed by Pindar, like the *aretē* described by Hesiod, is described in terms of difficulty and ease in *Isth.* 2. The necessity of money precludes the song's being composed "lightly" (*rhimpha*). It is necessarily arduous, and the poet must wait for a patron to sponsor him. On the other hand, when he is sponsored by an excellent host, his task is "easy." In verses 33-34, Pindar says that "There is no hill, nor is the path steep, if one brings the Muses' honors to the house of men of fair renown." It is interesting that in describing his song, Pindar uses road imagery, just as Hesiod had used it to speak of the ease and difficulty of *arete*.[54] In any event, Pindar presents epinician poetry as having the same ambivalence of "ease" and "difficulty" that attends every achievement in the present conditions of life.

Because of this ambivalence, wealth, too, appears both as an evil and a good. Wealth is at first presented as a degeneration from the past; the modern Muse—"silvered-over," "a hireling"—is portrayed in no very flattering light. On the other hand, within the diminished conditions, and by means of them, one achieves excellence. Thus, wealth is used for hospitality, and Pindar emphasizes the liberality of Xenokrates and Thrasuboulos in his praise (24, 30-32, 37-40).[55] The symposium and banquet, the activities of hospitality, are the excellences appropriate to a world of scarcity, where "wealth is the man." This is much the same conception of the symposium as was seen in the examples of symposiastic poetry considered above, but approached now from a different side.

Erotic verse—a spontaneous, free tribute to a beautiful boy—belonged to a different age, before work, need, and money became concerns. But now (*nun d'*, 9), song is necessarily taken up with these things, insofar as these are the present conditions of mortal life. Epinician, like erotic, is a tribute from one mortal to another, but it is a tribute shaped by the world where it occurs.

Thus, epinician is a descendant of erotic, but with certain differences from its ancestor. In this regard, we may consider briefly the other passage in the epinicians where Pindar discusses the earlier history of his verse, *Nem.* 8.50-51:

$$\mathring{\eta}\nu \ \gamma\epsilon \ \mu\grave{\alpha}\nu \ \epsilon\pi\iota\kappa\acute{\omega}\mu\iota\sigma\varsigma \ \mathring{\upsilon}\mu\nu\sigma\varsigma$$
$$\delta\grave{\eta} \ \pi\acute{\alpha}\lambda\alpha\iota \ \kappa\alpha\grave{\iota} \ \pi\rho\grave{\iota}\nu \ \gamma\epsilon\nu\acute{\epsilon}\sigma\vartheta\alpha\iota$$
$$\tau\grave{\alpha}\nu \ \text{'}\Alpha\delta\rho\acute{\alpha}\sigma\tau\sigma\upsilon \ \tau\acute{\alpha}\nu \ \tau\epsilon \ \Kappa\alpha\delta\mu\epsilon\acute{\iota}\omega\nu \ \mathring{\epsilon}\rho\iota\nu$$

Indeed there was encomiastic song from of old, and even before the strife of Adrastus and the Cadmeans.

"Of old" (*palai*) is the same word Pindar uses in the opening verses of *Isth.* 2 to describe the erotic poets. The word *eris* ("strife") is also significant, since it too is a word very closely associated with the distinguishing characteristics of the mortal condition.[56] The passage might, then, be a condensed version of what I have argued is found in *Isth.* 2.

That is, Pindar alludes to a time before *eris* (a golden age) and to a time characterized by *eris* (the present age); "encomiastic song" reaches back into that earlier era. However, *Isth.* 2 indicates that the encomia of that earlier time may have been different from the contemporary epinician ode. If the parallel to *Isth.* 2 is valid, they would be erotic songs. That Pindar in fact opens *Nem.* 8 with erotic motifs, describing the love of Zeus and Aegina, would seem to strengthen the parallel with *Isth.* 2.

I have considered three kinds of lyric poetry: symposiastic, erotic, and epinician. All three kinds have to do with the ties binding individuals together into a fellowship. Each one has its own light to shed on the nature of these ties. Symposiastic poetry suggests the separation of gods from men—that is, the disbanding of the old fellowship of mortal and immortal at a common table. The alliances and fellowship joining together the participants in a symposium gain greater definition by being distinguished from a fellowship no longer possible.

Erotic poetry is closely allied with symposiastic and deals with the affectional aspects of the fellowship celebrated at the drinking party. Erotic motifs are, in fact, common in songs of the symposium, and they can be used, like sympotic themes, to characterize the human condition. Thus, the *erotikon* celebrates the physical beauty of the *erōmenos* spontaneously, without mediation by money. However, the erotic poem does not respond, Pindar suggests in *Isth.* 2, to the particular nature of *aretē,* which is no longer something easy or purely given, like physical beauty. *Aretē* now involves work and wealth, and because it is no longer easy, no more can the song celebrating it be easy. As Hesiod says, individuals are now necessarily rooted in *eris* or competition with each other. While this *eris* can be good, it introduces a certain distance between individuals which cannot be willed away. Human ties are now necessarily mediated. It is this mediated tie that epinician song affirms and celebrates.

The consideration of erotic and symposiastic lyric has led us back to the myth of the golden age as presented in *Works and Days.* Briefly reconstructed, the golden age looks something like this: there had been a time when mortals and immortals shared the same table of fellowship. It was a time before the apportionment of honors to the several gods. It was also a time of prosperity, when mortals had immediately available to them everything they required for their sustenance. There was no differentiation of the sexes, and the relations among males were spontaneous and free.

The present era is the result of the separation of elements that had existed together. Immortals are now decisively distinguished from mortals, as males are from females. The distance set between the individual and his sustenance assures that humans must work for their living and are permanently disposed toward each other as competitors.

The distinguishing of things formerly indistinguishable has obvious connections with Greek cosmogonic accounts—for example, the separation of Gaia and Ouranos (Earth and Heaven), who had been joined in an endless coital embrace.[57] (It is also interesting that the division of Earth and Heaven was accomplished by the cunning of Cronus, just as the division of man and god has its origins in Prometheus's wiliness.)[58]

It has seemed worthwhile to refer the different kinds of lyric poetry to this mythic background. Sex and sustenance, as I argued in chapter 2, are two motifs characterizing the mortal condition. The mortal is fundamentally needy: he must have food, and he must have a mate. Symposiastic and erotic poetry can be referred to each of these needs. The sharers of the banquet commemorate the separation of mortal from immortal; the abundance of food and drink at their disposal is now "the best" joy available to them. It suggests the vanished era of plenty. Similarly the erotic song, at least as presented by Pindar, harkens back to a time when the society of men was not constrained by the need for ways to secure equity in the exchange of goods.

Such considerations imply that lyric poems, apart from being the work of individual poets, also have a traditional component. They grow from social institutions of long standing (e.g., the banquet) and show concerns and motifs that can be traced back to the myths. Rather than belonging to a separable literary realm of poesy, they participate in the broad currents of life around them.

In the final chapter, I will investigate in more detail the connections between epinician poetry and Greek myths and rituals. Pindar's odes are often described as documents of a waning aristocracy, and as attempts to shore up a class then ceding to the emerging bourgeoisie. While Pindar's odes do undoubtedly reflect the specific conditions of the first half of the fifth century and are tied to a particular class in a particular phase of its development, nonetheless their nature as songs of praise refers them to the broader, more permanent structures of Greek culture and society. It is the purpose of the next chapter to investigate some of the connections between Pindar's epinician odes and the institutions of archaic Greek culture.

4

The Return Home

One of the best known and most controversial of Pindar's poems is fr. 169 on *nomos:*

Νόμος ὁ πάντων βασιλεύς
θνατῶν τε καὶ ἀθανάτων
ἄγει δικαιῶν τὸ βιαιότατον
ὑπερτάτᾳ χειρί. τεκμαίρομαι
ἔργοισιν Ἡρακλέος·
ἐπεὶ Γηρυόνα βόας
Κυκλώπειον ἐπὶ πρόθυρον Εὐρυσθέος
]καὶ ἀπριάτας ἔλασεν

Nomos, the king of all mortals and immortals, leads us on, making just what is most violent with high hand. I call as witness the deeds of Heracles, since he drove the cattle of Geryon . . . and unbought to the Cyclopean doorway of Eurystheus.

The verse is cited by Callicles in Plato's *Gorgias* (484b) and interpreted by him as a statement concerning the "law of nature," whereby might is right.[1] This interpretation of *nomos* has found few supporters in modern times,[2] but scholars have yet to reach a consensus about the meaning of the word, and, with it, the interpretation of the poem. Lloyd-Jones distinguishes two groups of theories about the meaning of *nomos.*[3] The first group understands it to signify "custom" or "usage"; the second group takes it as the law of the universe, and especially the law of Zeus.[4]

The argument developed in the book so far indicates that any univocal definition of *nomos,* whether as "custom" or as "law of Zeus" is unlikely to prove adequate to Pindar's meaning. On the one hand, the gods' influence in men's lives is ambiguous, for they both uphold and disrupt men's notions of justice. Conversely, we have seen that a society's customary notions of right and wrong, while indeed crucial to the society and individual members of it, nonetheless do not enjoy an unfailing validity. Ambiguity attends both "divine law" and "social usage." We must expect that a word capable of meaning either of these will resist neat definition.

Pindar is dealing in this poem with irregularities in men's notions of right and wrong, as is clear from a later passage, where Pindar cites Heracles' theft of Diomedes' horses as another example of the powers of *nomos* to "make just what is most violent." Diomedes defended himself, Pindar says, not for reasons of greed but because of his *aretē* (15), and the scholiast adds, "It is the part of the courageous man, not the insolent one, to refuse to let his property go; it is Heracles who was unjust, in taking (the horses) away." Not only did Heracles steal the horses, but he also threw a man to the horses to be eaten, and Pindar dwells on the horrid consequences of Heracles' act (19–32).

Diomedes is praiseworthy; Heracles, in this instance, was blameworthy. Yet, thanks to *nomos*, the former is considered a villainous monster, who fed his horses on human flesh, while Heracles, the aggressor, the one who in fact threw a man to the horses, is held in high regard and honored by men.

The same is true of Geryon. As Pindar says in another poem (fr. 81), "I praise you, Geryon, in comparison with him (Heracles), but that which is not loved by Zeus I keep utterly silent." The scholiast to Aristides, to whom we owe the existence of the fragment, tells us that Geryon is being commended for offering resistance, when his property was being taken from him.[5] Since, however, it was Heracles, not Geryon, who was the favorite of Zeus, the encomiast will not continue his praise.

The passage is an interesting counterpart to *Nem.* 5.14–18, where Pindar alludes to the murder of Phocus by Peleus and Telamon. "I am ashamed to speak a great word, not hazarded in justice, how they [Peleus and Telamon] left the famous island [of Aegina] and what *daimon* drove the hardy men from Oenona. Not every truth (*alatheia*) is more profitable for showing its exact (*atrekes*) face." Peleus and Telamon were direct descendants of Zeus; Pindar covers in silence the evil deeds of those loved by Zeus. Conversely, he declines to praise those whom Zeus does not love, however praiseworthy their deeds might be.

The encomiast's role, then, is a circumscribed one. It is his duty to "praise the praiseworthy, blame the blameworthy," and failure to do this is very wrong. The imperative is not absolute, however, because it depends ultimately on whether the gods are benevolent or hostile to the person, and the gods' disposition is not subject to men's notions of right and wrong. The power to exalt or humble—even without regard to a person's "merits"—is a divine prerogative.[6] Scholars are right, therefore, to insist that *nomos* is divine, for the divinity of this *nomos* is shown precisely in its power to overthrow normal human notions of right and wrong. This divine *nomos* "makes the most violent just" not by using violence to serve, ultimately, justice;[7] rather, by virtue of *nomos*, violent deeds are understood by people as proper, and not deserving censure.

There is also a meaning of "custom" or "usage" that is important for an understanding of the word and the poem. In fr. 169, Pindar reflects on tradition, as he does elsewhere in the odes. When tradition tells of scandalous stories, Pindar's response is sometimes to be silent (as with the murder of Phocus in *Nem.* 5), and sometimes to emend the tradition, by claiming that the scandals are lies invented by the jealous (*Ol.* 1.46-52). By introducing this correction, Pindar maintains the distinction between just and unjust, and the infallible gods and fallible mortals. In fr. 169, however, his response to the stories of Heracles, Geryon, and Diomedes is quite different. Rather than correct tradition, to bring it into line with the customary distinctions of moral categories, he reflects rather on the power of *nomos* to make men hold contradictory beliefs, so that they revere what they condemn and condemn behavior (Diomedes') which they elsewhere commend.

The failure to give praise and blame where due is the great evil Pindar discusses in his poems; yet in this fragment, far from condemning the confusion of values (whereby the blameworthy person is revered), Pindar claims that *nomos,* which "makes just" what is violent, is "king of all mortals and immortals." If we take *nomos* as referring to the traditional, customary evaluation of heroes and villains, then Pindar is reflecting on the strange fact that our values are in contradiction with each other, since we praise both the just and Heracles.

While *nomos* is divine therefore, it ought not to be severed from connotations of men's beliefs and values. *Nomos,* men's esteem or hatred for the heroes, is based not only on human notions of commendable behavior but also on the gods' love for or hostility toward the hero. *Nomos* refers to men's beliefs and evaluations, but Pindar is showing how these beliefs and evaluations are grounded in the gods' activity of exalting and humbling and may even contradict men's own notions of what is praiseworthy.

The themes and ambiguities that find expression in fr. 169 will be explored in this final chapter. Having considered in the last two chapters some aspects of human societies and the ode as an expression of the ties binding members of a society, I will return again to the limitations placed on the ties and the code of values that safeguards them. The topic of this chapter is *nostos,* or the return home, in the odes, and the relationship of this theme, as it appears in the epinicians, to its occurrences in epic, myth, and ritual.

The victor's return home is made highly significant by Pindar; the purpose of the epinicians is to secure a proper reception of the victor upon his return to the community. Moreover, the movement out to the games and back again to the community suggests different aspects of victory. As argued in the second chapter, victory exists outside culture as

106

well as inside it. The athlete has had to leave his community to go out and win his victory—not only in a spatial but a moral sense as well, for he has left behind the system of rewards and redresses, which obtains within the city, and has gone out to the games, where his excellent actions may or may not "happen upon" (*tugkhanein*) victory, as the gods decide. The "journey home," then, suggests the movement back again to life within the considerations of moral distinctions, after the voyage away from the community, itself suggestive of the movement past the realm of clean distinctions and just retribution.

A study of the return home allows us to explore some of the manifold connections between the epinician and the myths and rituals of archaic Greek culture. Although the epinician is a highly formal work of art, distinguished by its peculiar repertory of commonplaces and stock motifs, it nonetheless grows from some of the most essential concerns of Greek culture in the archaic period. I will try to show some ways in which the epinician relates to the broad currents of life that surround and give rise to it.

Having treated the epinician as a cultural product, I will turn next to consider how it relates to life outside culture. Myths of failures in *nostos*—heroes rejected by their townsmen and forced to live in exile—should serve to illuminate *ex contrariis* the character of that social bond which is upheld in the odes. To enjoy renown and esteem within the community rules out other possibilities for glory, which are the prerogative of those in exile. The hero rejected by his townsmen for excessive violence ends as a figure of cult, honored by those who had rejected him. Conversely, the divinity of the exile is shut off for the one who is accepted and honored by members of his community. A consideration of the relationship between epinician poetry and cult may thus illuminate some of the problems presented by fr. 169, where Pindar deals with the contradictions in what people revere and praise.

Lastly, I will consider more closely an equivocation noted in chapter 2. Culture is set off against nature; the system of definitions and distinctions that make possible an orderly life for the community is itself distinguished from a realm of nature and necessity, where such distinctions do not obtain. Nonetheless, men form their *koinōniai* out of necessity; because sustenance has been made scarce by Zeus, the individual is no longer sufficient to himself, and, as we saw when considering *Works and Days,* a person's attempts to procure *bios* necessarily involve him with others. That is to say, culture is itself "natural"; the need for it is a need imposed on humans by the gods.

When a culture fails to maintain the differences between the praiseworthy and the blameworthy it badly compromises itself; Achilles, outraged at the loss of the prize he has deserved, refuses to have anything to do with the Achaeans. He can leave the society because it is but one among several kinds of life; he can return to his father in Phthia. The code of warrior life, discredited by the fallible mortals charged with safeguarding them, can be changed for another. Culture appears here, then, as mortal, relative, free, arbitrary. On the other hand, Achilles does not return to Phthia; to do so would mean an inglorious life, antithetical to Achilles' very being. The warrior society is, in a way, necessary and inescapable.

To cite another example, when Achilles, in defiance of the other Achaeans (cf. 24.650-58), wishes to persuade Priam to share a meal with him, he has at his disposal only the arguments that Odysseus, eager to reconcile Achilles to the society of Agamemnon and the Achaeans, had practiced on him.[8] Culture and society, for all their fallibility and arbitrariness, are necessary and inescapable.

This is similar to the point Herodotus seeks to make about *nomos.* It is arbitrary, to the extent that different societies hold different beliefs. Darius (Hdt.3.38) found that Greeks considered it the blackest impiety to eat the corpses of their parents (instead of cremating them, as was their *nomos*), while the Kallatiai, an Indian people, would take no amount of money to burn the bodies of their parents, for it was their *nomos* to eat them.[9] Despite the fact that a people's *nomoi* are not universal, however, they are still authoritative. It is a sign of the king Cambyses' madness that he outraged others' *nomoi* (Hdt.3.38).

Insofar as culture is natural and necessary, failures in it—that is, failures to praise and blame where due—show that culture *is* mortal and fallible (not that it is degenerate or worthless). Once again, we see how *nomos* is "king of all." Insofar as *nomos* gives evidence of the contradictions in men's beliefs, it shows the natural, necessary character of the system in which those contradictions exist, since contradiction is a characteristic of the nature imposed on men by the gods. While praise for the blameworthy and blame for the meritorious in one way represent an evil (a violation of the moral code), in another way they show that culture itself participates in a violent, contradictory world. A study of *Nem.* 7, in which Pindar deals with failures in just acknowledgment, should clarify these considerations.

i

The return of the athlete to his native city from the games is one of the most common of Pindar's themes. The odes are in part attempts to secure the victor's reception by his fellow citizens. Pindar occasionally begins his poems with a prayer that the athlete be "received" by the goddess who protects the city (*Ol.* 5, *Pyth.* 12); in *Pyth.* 8, he prays that

Hesychia—the calm that comes after a victory—"receive" the victor.[10] In *Nem.* 9, Pindar uses the departure from the games and arrival at home as a frame for the body of the poem. In *Pyth.* 9, Pindar lays stress on the fact that Telesikrates will be "received" by his city Cyrene when he returns from Delphi, just as the nymph Cyrene was once received by Libya when Apollo had chosen her for his mistress. *Pyth.* 4, another ode composed for Cyrene, is intended to secure the return home of Damophilos, a courtier who seems to have fallen afoul of the king Aristokleides. Pindar structures *Ol.* 6 around two journeys home: the one to Hagesias's ancestral home at Pitane (in the Peloponnese) and the other to Hagesias's home in Sicily.

Pindar uses the word *nostos* of the victorious athlete's return at *Nem.* 2.24: "Townsmen, celebrate Zeus for Timodemos, together with his return (*nostos*) in fair renown." The word is also found in description of defeat, as in *Pyth.* 8.81-86, where Pindar tells the victor, "You fell on four bodies from on high, planning evil; but for them no pleasant *nostos* was adjudged at the Pythian games, nor does sweet laughter stir up delight when they go to their mothers" (cf. also *Ol.* 8.69, *Pyth.* 1.35).

The victor's return is one of the most important motifs in Greek poetry. Its significance for the *Odyssey* is obvious, but it also plays an important role in the *Iliad,* where the warriors regularly discuss their battles and success in terms of *nostos.* In *Il.* 13.222-30, Idomeneus says to the disguised Poseidon that Zeus is giving victory to the Trojans so that the Achaeans will die far from their home in Argos. Poseidon then urges Idomeneus on to a renewed effort by saying, "Let the man who slackens in the fight today not return home (*mē . . . nostēseien*), but be a plaything for the dogs here" (13.231-33).

"To lose one's *nostos*" is synonymous with defeat. In 17.239, during the fight around Patroclus's corpse, Ajax says to Menelaus that he expects they will be killed. "I do not think that we two shall return home from war." It is perhaps this crucial significance of *nostos* that has shaped the episode of Hector's firing of the ships. The ships are the instruments of the return voyage; their loss would signal the defeat of the Achaeans. Achilles sends Patroclus out to prevent the catastrophe, with the command to "fall upon (the Trojans) with all your strength, lest they burn the ships with blazing fire and take away our own return home (*philon . . . noston*)" (16.81-82).

Warring seems to be understood in the *Iliad* as part of a cyclical journey out and back. The warrior leaves camp to fight, and his deeds come to their term in the successful return home to the camp. Thus, Hector says to the Trojans, "Just now I said that I would destroy the ships and all the Achaeans, and then return home" (*Il.* 8.498-99).

It is only by rejoining his fellows that the warrior can receive their

109

acknowledgment and honor. So, in the hard fighting over Patroclus's body, Ajax tells Menelaus that they must take the best counsel "how we may retrieve the body and at the same time bring joy to our own companions by our return" (17.634-36). In 24, when Priam brings Hector's body back to Troy, Cassandra reminds the Trojans of the great joy Hector's return from war used to bring (24.704-6; cf. *Ol.* 4.4-5).

For most of the warriors, the return home is the natural and proper conclusion for their deeds. For Achilles, on the other hand, *nostos* and renown (*kleos*) are mutually exclusive. He tells the embassy in 9: "If I stay here fighting beside the city of the Trojans, my day of return is ruined, but there will be a long life for me" (*Il.* 9.412-16). Achilles is like a negative version of the other warriors. They prove their mettle by fighting; Achilles proves his by refusing to fight, thus demonstrating to Agamemnon how badly the Achaeans depend on Achilles. "Return" for most warriors means the return to camp; Achilles, however, "returns" from his tents to the battlefield.[11]

Bereavement is regularly expressed in terms of the return home and the reception of the hero. Achilles tells Thetis that she will not "receive him on his day of return" (18.89-90). Thetis, too, tells the Nereids, "I raised him, like a plant in a garden's ground, and sent him on the beaked ships to Ilium, to fight the Trojans. I will not receive him back again, returning to the home of his father Peleus" (18.57-60). Andromache is also denied her "reception" of Hector (cf. 17.207-8; 22.440-46).

Achilles is, preeminently, the warrior who does not return home, and the *Iliad* is his poem. Odysseus is, preeminently, the warrior who does return home, and his story is told in the *Odyssey*.[12] Reception of the returned hero looms large in the latter poem; Odysseus and Agamemnon are distinguished mainly by the reception that greeted them at home. As we have seen, Penelope's role in the *Odyssey* seems analogous to that of the epinician poet, since each one plays a crucial role in securing a happy *nostos* for the returning victor/hero by receiving and welcoming him.

The importance of the athlete's or hero's return is not confined to lyric and epic poetry; it is a recurring motif in Greek myths as well.[13] When the hero returns, he comes with new powers or new knowledge, which may be either dangerous or beneficial to the community. He is not the same as when he set forth, and so his return is as uncertain in its outcome as the arrival of a stranger. The hero's strength threatens to overpower the society. When Heracles returned to Tiryns with the dead body of the Nemean lion, the king Eurystheus was so terrified that he hid in a bronze jar set in the earth, ordering Heracles henceforth to display his trophies outside the city gates. Oedipus's return to Thebes caused the death of the king Laius and a plague. Theseus was responsible for his

110

father's death, too; while returning from Crete, he forgot to hoist the white sail as a sign of his victory. Aegeus saw the black sail, assumed that Theseus's mission had been a failure, and killed himself.[14] Bacchylides gives us a vivid impression of the community's anxiety at reports of the hero's approach. *Bacch.* 18 is a dialogue between the Athenian citizens and king Aegeus, who informs them of a hero reportedly making his way to Athens:

> Just now there has come a messenger, having walked the long Isthmian road. He tells the unspeakable deeds of a mighty man. He slew the violent Sinis, the strongest of mortal men, the child of the earth-shaker, the Lytaean son of Cronus. He killed the man-murdering boar in the forests of Cremmyon and the overweening Sciron. He stopped Cercyon's wrestling, and Procoptes dropped the mighty hammer of Much-Woe, when he happened on a better man. I fear where these things will end (16-30).

Although Theseus is portrayed as a benevolent character, killing pests and evils, Aegeus nonetheless fears the consequences of his arrival in Athens. The hero's violent strength is not to be trusted.

In certain myths, however, the hero is a savior, the one who restores society; the violence is used for "just" purposes. Thus, Orestes slays his mother when he returns home, but this murder was demanded explicitly by Apollo. Perseus turns Polydectes and his minions to stone, but this was done to punish Polydectes for what he had done to Perseus's mother.[15] Odysseus slays his wife's suitors, who have outraged Zeus Xenios and the laws of hospitality. (It is worth noting, however, that the kinsmen of the slain do not admit the justice of the deaths and seek to destroy Odysseus.)[16]

The hero's return, then, can be a great boon to the community, although the hero's violence remains a troubling aspect of his benevolence; to set matters straight, Perseus destroys an entire population. Nonetheless, to the extent that the hero's return is beneficial to the community, we may compare it to certain myths about the gods. In these divine myths, a god's departure brings barrenness and scarcity, while his or her return signals the restoration of fertility. Thus, Demeter goes away out of anger at the loss of her daughter Persephone. It is not until she has been appeased by the gods that Demeter returns and the earth is once again made productive. The story has parallels in Hittite myths, and seems also to have shaped the story of Achilles' wrath—that is, Achilles goes away in anger and, by refusing to fight, causes a great destruction among the Achaeans. Not until he returns to battle can the Achaeans stave off the Trojans.[17]

The returning hero is an ambiguous figure. He is not a stranger to the

111

community, but neither is he a member, since he is no longer the person he was when he departed; he has been changed during his absence. In *Pyth.* 4, Jason returning to Iolcos from his childhood in the mountains is described as being "like a stranger (*xenos*), although a townsman (*astos*)" (78). It is perhaps this ambiguous, or "liminal"[18] character of the returning hero that accounts for the prevalence of *nostos* as a motif in poetry and myth. The returning person is problematical because he is not easily classified, being neither one thing nor the other. He thus becomes a richly suggestive theme in songs and stories.

It seems worthwhile to consider a community situation that may have helped shape stories of the returning hero. I refer to rites of initiation of the young into the life of the society. Such rites are necessary because of the ambiguous status of the young person, who is neither child nor adult, neither within the community nor outside it, neither a member nor a stranger. Van Gennep has compared society to a house with many rooms and corridors; to pass from one room to another is fraught with danger.[19] Mary Douglas writes:

> Danger lies in transitional states, simply because transition is neither one state nor the next; it is undefinable. The person who must pass from one to another is himself in danger and emanates danger to others. The danger is controlled by ritual which precisely separates him from his old status, segregates him for a time and then publicly declares his entry to his new status. Not only is transition itself dangerous, but also the rituals of segregation are the most dangerous phase of the rites. . . . To say that the boys risk their lives (during the period of segregation) says precisely that to go out of the formal structure and to enter the margins is to be exposed to power that is enough to kill them or make their manhood.[20]

To what extent rituals of initiation can be found among the Greeks must remain controversial, and the following observations, therefore, can lead only to tentative conclusions.[21] Nonetheless, the connections between such rituals and narratives of the hero's journey out to confront mortal risks, followed by his return, seem striking enough to merit attention. In the following account, I draw for the most part from Angelo Brelich, whose treatment, together with extensive references, should be consulted.[22]

These rituals have as their purpose the initiation of young people into the normal life of society, with its responsibilities and privileges.[23] Birth does not confer membership in the community; the child, strictly speaking, is not a member. Only when the young person gives proof of his strength and ability to withstand hardship is he accepted into the society. The initiate is regularly segregated from the community. In

112

several cultures, we hear of mock struggles wherein the adult males wrest those to be initiated from the women's side, while the women make as if to resist.

During the period of segregation from the community, the young person may follow a special diet or wear a distinctive garment. It is often a time of duress. The initiate undergoes abuse and even torments of various kinds—for example, extremes of heat or cold, beating, circumcision, subincision, extraction of teeth, confinement in an uncomfortable position. Abuse is meant to prove the young person's strength, but it seems to have a magical element as well. That is, by means of violent and stressful rituals, the former self dies and a new person is born into the community. Furthermore, since the initiation serves as a means by which the culture perpetuates itself, there is often a pedagogical element in the rites: the young are taught dances, or tribal traditions, or the lore of hunting or farming, or norms of conduct.

The life outside the community overthrows the familiar ways. Not only is the regime far more austere, but the normal codes of behavior are violated. In Sparta, for example, where it seems certain that we may speak of initiation rites, boys were encouraged to steal. While skill in theft may have had some educational value for the future soldier, the practice need not be confined to pedagogical uses; we may see here a deliberate inversion in standards of behavior. Antisocial behavior is permitted, even enjoined, as an expression of the youth's exclusion from society. Initiatory murder may be found in Sparta as well, in the *krupteia*. This was a custom whereby a youth was separated from the city for a year, ordered to roam day and night without shoes or cloak, and to go unattended by servants. (The institution was called *krupteia* because the youth was to go unseen; he was never to sleep soundly for fear of being caught.) During his travels the youth was to attack and kill helots. Vidal-Naquet has shown how such a regime represents a striking inversion of the customs and ideals of hoplite life and warfare.[24]

The common use of transvestism during the exile also suggests an inversion of normal standards. By these means, the young person is sundered not only from his community, but all community and all culture. The one who presents himself to the community for membership, therefore, is a new person. His "return" to the community is, in another sense, a first approach.

The "birth" of the new person is represented in different ways. The body is painted, hair is cut, tattoos are sketched. Combats, found in a variety of religious contexts, are also common during the initiation. The outcome may be determined (e.g., the initiates must be defeated by their elders). In other societies, the contest is not predetermined and serves as a proof of strength.

There are ceremonies—for example, dances or banquets—to mark the return from segregation. A new costume or name may be given to the young person. Initiates may stress their "new-born" status by showing themselves unable to speak or walk or recognize their family. Among certain peoples, moreover, initiation confers on the subjects a power that can at first be excessive or dangerous; they remain, therefore, on the fringes of the community for a while.

The initiate's experience matches the hero's at several points. Both depart from the familiar to encounter a wild and threatening world, finally to return again to their native place. The monsters confronted and killed by the hero suggest the sense of danger and ordeal associated with the ritual.[25] The inversion of mores in the period of segregation has its analogs, too, in mythic narratives. Detienne has discussed the inversion of sexual roles that is associated with the hunt and the countryside in Greek myths.[26] Adonis is an effeminate hunter; Atalanta is a woman who excells in masculine activities. The panionic feast of the Apatouria, which included a puberty rite (on the day called Koureotis, or "cutting of hair"), had associated with it at Athens a tale of the hero's deceit (*apatē*) in which the Athenian youth Melanthus ("Black") defeated the Boeotian king Xanthus ("Blond") by tricking him into looking behind him and taking advantage of the king's inattention. The use of such treachery may be felt to be the direct opposite of the behavior recommended to young people about to become full members of their phratry.[27] Finally, the return of the hero, and the prodigious, possibly threatening powers attending him, recall the dangerous powers that were sometimes felt to surround initiates, once they had returned from the wild and formless marginal world.

The festivals at which Greek athletes won their victories were in several instances closely associated with rites that appear to involve initiation. The Arcadian ceremony in honor of Lycaean Zeus is a striking example. Youths met at night to share a meal; the innards of beasts and, it was said, of humans, were cooked together and then eaten by the assembled company.[28] Pausanias (6.8.2) writes of the athlete Damarkhos that he was transformed into a wolf at this sacrifice, and remained that way for ten years. Elsewhere (8.2.6) he says that at every sacrifice to Lycaean Zeus, from the time of Lycaon, a man has been turned into a wolf and remains that way for ten years. If, during that time, he has refrained from tasting human flesh, he will be restored to his humanity; otherwise, he must remain a wolf forever. The secrecy of the proceedings, the assembly of young people, the overthrow of moral codes, as well as the "transformation" of some participants into wolves who must roam the countryside for ten years all indicate that an initiation ritual is in question. Near the site of the sacrifice were a stadium and hippodrome, where an athletic contest was held after the sacrifice. The contest is mentioned several times in Pindar's odes and was reputed to be the oldest of athletic festivals. The prize was a bronze tripod.[29] Burkert argues that the secret meal and the games form a coherent sequence, by which youths are segregated from the community and then reunited with it.[30]

In Sparta, the contest of the youths called *sphaireis* sounds more like an initiatory trial than a contest. Two groups approached an island from different sides and then fought each other; kicks, bites, and eye gouging were permitted.[31] They fought one-on-one and also in groups; the object was to push the opponents in the water. The night preceding the contest saw the sacrifice by each team of a dog to Enyalius, the war god. After the sacrifice, the sides pitted tame boars against each other, and the side whose animal won was thought likely to have the victory on the following day.

There is also a marked agonistic character to the rites in honor of Artemis Orthia. One group of youths tried to steal as many cheeses as possible from the altar of Artemis, while another group whipped them. We also hear of contests of young people at this festival, in which the prize was an iron sickle.[32]

As a final example, we may cite the Oschophoria, which was celebrated during the Attic feast of the Pyanepsia. The Oschophoria consisted of a procession from a sanctuary of Dionysus in Athens to the shrine of Athena Sciras at Phaleron.[33] The two young men led the procession, dressed in women's apparel. They also carried vine branches with clusters of grapes; these were called *oskhoi* and gave their name to the festival. A chorus followed the two leaders and sang songs. There was a running race, in which youths from the best families in all the tribes competed. The winner was given to drink a potion made from olives, wine, honey, cheese, and barley.

The events contained much that was strange. The herald who accompanied the procession did not wear a crown, as was normal practice; instead, the crown was placed on the herald's staff. While the libations were poured, those present shouted *"Eleleu, iou, iou."* Assisting at the feast were women called *deipnophoroi* ("dinner bearers"), who carried food and participated in the sacrifice—an unusual practice, since women were normally excluded from public banquets. Plutarch tells us that stories were told by the women during the banquet.[34]

Lending support, perhaps, to my suggestion that initiation and the *nostos* theme are connected is the fact that the story of Theseus's return (*nostos*) was invoked to explain the cultic practices of the Oschophoria.[35] Thus, the *deipnophoroi* represent the mothers of the Athenian youths sent to Crete, and the stories told at the feast

115

were thought to commemorate the stories the mothers told their children, to cheer them before their hazardous voyage. The two youths dressed as girls represented the two youths whom Theseus dressed in women's garb, to deceive Minos. The cry of *"eleleu iou iou"* was explained as a combination of cries of triumph (*eleleu*) and confusion (*iou iou*). This combination of joy and sorrow was thought proper to the occasion, for after Theseus had landed in Attica, it was reported that his father Aegeus had jumped to his death; Theseus and his company thus returned to Athens with mixed cries of joy and grief. The herald, too, marked his grief by not wearing a crown.[36]

The occurrence of transvestism, the ambiguous cry (joyful and sorrowful), perhaps even the presence of "mothers" who send their "children" off on the adventure all suggest that the Oschophoria is a descendant of an initiation ritual and retains several vestiges of it.

In all of these examples, we find athletic contests in close proximity to rituals at least suggestive of initiation. Thus, it is not surprising that we find in the victory odes several motifs—apart from *nostos*—which imply connections with initiation rituals.

For example, there are in the odes a number of tales concerning a birth in the wilds, or a movement from the wilds into the city. As we have seen, the initiate is received back from his sojourn outside the community as though he were new-born. The return from his segregation is a return from the asocial activity associated with life outside culture, to take up once again the patterns and codes of his society.

In *Ol.* 6, an ode taken up with home and the return home, Pindar tells the story of Iamus's birth in the wilds. The name his mother gives him—Iamus—alludes to his birth outside the city, as Pindar suggests by a number of puns. Two snakes nourished the baby with honey, which Pindar calls the "blameless venom of bees" (*amemphei iōi melissān*). *Ios* here seems to suggest *Iamus.* Later on in the poem, in describing the people's ignorance of the child's whereabouts, Pindar says Iamus was "hidden in rushes and unbounded bramble; its soft body was steeped in the tawny and dark rays of violets (*ioi*)" (54-56). The violets (*ioi*) that form his bed and the "blameless poison" (*ios*) that constitutes his food are aspects of the hero's birth outside the city and seem to be crystallized in his name.[37] Thus, the myth parallels aspects of the initiation ritual. The initiate is "new-born"; he is given a name to signify his time in the wilds, just as initiates are often given new names. Moreover, the "child" has special powers: Iamus is welcomed into the city when it is learned from the oracle at Delphi that his father is a god (Apollo), and that the child and his descendants are to be prophets.

In *Pyth.* 9, Cyrene is another "nature child." She is a descendant of Heaven (Ouranos) and Earth (Gaia) and has forsaken the city and the normal social role of women to be a huntress in the mountains. The inversion in sexual roles suggests initiation rituals. Moreover, Apollo, who falls in love with her, will marry her and bring her to Africa, where the nymph Libya will "receive" her (55-56). There she will give birth to Aristaeus, who will be a guardian spirit for shepherds (59-65). In *Pyth.* 9, as in *Ol.* 6, there is a movement from the wild countryside to the city;[38] it is interesting that in both cases, Apollo, the god most closely associated with culture for the Greeks, is responsible for the passage. It is clear that this movement from the wilds into the city is significant for the athlete Telesikrates as well, in whose honor the poem was composed. He, too, has been looked upon favorably by Apollo, as is shown by his victory in the Pythian games; like Cyrene, he will journey from the mainland to north Africa.

In *Pyth.* 4, the motif of the new-born once again occurs. Jason was spirited away from Iolcus when still a child, for fear of being killed by the usurper Pelias. Jason was educated on the mountainsides by the centaur Chiron. It is in the wilds that youths, segregated for purposes of initiation, are educated (this motif is found in *Nem.* 3.53-54 as well, where Achilles is educated by Chiron in his cave.) When Jason returns as a young man to Iolcus, the citizens do not recognize him, although they compare him to Apollo, Ares, Otus and Ephialtes, and Tityos; that is, to gods and to heroes capable of threatening the gods. Pelias recognizes him as the one who will ruin him. In all of this, we find an emphasis on the special powers of the person returned from the wilderness. The people's failure to recognize Jason, moreover, parallels the initiate's failure to recognize his family, and, just as the initiate is often given some special sign, so does Jason arrive wearing but one sandal (74-75, 95-96).

Another feature of the odes that suggests a connection with tribal initiation is the interest in the athlete's relation to his parents. To set out to participate in the contests is to depart from mother's side. In *Pyth.* 4, we find one of the most striking instances of this motif. Jason must gather a crew to accompany him during his quest for the golden fleece. Hera aids him by awakening in the breasts of several heroes "an all-persuasive, sweet yearning (*pothos*) for the ship Argo, so that no one would stay back, digesting a life-time without danger by his mother's side, but that (each) might find the finest drug for death in his own excellence, at the side of his contemporaries" (184-87). Life with one's parents must be rejected in favor of an expedition with contemporaries.[39] The reference to contemporaries here may perhaps reflect the significance of age groups in rituals of initiation, since youths of the same age, or at least within the same age group, often go through the rigors of initiation together.[40] In any event, Pindar suggests here that it is only by abandoning the home and family that the young person can come to grips with his own life.

The crucial importance of the departure from home emerges most clearly from this passage. That the departure thus represents a crisis in the young person's life may account for the interesting ambivalence in the attitude toward parents, who are presented in the odes as both hostile and beneficial to the youngster's interests. The parents need the youngster to mature and grow into his full excellence, since their own life may be continued in this way (cf. *Ol.* 10.86ff., *Ol.* 8.70-71). On the other hand, they themselves represent one of the hurdles to be overcome if the child is to grow and flourish. In *Nem.* 11, for example, Pindar blames the parents' "too hesitant hopes" (22), for discouraging Aristagoras's participation in the most important athletic festivals. Earlier in the poem, however, he congratulates the father, and the praise he offers seems deliberately ambiguous; it can be applied either to father or son:

ἄνδρα δ᾽ ἐγὼ μακαρίζω μὲν πατέρ᾽ Ἀρκεσίλαν,
καὶ τὸ θαητὸν δέμας ἀτρεμίαν τε σύγγονον   (11-12)

I count the father Arkesilas a blessed man, for his handsome frame and inborn courage.

The father both resembles the son (or, at least, shares the praise for the son's victory)[41] and holds the son back. The concern with home and its ambivalence is introduced in the poem by the prayer to Hestia, the guardian of the hearth and center of the home. Pindar presents both the continuity and discontinuity in the succession of generations. The children continue the father's *aretē* on the one hand, and on the other, either surpass or fall short of it. So, in the last part of *Nem.* 11, Pindar compares a family's innate and enduring (*arkhaiai*) excellences to a field that is productive in some years and not in others (37-43); cf. *Nem.* 6. 8-22.

The father-son relationship can be of a simple, uncomplicated kind—most notably in *Pyth.* 6, an ode in honor of Xenokrates, addressed to his son Thrasuboulos. Pindar recounts there the story of Antilochus, who gave his life for his father Nestor at Troy. "The godly man purchased with his death the rescue of his father" (38-39). If the parent-child relationship is so uncomplicated here, this is partly due to the fact that Antilochus and Nestor are companions in war; the father too seeks a return home. Similarly, Thrasuboulos has not had to leave his parents to go off to the games, for Xenokrates, the father, was himself the victor in the games.

In *Pyth.* 8, Pindar describes the losers' plight in terms of the return to the mother. "Nor does sweet laughter stir grace while they go to their mothers" (85-86). In *Pyth.* 12, Perseus returns to save his mother and take vengeance on her persecutors; in *Pyth.* 11, on the other hand, Orestes returns home to murder his mother Clytaemnestra. Here, too, then, the ambivalence of the parent-child relationship is evident.[42]

In *Pyth.* 4, finally, Jason encounters both benevolence and hostility among his blood kin—that is, Aeson (his father) and Pelias (his uncle). Pelias, as a close relative and a figure of authority, is a kind of parental figure; furthermore, the relationship between Pelias and Jason—the older man and the younger, who comes to unseat him—resembles that between several fathers and sons in Greek myths. In *Bacch.* 17, cited above, Aegeus fears the approach of the unknown stranger, whose prodigious strength threatens to harm Athens; the irony is that Aegeus does not realize the hero is his own son. Laeus had cast out Oedipus because of a prophecy that the child would kill him; when the son returns (from Delphi, and, before that, the wild countryside), he does indeed kill his father. Pelias, then, is a kind of displaced father-figure.

In Colchis, Jason must contend with yet another paternal figure— Aeetes, Medea's father, who obstructs the fulfillment of Jason's and Medea's wishes. In this context of the athlete and his parents, the several myths that tell of contests where a young woman is the prize take on a new light. Not only do such myths present competition as a form of *erōs,* but they emphasize the connection between competition and maturing; the athlete leaves his mother's side and, by entering the contest, wins a wife.

The initiate's departure is incomplete by itself; it is only the first part of a cyclical voyage out and back. The youth to be initiated is sent out of the community, only so that he might reenter and become a full member. In *Pyth.* 4, we find something similar. The usurper Pelias craftily agrees to restore the scepter to Jason, the rightful heir, but requests that the young man first go and retrieve the golden fleece and the soul of Phrixus. "For Phrixus orders us to go to the chambers of Aeetes and rescue (*komixai*) his soul and to bring the ram's deep-fleeced skin" (159-61). Therefore, when Jason goes away to Colchis with the Argonauts, it is done precisely in order that he might return once again, bringing Phrixus's soul to its home and reclaiming the throne for himself. At Colchis, Medea is made to fall in love with Jason, and her love is expressed, significantly, in terms of Jason's homeland. That is, Aphrodite sends a love charm and teaches Jason prayers and incantations "so that he might take from Medea the fear of her parents, and that Hellas, yearned for [by her], might whirl her burning heart with the whip of Persuasion" (218-20).

Everything about Jason's voyage out, therefore, points to the journey back again to home. It is as though to live within the society, one had to prove first his ability to live outside it. The young person must leave the family and home if he is to come into possession of the innate excellence of the family; thus, in *Nem.* 11, Aristagoras has been deprived of "his own goods" (*oikeia kala,* 31) by an "undaring spirit," which kept him from going to Delphi and Olympia. As among peoples who have initiation rites, the ancestral traditions and prerogatives do not belong to the person by virtue of his birth; they must be earned through the rigors of competition.

It seems, then, that the athlete is presented in Pindar's odes along lines suggestive of the young person being initiated into the tribe. This is not to suggest that competition in the games was a form of initiation, nor that the athletes all belonged to a particular age group (which would be obviously false), but to point out the similarity of the victor and the youthful initiate. Both are fraught with ambiguities. As we have seen, victory stands both outside the culture and within it. It is neither wholly human nor wholly divine; it both violates and respects the injunction to be content with what one has. The victor is a man apart from his fellows and indeed entered the contests so that he might be set apart (*kritheis;* cf. *Nem.* 7. 7); on the other hand, he needs to be *with* his fellows if his works are to enjoy a permanent renown. The relationship of the victor and the community, therefore, is problematical, like the relationship between the young person and the community.

Pindar claims in his odes to do something similar to what rituals do. The epinician reasserts and strengthens the ties among people by welcoming the athlete back into the community and awarding him the praise which is his due. The poet confounds the jealous, who hasten to obscure the deed and its significance, and, in doing so, compromise the culture's claim to distinguish between the praiseworthy and the base. Both epinician song and ritual, therefore, are rooted in the community and devoted to maintaining it; both are prompted by situations when the ties binding members of a *koinōnia* are obscured or threatened.

It may well be that the crucial significance of praise functions more as a poetic fiction in the odes than as a felt, social need. We may doubt, for example, that Pindar's athletes would kill themselves, if, like Ajax, they were cheated of their proper meed of praise. The odes belong to a far more complex society than do the initiation rituals and reflect the contemporary society in a variety of fundamental ways. The poet was a professional, and his relationship to the athlete had a contractual aspect. Choral lyric of the historical period is unthinkable without the new wealth, and the colonial expansion and social unrest that followed in its train. Aristrocrats and tyrants consolidated their political strength partly through patronage of the arts. The odes of Pindar are closely associated with the ideals of the aristocracy and must have seemed faintly antique in the era of Athenian democracy and expansionism.[43] Nonetheless, the comparison with initiation rites or the vestiges of these seems worthwhile, in that it shows the possible backgrounds for the ways in which Pindar presents his encomium and its significance.

The victory ode, as I argued in the last chapter, purports to be an effective kind of poetry: it satisfies the victor's need to have the victory completed by others' acknowledgment of it. I now add to this that the ode effects this praise by reintroducing the victor into the *koinōnia* of good men that he left behind in order to compete. To offer praise is to include the athlete in a community; the epinician is an "act of inclusion."[44] The ode does what Athena's praise of Odysseus does in book 8 of the *Odyssey:* it inaugurates a warm and mutual *philotēs* between the society and the hero/athlete. The ode binds the victor into that *koinōnia* which, as shown in the last chapter, is described in terms of table fellowship and erotic attachment.

Insofar as it is a means of inclusion, however, the ode necessarily excludes; there are things the victory ode cannot do and things it rejects. So, for example, in *Nem.* 8.44-48, Pindar confesses that he cannot "rescue" the soul of the deceased Megas; the most the poet can do is erect a "musical monument" to the dead man's homeland and family. In *Pyth.* 3 Pindar spends the first half of the poem explaining why he cannot restore Hieron's health. Immortality and an untroubled life are excluded by life in the community.

In the next section, I will consider life outside the community, and the possibilities of divinization associated with exile and rejection by the community. I will argue that in offering praise which binds the athlete into the community, Pindar necessarily excludes the apotheosis and immortality that can be bestowed upon the exile.

Pindar is aware of the limits of his song and its power. Comparison with Hesiod and *Works and Days* is suggestive. Like the *Works,* Pindar's odes are persuasive and effective; both Hesiod and Pindar hope to affect the course of events by means of their songs. On the other hand, Hesiod's song is wholly adequate to his purposes. He seeks to persuade his brother with honeyed words to work and behave in a just manner. Whether or not Perses took the advice is unimportant; poetry is fully *capable* of persuading him. Pindar's odes, however, are quite explicitly not able to achieve the poet's wishes. If Pindar were to bring a new Asclepius to Sicily to cure Hieron, he would be a light brighter than any star's (*Pyth.* 3.72-76); however, this is beyond the scope of poetry, and so Pindar rejects the notion of bringing health to his patron. Pindar characterizes the effectiveness of song negatively: the poet persuades others of the athlete's praiseworthiness because he is incapable of securing personal immortality for the athlete.

In the next section, I will also explore the limits of song as a means of strengthening *koinōnia*. Throughout this study, I have stressed the limitations placed on those mortal notions and guarantees of fairness that are essential to the life of a community. Song, too, suffers these limits, for, as I have tried to show, it is intimately associated with *koinōnia* as a means of stabilizing and maintaining it.

ii

Nostos would not be of much interest if it were a safe, guaranteed passage; it is anything but that. The *Odyssey,* and the several stories of *nostos* recounted in it, are the most obvious examples of the inherent interest of the return home. The hero in Greek myths does not always succeed in returning home; or, if he does return, he does not take up the normal life of the community. A good example of this is the story of Orpheus, who returned from the underworld, but, having lost Eurydice, refused to have anything to do with women. He was said to have introduced homosexuality to mankind, and, in consequence, was torn apart by the Thracian women.[45] Again, Oedipus returns to Thebes, but cannot remain; the pollution he brings upon the city causes him to go off in exile. Moreover, there is a group of stories, known to us mainly from Pausanias, dealing with the returned athlete and the community's rejection of him. A consideration of these myths will illuminate archaic conceptions of what lies beyond the community, and the values and beliefs associated with exile. A comparison of society and exile should define epinician song more clearly, by showing what exists beyond the reaches of poetic acknowledgment.

Pausanias recounts the stories while describing the statues of victors at Olympia. Some of these athletes actually lived, but there is no reason to deny that the stories told about them qualify as myths. Fontenrose has shown how the recurrent motifs in these stories are found also in myths about heroes.[46] He shows certain connections between the athlete stories and combat myths, in which a hero challenges a monster ravaging the land. Let us consider a few of the stories.

1. Oibotas of Dyme was said to be the first Achaean to win an Olympic victory. He was a sprinter, and his victory was dated to 756. His fellow Achaeans, however, did not give him a *geras*, or honor, as was his due. Oibotas cursed the Achaeans, and in consequence no Achaean won an Olympic victory for about 300 years. At length, they consulted the Delphic oracle and were instructed to erect an image of Oibotas. Soon

thereafter, an Achaean boy won in the stadium race (460 B.C.). Achaean athletes now sacrifice to Oibotas before competing.[47]

2. Kleomedes of Astypalaea, a boxer, killed his opponent Ikkos of Epidaurus in a brutal way during the contests. The judges (Hellanodikai) denied him the victor's crown and fined him four talents. Kleomedes went mad and, having returned home, he broke the pillar supporting the roof of the schoolhouse and thus killed the boys and their teachers inside. The citizens stoned him, but Kleomedes escaped into a temple, where he climbed inside a chest and shut it after him. When the Astypalaeans broke into the chest, they found nothing. They were told by the Delphic oracle to honor Kleomedes with sacrifices, since he was no longer a mortal.[48]

3. Euthukles of Locri was a victor in the pentathlon. He served on an embassy in his city's behalf and returned to the city with mules given him by a friend. The townspeople accused him of having taken a bribe, then convicted and imprisoned him. Not only did Euthukles die in prison, but the Locrians abused his statue as well, until a blight came upon the land. Again, the Delphic oracle advised them to honor the statue, and thus the land was restored to fruitfulness.[49]

Despite the considerable variations in these three stories it is clear that each deals with the encounter of the athlete and his community. The story of Oibotas, refused a *geras* by the citizens, is most obviously parallel to the situations described in some of Pindar's odes, where an athlete is deprived of his due by the jealousy or ignorance of others. The clear-cut moral distinction between the worthy Oibotas and the perverse Achaeans is similar to the distinction drawn in the epinicians between the victor and the jealous. These moral distinctions are not important in the story of Kleomedes, which emphasizes rather the threat posed by the hero's strength. Kleomedes is guilty of manslaughter at the games, and his madness takes the lives of several Astypalaeans. Nonetheless, Kleomedes' story resembles Oibotas's, in that Kleomedes does not receive a prize and a great loss is the result; both Oibotas and Kleomedes are honored, finally, in cults. It does not matter whether the athlete is justly or unjustly rejected by the people; in either case, the athlete has a cult established in his honor. What seems significant is that the athlete remained an outsider, and was never reassimilated into the community from which he had set forth.

Euthukles falls afoul of the citizens when he returns from an embassy, rather than from the games; nonetheless, the situation resembles that found in the above two stories, since it deals with an athlete's return and the response by the townspeople. As in the story of Oibotas, the citizens' behavior is unjust. Moreover, Euthukles' confinement in prison is perhaps a rationalized version of the chest into which Kleomedes escapes. In each story, the athlete is removed from public view. The disappearance of the hero is connected with the plague or plight that results from the people's treatment. (This connection between disappearance and destruction is also found in the story of Demeter, whose disappearance causes the earth to wither.)

In outline, these three stories tell of an athlete-hero, denied recognition, who disappears and brings destruction until a cult is established in his honor. The outcast ends by becoming sacred. This same outline can be traced in the account of Neoptolemus, as presented in *Nem.* 7.

There are several versions of the story of Neoptolemus's death at Delphi.[50] In some, he comes to Delphi in hostility, either to demand reparation from Apollo for Achilles' death, or to plunder the temple, in order to finance his attempt to conquer the Peloponnese. In others, Neoptolemus comes to consult the oracle about the barrenness of his wife Hermione, or—as in *Nem.* 7—to offer to Apollo the spoils of his victory at Troy. While at Delphi, Neoptolemus was killed. Again, the sources differ about the assailant. In some versions, a Delphian priest called Makhaireus ("Knife"), son of Daitas ("Apportioner," "Banqueter"), kills the hostile Neoptolemus, who was plundering the temple. In other versions, Apollo himself kills the man guilty of outraging his sanctuary. In yet other versions, Orestes, who had been promised Hermione in marriage, kills Neoptolemus, who had actually been given Hermione. In the version found in *Nem.* 7, Neoptolemus quarrels over the sacrificial meats and is killed during the fight by a dagger (*makhaira*). Pindar does not name the killer, but by specifying the instrument, he seems to allude to versions in which Makhaireus appears.

The story of a fight over meat seems to reflect ritual practice at Delphi. We learn from a papyrus (*P. Oxy.* 1800 fr. 2ii.32-46) that when someone offered sacrifice at Delphi, the Delphians stood nearby with concealed daggers (*makhairai*). When the priest had slaughtered and flayed the victim, and had removed the innards, those who were nearby cut off whatever portion of the meat they could, and having done so, went away. The person offering the sacrifice often received no share in the meat, as a result.

Such a ritual clarifies the nature of Makhaireus, son of Daitas. The apportionment (*dais*) of the meats is determined by strife among the participants, all of whom wield a *makhaira*. The shared meal, a normal part of Greek sacrifices, is replaced here by fighting. The two different practices, however, seem merely to emphasize one or other aspect of the complex relations among the participants in any banquet. As I argued in chapter 3, the sacrificial meal is expressive not only of the participants' fellowship, but also of their distance from the gods; the fellowship of mortals must respect the competition or *eris* necessarily existing among individuals as a result of the distance between men and gods. The sacrificial practice at Delphi may be understood as emphasizing this competition by establishing strife or *eris* among the participants.

Pindar's account of Neoptolemus in *Nem.* 7 is as follows:

ᾤχετο δὲ πρὸς θεόν,
κτέατ᾽ ἄγων Τροΐαθεν ἀκροθινίων·
ἵνα κρεῶν νιν ὕπερ μάχας
  ἔλασεν ἀντιτυχόντ᾽ ἀνὴρ μαχαίρᾳ.
βάρυνθεν δὲ περισσὰ Δελφοὶ ξεναγέται.
ἀλλὰ τὸ μόρσιμον ἀπέδω-
  κεν· ἐχρῆν δέ τιν᾽ ἔνδον ἄλσει παλαιτάτῳ
Αἰακιδᾶν κρεόντων τὸ λοιπὸν ἔμμεναι
θεοῦ παρ᾽ εὐτειχέα δόμον, ἡροΐαις δὲ πομπαῖς
θεμισκόπον οἰκεῖν ἐόντα πολυθύτοις   (40–47)

He went to the god [Apollo], bringing possessions from the first-fruits of Troy. There [at Delphi] in a battle over meats, a man ran him through when he fell on a dagger. The Delphic hosts mourned exceedingly, but what had been fated came to pass. It was necessary that one of the mighty Aiakids be forever within the ancient grove by the well-walled house of the god, and dwell there as an overseer for the sacrificial processions in heroes' honor.

In *Paean* 6, Pindar also tells the story of Neoptolemus at Delphi. There Apollo is said to kill Neoptolemus, and the episode is described this way:

ἀμφιπόλοις δὲ
κ]υριᾶν περὶ τιμᾶν
δηρι]αξόμενον κτάνεν
⟨ἐν⟩ τεμέ]νει φίλῳ γᾶς παρ᾽ ὀμφαλὸν εὐρύν.   (117–20)

[Apollo] killed him while he fought with the attendants over lordly honors, in his own sanctuary by the broad navel of the earth.

The wrangling, as presented in *Paean* 6, is an attempt by Neoptolemus to wrest *timai* or honors from the Delphians. The hero is killed but subsequently becomes an immortal, officiating at the sacrificial rites. As told by Pindar, the story bears a certain resemblance to the myths of the returned athlete. Neoptolemus, like the athletes, dies after being denied his proper honors, and he becomes a figure of cult.

It is true that Neoptolemus, in going to Delphi, is not returning home. Nonetheless, he resembles the athletes to the extent that he is an exile, since he never succeeded in returning home from Troy; he wandered until settling finally in Ephyra (*Nem.* 7.36-37). The stories of the returned athlete indicate that, as far as the inauguration of Neoptolemus as a cult figure is concerned, it matters little whether he is an enemy of Apollo (as in *Paean* 6) or piously disposed toward the god (as in *Nem.* 7).[51] What is most important, rather, is his death in a dispute over the apportionment of honors, and the fact that he is not accorded his due by others.

The resemblance of the Neoptolemus story in *Nem.* 7 and the myths of the returned athlete emerges clearly from a consideration of the logical development of the poem. Pindar begins *Nem.* 7 by reflecting on the sameness of all men's beginning and end; only during their lifetimes can mortals distinguish themselves from other people. The purpose of song is to preserve these distinctions against the time when the man is dead and no longer distinguished from others; cf. *Nem.* 7.1-20. This passage was discussed in chapter 2 and compared there to Achilles' speech in *Il.* 9, where the hero protests the Achaeans' failure to distinguish between the good and the base. Pindar, too, in *Nem.* 7.20-30, considers the possibility of failing to recognize merit and of praising the undeserving:

> I expect that Odysseus's story (*logos*) is more than his experi-
> ence (*patha*) thanks to Homer's sweet words, because there is
> something holy in his falsehoods and winged craft. Wisdom cheats,
> seducing with its words. The crowd of men has a blind heart. For
> if it were able to see the truth, the mighty Ajax would not have
> fixed the smooth blade in his breast, furious over the armor [of
> Achilles]. Apart from Achilles, Ajax was the greatest man in battle
> that the guides of straight-blowing Zephyr bore in swift ships to
> Troy, to bring back his wife to blond Menelaus (20-30).

Homer is presented as an encomiastic poet, who exaggerates Odysseus's merits; the resources of poetry (*sophia*) are used to win a spurious renown. The poet, like the Muses in the poem to Hesiod's *Theogony,* can say "false things like the truth." Pindar emphasizes the possibility of success that the deceitful poet enjoys. Lies are believed since "the crowd of men has a blind heart."

Odysseus, the subject of Homer's song, is no less illustrative of the possibilities of deceit having success. Odysseus, like Homer, has "sweet words" and persuades the Achaeans to award him the armor, which should go to Ajax. The wisdom (*sophia*) of Odysseus, which leads astray (*paragoisa*) the Achaeans, is like that of Homer, whose art has falsely persuaded the Greeks of Odysseus's eminence.[52]

When the distinctions between good and bad are obscured, the society is discredited and action within it becomes pointless. Thus, Achilles refused to fight; Ajax, more dramatically, killed himself. I argued above that the culture which fails to maintain distinctions is indistinguishable

126

from a state of nature; the differences among mortals that are upheld by culture yield to the one great difference between mortal and immortal, which is our natural condition. Thus, Pindar concludes his portrayal of Ajax with reflections on men's common mortality. "Hades' wave swells everywhere; it falls alike on the glorious and the inglorious" (30-31). Nature resembles the failed culture in that both are indiscriminate.

In the next verses, however, Pindar reflects on the possibility of *timē* even within the considerations of a universal mortality and the scandal of undeserved praise:

$$\tau\iota\mu\grave{\alpha} \; \delta\grave{\epsilon} \; \gamma\acute{\iota}\nu\epsilon\tau\alpha\iota$$
$$\mathring{\omega}\nu \; \vartheta\epsilon\grave{o}\varsigma \; \dot{\alpha}\beta\rho\grave{o}\nu \; \alpha\mathring{\upsilon}\xi\epsilon\iota \; \lambda\acute{o}\gamma o\nu \; \tau\epsilon\vartheta\nu\alpha\kappa\acute{o}\tau\omega\nu. \qquad (31\text{-}32)$$

They have honor (*tima*) for whom after death god raises up a splendid word.

The *logos* Pindar discusses here does not have its origins in mortals, but in the gods. Poetry is no longer the ultimate agent of a man's fame but an instrument in the hands of a being more powerful than fallible mortals.

The story of Neoptolemus, which now follows, is presented so as to show the gods' responsibility for his *timē*. Sad events have fortunate outcomes. Neoptolemus was lost on the way back to Greece and did not reach his home; nonetheless, he became a king at Molossia, where he touched shore. The honor (*geras*) of kingship continues to be paid to him by the people (36-40).[53] Again, Neoptolemus was killed at Delphi, but he became a *themiskopos* there; as a result, his descendants have a sure witness (Neoptolemus himself) for their deeds (40-50).[54]

In both episodes, Pindar illustrates the truth of the aphorism "They have honor for whom after death god raises up a splendid word." First, the change from misfortune to good fortune suggests the gods' responsibility for Neoptolemus's *timē*. Second, his honor is largely posthumous; it is a matter of his cult at Delphi and his continuing prestige in Molossia.[55]

It is worth remarking that the word *timē* can mean the honor a god or hero receives in cult. This *timē* may be distinguished from renown (*kleos*) secured by poetry, the fallibility of which has been exposed in the earlier passages of the ode.[56] The responsibility for Neoptolemus's *logos* belongs to the gods, who established a cult for the hero; his renown among men, Pindar suggests, is based on the cult and the kingship the gods have bestowed on him.

The progression in *Nem.* 7, then, resembles the myths about the returned athlete. In those myths the athlete, spurned by the city (whether justly or unjustly), ultimately becomes a figure of cult. In *Nem.* 7, Pindar begins with the importance of acknowledgment in securing the athlete's

127

goals, next considers the possibility of failure to award due acknowledgment, and then presents the heroic cult that is established by the gods.

Insofar as cult is imposed by the gods, as it clearly is in the myths of the returned athlete, it belongs to the realm of nature, where moral distinctions are less important than the separation of mortal and immortal. It is consequently less important whether the hero is just or unjust; what matters is that he must be honored in cult if the plague or some other evil is to cease.

In being rejected by the society of his fellows, the hero is placed outside the normal conditions of mortal life. Aristotle says that to live without a community is to exist as a god or a beast. There is much in Greek rituals and beliefs that bears this out. As we have seen, whenever the sinister rites of Lycaean Zeus were celebrated, at least one of the participants became a wolf, after partaking of the sacrificial—and, reputedly, human—meat, and was forced to live outside human society for a time. We have seen that in the Spartan *krupteia,* too, the youth in exile was supposed to live unseen and to take human lives—a program at least suggestive of the animal's existence.

Dario Sabbatucci has described the way those who longed for immortality—that is, a godlike existence—deliberately set themselves apart from the city and its ways.[57] For example, Orphic prohibitions against the eating of meat distanced the individual from the culinary habits of those in the city. Meat was eaten, for the most part, on the occasion of an animal sacrifice, and it was easily associated with Prometheus's trick and the consequent distance set between mortals and gods. To eat meat, therefore, is not only to participate in a communal act but to acknowledge the mortal condition of that community and its participants.[58] Vegetarianism is a way of rejecting the communal acknowledgment of mortality. To live as an immortal, one must set oneself apart from the city's confession of mortality. A life outside the community, then, might be deliberately sought; as Sabbatucci argues, those who sought to secure an immortal life did so by establishing their exclusion from the city.

In the above examples, the two forms of exile—bestiality and divinity—are both closely associated with cuisine. To eat human flesh leads to life as an animal; to abstain from all flesh leads to life as a god. There is a certain kinship between cannibalism and vegetarianism in that both are opposed to the dietary codes of the city—in particular, the eating of cooked animal flesh. By extension, there is a certain kinship between the animal kingdom and the gods; both god and beast are nonhuman and observe from the outside the sorrows of human mortality. This emerges clearly from the scenes with Achilles' horses in the *Iliad.* In book 17.443-47, the horses weep for the slain Patroclus, and Zeus says, "Sad things, why did I give you to King Peleus, a mortal, you who never age nor die,

128

so that you share griefs with wretched men? Of all creatures that breathe and move on earth none is more miserable than a man." Later on, in book 19 (404-17) the horses are given a voice to speak and they prophesy to Achilles concerning his approaching death. God and animal are allies from the point of view of mortal man and enjoy a deep sympathy with each other. Zeus pities the horses; the horses have the divine office of prophecy.[59]

The connections between beast and god, and between bestiality and immortality, illuminate the stories of heroes who lived violently, even insanely, and became figures of cult. That is, heroes who act in a subhuman way (as judged by the city and its notions of proper human behavior) end as superhuman. Kleomedes, in the story above, went mad and killed a houseful of children, then was later honored with sacrifices by the Astypalaeans. Several heroes celebrated in Pindar's odes have similar stories. Tlepolemus, who came to Rhodes as an exile after murdering Lycymnius, enjoyed a cult in his honor on the island (Ol. 7.25-38, 77-80). Pindar concludes Ol. 9 with a description of the cult in honor of Ajax Oeliades, who died because he boasted that the gods had no responsibility for saving his life.[60] In denying the gods' influence on men's lives, Ajax invited destruction. But his destruction by the gods has the paradoxical effect of identifying him closely with them, so that he becomes the object of cultic worship.

In Isth. 4 we hear of a cult in honor of Heracles' children (Isth. 4.79-81). These were the children whom Heracles killed in an insane rage, although Pindar seems to soften this by implying that the children were in fact adult warriors at the time of their death. Alcmaeon, the guardian of Pindar's goods, who appeared to Pindar when he was going to Delphi (Pyth. 8.56-60) murdered his mother. Pelops, the cult hero at Olympia, cheated in the famous chariot race; he bribed Oenomaus's charioteer Myrtilus to sabotage the chariot. Oenomaus was killed when the wheel fell from the axle; entangled in the reins, he was dragged to his death.[61]

Rejection by society is ambivalent. The outlaw is, in one way, simply a villain, one who violates the communal notions of right and wrong. However, since the distinctions between right and wrong, or between praiseworthy and blameworthy, are ultimately of a limited validity, the outlaw is, in another way, the one outside the reach of human law and the distinctions it draws. That what has been condemned by the community as "bestial" (e.g., Kleomedes) may be later revered by it as immortal indicates the limited validity of the community's laws and judgments.

We may distinguish two kinds of renown: that accorded by and within the community and that accorded outside it. The praise Pindar offers in his song rewards the athlete who observes justice and moderation, and it welcomes him back into the community from his successful journey to the games. For example, it is precisely on the grounds of Damophilus's cooperative excellences that Pindar urges he be accepted once again into the city (*Pyth.* 4.281-99). The epinician upholds the validity of culture and the community by according praise to the meritorious and blame to the blameworthy. The gods protect the laws that make communal life possible, and the one who violates them—by greed or arrogance, for example—will be punished.

In the myths, on the other hand, we hear of athletes who have been rejected by the community. The gods no longer appear as the upholders of morality, nor are the athletes particularly moral. Renown is secured by cult, which is established in recognition not of the person's community-promoting *aretai* but rather of his exiled state, which removes him from both the prerogatives and limits of the human condition. Exile does not "call for" or demand cult, in the way that victory demands song. Exile does not lead inevitably to cult, for there is no sense of reciprocity and equity in exile and nature. But precisely because he exists beyond communal notions of what is right, the exile serves to mark out the limits of those ideas. Life outside society thus becomes easily associated with divinity, for both of these mark off the boundaries of community and culture.

To live in society and to be celebrated in song are desirable but also limiting, for they cut off the possibilities of immortality associated with exile. Certain equivocations in the odes seem to originate in this split between the rewards possible within a society and the kinds of honor associated with exile. In *Ol.* 9.27ff., for example, Pindar pays tribute to the victor's city and comments on the divine origins of human *aretai.* "Men become good and wise through the daemon. For how could Heracles have shaken his club at the trident, when, taking his stand by Pylos, he pressed Poseidon hard; Phoebus Apollo pressed Heracles hard, battling with his silver bow, nor did Hades hold his staff unmoved, the one with which he brings mortal bodies down to the hollow road of the dead. Mouth, throw this speech away! To slander the gods is a hateful wisdom (*sophia*) and unseasonable boasting sounds harmony with madness" (*Ol.* 9.27-39).[62]

Excellence comes from the gods and makes humans resemble them. Myths express this by recounting tales in which the hero is actually a match for the gods. Pindar rejects the story of Heracles' fight with Poseidon, Apollo, and Hades as "hateful" and almost "madness." It is significant that he rejects the story immediately after the description of Hades' staff, by which men are led down to the realm of the dead. The theme of mortality leads Pindar to reject the amoral tales of heroes who contend with gods. A tale of heroic defiance and overweening strength is decisively rejected in favor of a communal ethic of resignation and respect

130

for the gods. Madness, a frequent characteristic of heroes in myth, is here condemned as an evil.

Nonetheless, Pindar's rejection is not as complete and decisive as it may seem. For the ode ends with an address to Ajax Oeliades, whose altar has been adorned with the athlete's crowns (108-12). This Ajax was a *theomakhos* even more foolhardy than Heracles. Having been saved from the seas while returning from the Trojan War, he insisted that Poseidon had had nothing to do with his rescue. While at Troy, he had outraged Athena by dragging Cassandra from her sanctuary, in order to rape her.[63] In punishment, Poseidon sent him tumbling into the sea, where he drowned. Ajax Oeliades behaved in a way that Pindar has called hateful and mad; yet *Olympian* 9 was quite possibly performed at a festival in his honor. Pindar seems to invite comparison of the earlier Heracles passage and the final reference to Ajax Oeliades by placing both in the context of gnomic passages on the gods' responsibility for mortal excellence; cf. 100-108, 27-29.[64]

There seems to be no way of reconciling the breach between the implications of the two passages. Heroes and cult figures behave one way; mortals within a community behave in quite a different way. I argued in an earlier chapter that culture necessarily respects nature and incorporates it in its institutions. On the other hand, there remains a contradiction between culture and nature that cannot be bridged or synthesized. In *Olympian* 9, the athlete honors a hero whose behavior he himself must avoid.

Another example may be found in *Pyth.* 10, where Pindar comments on the limitations of human achievement. "Neither in ships nor going on foot could you find the wondrous road to the assembly of the Hyperboreans" (*Pyth.* 10.29-30). The passage is a straightforward warning on the need for moderation. Pindar seems, however, to contradict himself immediately by saying that "With the Hyperboreans, Perseus, the leader of men, dined, having gone to their houses. . . ." (31-32).

Köhnken has argued that the description of the Hyperboreans that follows is intended to illustrate the delights afforded by poetry; that is, life among the Hyperboreans is offered as a metaphor for poetic renown and immortality.[65] The argument sketched in this chapter, however, would indicate that the passage describes a life impossible to mortals, and its impossibility is upheld and insisted upon by Pindar's song. Pindar may indulge the athlete's fancy with the resources of his poetic art—we may agree with Köhnken so far—but ultimately the vision must be dismissed. "Stay the oar; hurry and pitch the anchor from the prow into the earth, to guard against the rocky reef" (51-52). Ultimately Perseus and the athlete are not alike. Perseus was an outcast, without a home. When he returned to his island, it was to punish the inhabitants by turning them to stone (46–48); the athlete Hippokles, on the other hand, is very much part of a family and a community (cf. 64–72).

Heracles, the mortal who died and became a god, is the most striking contradiction of Pindar's insistence that mortals refrain from "trying to be god." In *Nem.* 1, Pindar devotes the latter half of the poem to a description of Heracles' birth, where remarkable features already distinguish him from other men (cf. *Nem.* 7.1 ff. on the sameness of men's births and deaths). The infant throttles the twin snakes sent by the jealous Hera to attack him. Tiresias arrives to predict the child's apotheosis and immortal life with Hebe ("Youth") for his wife. The poem concludes with the description of Heracles at the banquet of the gods. Pindar lets the fantasy stand; he does not append warnings about moderation or the folly of trying to be like the gods.

Nem. 1 is an unusual poem in that it ends not with final praise but with the myth, usually found in the center of the ode. Moreover, although the description of Heracles' life among the gods is cast as a prediction by Tiresias, standing beside the infant's cradle, yet Pindar avoids any closing formula, such as "Thus Tiresias spoke." The poem concludes, as it were, in midsentence.[66] The conclusion of *Nem.* 1 has been made as indefinite and open ended as possible. Pindar says in a passage just before the myth, "Common are the hopes of much-laboring men," and the story of Heracles' infancy and apotheosis seems to represent such "hopes." In *Nem.* 1, Pindar does not deny or upbraid such fantasies, even though they run counter to the ethic of resignation that he usually emphasizes. Heracles is a figure of contradiction in the odes. The "pillars of Heracles" represent the limits of human happiness beyond which one cannot go; yet Heracles himself is bound by no limits. Pindar does not bridge the contradiction. As a rule, he insists on mortality, moderation, and piety, while also insisting on the limited validity of these. But precisely because the ethic is limited, however necessary it may be for the functioning of society, Pindar occasionally looks beyond and allows his athletes fantasies of a life outside the community and at odds with the ethic he urges.

Despite these fantasies, Pindar is committed to the ethic of the community. The voyage out is intended, as a rule, to be completed by the journey home. *Nostos* comes to stand for *sōphrosunē* or moderation; the athlete realizes the limitations placed on human accomplishment and therefore turns back once he has touched the limits (cf. *Ol.* 3.44; *Nem.* 3. 20–21; *Isth.* 4.12). The framing structure of the return home in *Nem.* 9 opposes the outward movement of the ill-fated expedition against Thebes. Like the athlete, the poet too "returns" to the occasion at hand after venturing out onto the ocean of the numberless praises he could offer (*Nem.* 4.69–72).

132

Sometimes the voyage out is itself the voyage home. In *Ol.* 12, for example, Pindar says that Ergoteles would have gone without renown had not civil war deprived him of his fatherland (13-16). Ergoteles left Crete and came to Sicily, which is now his new home; Pindar refers to the victor's *oikeiai arourai* (ancestral fields) in Sicily (19). *Ol.* 6 was composed in honor of Hagesias, whose family came from Arcadia, and who lived in Syracuse. Pindar "journeys" (cf. 22-25) first to the Arcadian homeland and tells the story of the birth of Iamus, Hagesias's ancestor. The poem ends with the journey to Sicily, and Pindar prays for fair winds and a hospitable reception (101-5). The journey goes "from home to home" (*oikothen oikade*, 99).

The importance of home is emphasized in *Pyth.* 3, where Pindar refuses to set out on the high seas for Sicily:

Do not, my soul, hurry after immortal life; drain dry the means in your power. If prudent Chiron still dwelled in his cave, and our sweet-voiced songs put some charm in his heart; I would have persuaded him to provide good men with a doctor for their fevers, called Son of Leto, or of the father [Zeus]. Then I would sail in ships, slicing the Ionian sea, to the fountain of Arethusa, to the side of my Aetnaean *xenos,* the king who rules Syracuse. . . . If I came, bringing a double grace—golden health and a celebration bright with crowns from the Pythian games, which victorious Pherenikos won at Cirrha—I declare that having crossed the deep sea, I would have arrived as a light brighter than a star in the skies. But I want to pray to Mother, the revered goddess celebrated along with Pan at night by the maidens, beside my door (61-79).

To sail away is characterized here as a foolish, hubristic act, for it implies the hope to bring some cure for mortality; to sail the seas is to hope for things "far away." Elsewhere in the odes, departure is a good, but potentially dangerous, thing. It suggests the possibility of hubris, but no more than that. In *Pyth.* 3, the presentation of the voyage is simplified, so that it seems to be simply hubristic. Conversely, Pindar's intention to stay home expresses his resignation and moderation. The more complex presentation of home in other odes—as the place from which one must depart and to which one must return—is simplified in *Pyth.* 3: to stay home is an expression of *sōphrosunē.*

The themes of home and parents may explain why Pindar prays to "Mother." The passage is not necessarily evidence for a shrine to Rhea in Pindar's immediate neighborhood, nor does it indicate that this goddess was associated with illness or curing.[67] The mother and the home are closely associated in the odes; the young athlete must leave both. Pindar is playing a variation on this theme. The mother becomes the

Mother (Rhea); the motif of "remaining by mother's side" appears as "dwelling in the vicinity of Mother's precinct." Pindar's pious attitude to the goddess suggests once again his observance of the proper relations between gods and men.

The neighboring sanctuary occurs a few times elsewhere in the odes. In *Pyth.* 8, Pindar speaks of Alcmaeon as his "neighbor" (*geitōn*) and the guardian of his goods (58). In *Nem.* 7, Sogenes is said to have his house in the sanctuary of Heracles (93-94). The proximity of athlete and god is a bond between the two, and Pindar seems to ground the god's benevolence to the mortal in the fact that the two are neighbors. Alcmaeon appears in a vision to Pindar because of the connection between them (*Pyth.* 8.59-60). Heracles is asked to watch over Sogenes' life, since Sogenes dwells in his sanctuary, "as in the yoke of a four-horse chariot" (*Nem.* 7.93-94). This bond is a stable, enduring one and thus contrasts with the singular, momentary conjunction of god and man that victory represents. The proximity of the two, moreover, is set within the city, and this too distinguishes it from victory in the contests outside the city.

The significance of this last item may be clarified by a consideration of *Nem.* 7 and its closing passage, where Pindar describes Sogenes' house within the arms of Heracles' sanctuary. Callistratus (Dr. IIIp. 136 *ad Nem.* 7. 150a) suggested that the allusion to Sogenes' dwelling place recalls the earlier description of Neoptolemus's dwelling place in Delphi (44-47). The comparison is apt, but surely it is the differences between the two passages that are more interesting. The "dwelling place" of Neoptolemus is outside the city. He never succeeded in returning to Scyrus, nor did he return to his new home Molossia from Delphi. Neoptolemus enjoys honor (*timē*) there, but it is the honor of cult, which the gods raise up for those who have died. Sogenes, on the other hand, has his home within the city, and the honor he received comes from his fellow mortals while he is still alive.

Throughout the final passage of *Nem.* 7, Pindar lays stress on the home and on the several connections among mortals within the city. "If man has taste of man," Pindar says, "we would say that a neighbor who loves with a straight mind is a joy worthy of everything to his neighbor" (εἰ δὲ γεύεται ἀνδρὸς ἀνήρ τι, φαῖμέν κε γείτον' ἔμμεναι νόῳ φιλήσαντ' ἀτενέι γείτονι χάρμα πάντων ἐπάξιον 86-89).

"If man has taste of man" is a strange expression. Metaphorically, *geuesthai* means "to have experience of." (The metaphor is similar to our English expression "get a taste of.") When the verb is followed by an object suggesting an experience of one sort or another, the whole expression offers no problem. When Pindar speaks, for example, of "tasting" crowns or songs or strength or liberty, his meaning is clear.

Is it possible, however, to specify what might be intended by "one man getting a taste of another"?

In *Od.* 17.411-13, the disguised Odysseus is said to "get a taste of the Achaeans" by asking the suitors for food while they banquet. The metaphorical use of *geuesthai* seems natural here, because of the context—the suitors' feast. As we saw in the last chapter, the shared meal or drinking party is a way of coming to know or of testing people. It is just this sense of "coming to know" or "testing" that explains *geuesthai* here. The metaphor, therefore, may derive partly from the ethics and codes of the banquet.

Geuesthai is also found when men make trial of each other in battle. In *Iliad* 21, Achilles is perplexed when he encounters Lycaon on the battlefield, since he had once before captured and sold him into slavery. "Come, let him taste the point of my spear, so that I might see in my heart and learn whether he will return even from death, or whether the life-sustaining earth will hold him" (21.60-63). Once again, we find *geuesthai* used in a context in which one person tests another. (Of course, it is a natural image to speak of the victim shot by spear or arrow as "tasting" the weapon. The victim "ingests" the instrument of his death.)

In the *Odyssey*, we find passages in which the contexts of banquet and battle are mixed. In 20.178ff., for instance, Melanthius, one of the suitors' lackeys, threatens the disguised Odysseus. "I do not think, now, we shall part before tasting fists" (*prin kheirōn geusasthai*). He objects to the stranger's behavior at the banquet. ("Do you still roam through the house begging?"). The suitor Antinous was destined to be the first to "taste" Odysseus's arrow (21.98), while he raised a cup of wine to his lips (cf. 22.8-14).

In Homer, the metaphorical uses of *geuesthai* are confined to these contexts of feasts and war. This is not accidental. Not only are these two institutions means by which people test each other, but we have seen how closely intertwined are the motifs of the community (as celebrated in the feast) and *eris* (which finds its most vigorous expression in war).

If a man "has taste of" another, then, this means something more specific than "have experience of." The verb may suggest coming to know the person through particular social institutions, closely associated with the trial of others' character or strength. This seems significant in the context of *Nem.* 7, because Pindar is at pains to insist that Sogenes is recognized and praised by just such an institution—viz., epinician song. After showing the fallibility of men's praise, and the limitation on human culture in the first part of the poem, Pindar insists that in this instance, the victor is duly recognized by his fellows and is celebrated by a poet worthy to do so.

135

In 61-63, Pindar says, "I am a *xenos*. Holding off dark blame, like one bringing streams of water to a friend (*philos*), I will praise his true renown. This is the pay belonging to good men." Pindar takes care to distinguish himself from poets like Homer and liars like Odysseus. His good will upholds the validity of *xenia* and *philotēs*.

The passage following these verses is a controversial one. In it, Pindar seems to refute accusations of being a blame-monger. The scholiast (Dr. III p. 137 *ad Nem.* 7. 150a) tells us that Pindar had come in for criticism because of his pejorative treatment of Neoptolemus in *Paean* 6. When fragments of this paean (*P. Oxy.* 841) were published, the truth of the scholion seemed to be confirmed, since in that poem Pindar says that Apollo killed Neoptolemus in punishment for the latter's slaughter of Priam. More recently, scholars have tended to interpret the verses according to Bundy's method, and argue that the passage is simply an instance of typical encomiastic motifs.[68] The passage reads:

> The Achaean man who dwells beyond the Ionian sea will not blame me when he is near, and I have put my trust in the *proxeny;* among the citizens, my glance is bright. I do not overshoot, and draw all violence far from my foot. May the remaining time come benevolent. Anyone who has learned will say if I come speaking a crooked song out of tune. Sogenes, of the Euxenid clan, I swear that in stepping forth toward the marker, I did not wield my tongue like the bronze-cheeked javelin which sends the neck and strength [of a losing candidate] from the wrestling matches before the limbs stumble in the blazing sun.[69] If there was toil, joy follows after, all the greater (64-74).

The more recent critics of the poem are right to point out that Pindar's insistence on his good will and the comparison of himself to the athlete are motifs found elsewhere in the poems, and belong to the *genre* rather than to a particular historical situation. To this extent, the lines do not lend support to the scholiast's statement that Pindar here alludes to a particular offense.

Still, it is surely unusual and worth remarking that Pindar lays such stress on his good will. Nowhere else in the epinicians do we find Pindar lingering for so long over these motifs. The extraordinary emphasis seems to serve a structural purpose in the ode. After exposing the fallibility of men's praise, Pindar needs a very strong statement as a counterbalance, to assert that this ode, within the limits that have been sketched, is a valid and enduring tribute to the victor. Pindar even acknowledges his own fallibility, but he still claims that this does not discredit the power of song to acknowledge and ratify the victor's success.

The passage also stresses the difficulty of giving adequate praise. Pindar compares song to the pentathlon (in which Sogenes won his victory), and his language highlights the sweat, the heat and exhaustion of effort—whether athletic or poetic. The ties binding the poet and athlete and, more generally, man and man within the city require effort and entail risk—like the athletic contest outside the city.

What the athlete returns to is, in a way, a continuation of the struggle encountered outside the city. The return home is not a conclusion but simply a phase in an ongoing story of challenge, victory, or defeat. Narratives of the return home seem to stress the continuity of challenge and effort. Jason no sooner returns to Iolcus from the countryside than he sets out again; in the *Odyssey*, Odysseus leaves Penelope the day after his reunion with her, in order to seek out his father; Theseus returns to Athens but soon sets out to save the Athenian maidens from the Minotaur. These heroes return only to leave, but even those who take up life within a community must face continuing challenge. In *Pyth.* 4, Pindar says that governing a city is "hard wrestling" (*duspales,* 273) and that to succeed in it requires the gods' help. The struggle the athlete encounters in the games exposes the difficult, competitive base of all mortal life, even within the city.

The reason human bonds are difficult is that the persons participating in them are fallible. Far from discrediting the worth of these ties, however, the fallibility and difficulty make them more precious. "If there was toil, joy follows after all the greater," Pindar assures Sogenes. *Nem.* 7 could be understood as a response to Achilles' speech in *Iliad* 9. The fallibility of culture, Pindar seems to argue, shows that it is human, not that it is worthless.

In the final passage in the poem, Pindar offers several examples of human ties. Aeacus is a brotherly *xenos* to Heracles (86). Pindar prays that Sogenes cultivate a gentle spirit toward his father Thearion (91). These pairs exemplify one man "tasting" another, and each of them is meant to show that a neighbor who loves and deals squarely with his neighbor is a "joy worthy of everything." But precisely because this bond is so valuable, it is inextricably bound to the *ponos* that goes before it and makes the bond all the sweeter. The bond resembles athletic effort in that it mingles *olbos* and *ponos.* Furthermore, a god must bless men's efforts at maintaining the ties between them, just as the gods must look favorably upon the athlete's efforts if he is to succeed. Pindar says that "If god should uphold this, through you [Heracles], who tamed the Giants, may Sogenes wish to dwell with fair fortune on the rich and godly path of his ancestors, cultivating a gentle spirit toward his father" (89-92).

The parental motif stresses the fact that Pindar is dealing with the relationships that the returned and readmitted athlete takes up. The athlete leaves the family behind in order to return to them.

The prayer to Heracles continues: "It is for you [Heracles] to persuade Hera's husband and his grey-eyed daughter. You can give to mortals strength against obstacles hard to surmount. For if you weave, fitting together for him a life steady in strength and happy in bright youth and old age, his children's children would always have this present honor and better hereafter" (95-101).

The prayer on Sogenes' behalf recalls the story of Neoptolemus; not only do both dwell in sacred precincts (cf. 44-46, 93-94), but both are to enjoy a perennial *geras* (39-40 and 100-101). But again the distinctions are more interesting. Sogenes is to be blessed within the confines of the city. It is a life within the community that a god is asked to uphold and increase. The gods no longer stand over against culture, to mark out its limits; rather, they work within it in order to maintain it.

The thematic movement of *Nem.* 7 is such that it explores various aspects of *nostos* and the connections between culture and nature, or between mortals and the gods. The ode begins with a description of men's efforts to distinguish themselves, and their dependence on the praise of others. Pindar draws attention to the undependability of mortals, however, and, in so doing, traces the limits of culture and of epinician song, which upholds and strengthens that culture. It may seem that the city of men is not worth returning to. Pindar next turns from the (unreliable) recognition accorded by men to that raised up by the gods outside culture for the hero outside the city. In the final part of the poem, however, Pindar struggles to vindicate the worth of culture, recognition, and human praise. The community is fallible, but this does not undermine its worth. It merely shows that society as a whole, like any individual enterprise, is subject to the laws of struggle and uncertainty, and depends, just as much as the lone athlete, upon the benevolence of the gods.

# Notes

CHAPTER 1

1. The evidence for polarities in Greek thought is amply set forth in G. E. R. Lloyd, *Polarity and Analogy*, pp. 31-35.

2. Arist. *Metaph.* 986a22-b8.

3. References are to the Bruno Snell, Herwig Maehler text of Pindar's odes, 5th ed. (Leipzig, 1971).

4. Albin Lesky, "Die Göttliche und Menschliche Motivation bei Homer," and "Decision and Responsibility in the Tragedy of Aeschylus," pp. 78-85. See A. W. H. Adkins, *Merit and Responsibility*, on "Free Will and Compulsion."

5. E. R. Dodds, *Greeks and the Irrational*, p. 7.

6. Cedric H. Whitman, *Homer and the Heroic Tradition*, p. 229.

7. Hermann Fraenkel, *Dichtung und Philosophie des Frühen Griechentums*, pp. 83-94.

8. James M. Redfield, *Nature and Culture in the Iliad*, p. 21.

9. See the second chapter and especially pp. 82-91 in Redfield, on the usefulness of Aristotle's *Poetics* for an understanding of the *Iliad*. John Jones, *Aristotle and Greek Tragedy*, pp. 11-62, shows how modern interpretations of Greek tragedy have been hurt by the failure to understand Aristotle's insistence on the primacy of action over character.

10. In *Po.* 1454a4-9, Aristotle says that the plot in which a contemplated murder is averted by a timely recognition is superior to that in which recognition (for example, of a son by the mother) occurs only after the killing. Aristotle's preference for a "happy ending" seems to conflict with 1453a13-17, where he says that the change must not be "to good fortune from misfortune (*dustukhia*), but on the contrary, from good fortune to misfortune." Jones (*Aristotle and Greek Tragedy*, pp. 46-47) concludes from this discrepancy that Aristotle was indifferent to the happiness or sadness of the conclusion.

The contradiction is less glaring if we recall that Aristotle is discussing different plot devices in the two passages. In the kinds of plot discussed in chapter 13, peripety—or change in fortune—is featured most prominently; a plot that makes use of peripety must show a change from good to bad fortune if it is to have the proper tragic effect. In chapter 14, on the other hand, the plots under discussion emphasize recognition (*anagnōrisis*)—that is, a movement from ignorance to knowledge, rather than from good to bad fortune. Aristotle states, for reasons not altogether clear, that in plots involving recognition, the optimum tragic effect may be had when a character passes from ignorance to knowledge before committing a deed planned when the character was still ignorant. The plots discussed in chapter 13 lay stress on what the character undergoes (*pathos*); in chapter 14, the plots concern rather the character's

139

deliberate action (*praxis*). *Praxis* and *pathos* are intertwined in both kinds of plot, but the emphases in each are different.

11. On *hamartia* as "error," see J. M. Bremer, *Hamartia*. On pp. 93-97, Bremer lists the modern scholars who have objected to the moralistic interpretation of the word as "flaw." See, more recently, Suzanne Saïd, *La Faute Tragique*, especially pp. 9-37. Saïd shows the complexity of *hamartia*, which is necessarily simplified in the present, brief treatment.

12. On the poet as athlete, see *Ol.* 6.22-25; *Pyth.* 2.84; *Nem.* 4.93-96, 5.19-20, 7.70-74; and *Isth.* 2.1-3. On metaphors of the road, see O. Becker, *Das Bild des Weges und Verwandte Vorstellungen im Frühgriechischen Denken.* On the poem as a boat, see Jacques Peron, *Les Images Maritimes de Pindare.* On the poems as a martial-athletic enterprise, see Michael Simpson, "The Chariot and the Bow as Metaphors for Poetry in Pindar's Odes," pp. 437-73.

13. On the conventions of the genre and the poet's use of these in composing his odes, see Elroy L. Bundy, *Studia Pindarica* vols. 1 and 2. Bundy's work was preceded by Wolfgang Schadewaldt, *Der Aufbau des Pindarischen Epinikion.* Since Bundy, see Erich Thummer, *Pindar: die Isthmischen Gedichte,* vols. 1 and 2, and Richard Hamilton, *Epinikion.*

14. Pindaric scholarship of the nineteenth century was concerned to find the essential "idea" of the poem and to show how the idea was expressed or developed in all parts of the ode. See David C. Young, "Pindaric Criticism," pp. 584-641.

15. Hamilton, *Epinikion.* A somewhat similar attempt to map out a "morphology" of the Pindaric ode and archaic choral lyric in general is that of Carlo Pavese. See, for example, his articles "Semantematica della poesia corale greca," pp. 389-430, and "Le Olimpiche de Pindaro," pp. 65-121.

16. Hermann Fraenkel, *Wege und Formen Frühgriechischen Denkens,* pp. 368-69.

17. W. J. Verdenius, "Pindar's Twelfth Olympian Ode, A Commentary," pp. 332-41; Frank J. Nisetich, "The Leaves of Triumph and Mortality: Transformation of a Traditional Image in Pindar's Olympian 12," pp. 235-64. On the historical background, see W. S. Barrett, "Pindar's Twelfth *Olympian* and the Fall of the Deinomenidai," pp. 23-35. On the nautical language that figures so importantly in the ode, see Peron, *Images Maritimes,* pp. 122-37.

18. Verdenius, "Pindar's Twelfth," p. 333. See Hans Strohm, *Tyche. Zur Schicksalsauffassung bei Pindar und den Frühgriechischen Dichtern.*

19. Verdenius, "Pindar's Twelfth," p. 332.

20. Verdenius, "Pindar's Twelfth," p. 334, cites *Pyth.* 4.274 and 5.122; Heracl. B41; Parm. B12.3; Diog. Apoll. B5. See also Pietro Janni, "Σώτειρα e σωτήρ in Pindaro," pp. 104-9.

21. Nisetich, "Leaves," p. 240.

22. *Ibid.*, pp. 243-44, on *elpis* and *telos*, and pp. 245-47, on hope and mortality.

23. On the "orchestration" of motifs in the odes, see Bundy, *Studia Pindarica.* He uses terms like "crescendo" or "foil and cap" in discussing the structure of the odes.

24. On the Pindaric ode as "argument," see W. J. Slater, "Doubts about Pindaric Interpretation," pp. 193-208.

25. The antithesis of joy and its opposite, which has shaped the poem, is argued in detail by Eilhard Schlesinger, "Pindar, *Pyth.* 12," pp. 275-86. Adolf Köhnken establishes the relevance to the surrounding material of the mythic narrative concerning Perseus's adventures in *Die Funktion des Mythos bei Pindar,* pp. 120-47. See also his article "Perseus' Kampf und Athenes' Erfindung (Bemerkungen zu Pindar, Pythien 12)," pp. 257-65, and his note on *Pyth.* 12.9-12 in *Bulletin of the Institute of Classical Studies* 25 (1978), pp. 92-93.

26. For a recent treatment of the ode, see Mary R. Lefkowitz, "Pindar's *Nemean XI*," pp. 49-56.

27. On Pindar's reasons for including mention of the father's diffidence, see chapter 4, first section.

28. See above, note 24.

29. Mary R. Lefkowitz, "Pindar's Pythian 8," pp. 209-21. See also her article, "The Influential Fictions in the Scholia to Pindar's Pythian 8," pp. 173-85.

30. cf. *Nem.* 1.70 and 9.48; *Paean* 2.33.

31. For a criticism of the view that the Greek conception of Zeus "evolved" in a moral direction, see Hugh Lloyd-Jones, *The Justice of Zeus*.

32. Dodds, *Greeks and the Irrational*, p. 32.

33. The reading of these verses is very troubled. I accept the Snell-Maehler text here, which reads:

$$\delta\alpha\acute{\iota}\mu\omega\nu \; \delta\grave{\epsilon} \; \pi\alpha\rho\acute{\iota}\sigma\chi\epsilon\iota\cdot$$
$$\ddot{\alpha}\lambda\lambda o\tau' \; \ddot{\alpha}\lambda\lambda o\nu \; \ddot{\upsilon}\pi\epsilon\rho\vartheta\epsilon \; \beta\acute{\alpha}\lambda\lambda\omega\nu, \; \ddot{\alpha}\lambda\lambda o\nu \; \delta' \; \grave{\upsilon}\pi\grave{o} \; \chi\epsilon\iota\rho\tilde{\omega}\nu,$$
$$\mu\acute{\epsilon}\tau\rho\omega \; \kappa\alpha\tau\alpha\beta\alpha\acute{\iota}\nu\epsilon\iota\cdot \; [\grave{\epsilon}\nu] \; \mathrm{M}\epsilon\gamma\acute{\alpha}\rho o\iota\varsigma \; \delta' \; \ddot{\epsilon}\chi\epsilon\iota\varsigma \; \gamma\acute{\epsilon}\rho\alpha\varsigma \ldots \qquad (76\text{-}78)$$

The first problem is that verse 78, as found in our MSS, does not fit the meter, and editors either write καταβαίνει and omit ἐν (correctly, I think), or they write μέτρῳ κατάβαιν'· ἐν Μεγάροις .. This latter is then translated "Enter the contests in moderation," as though too much competition would be hubristic. See, for example, Lewis R. Farnell, *A Critical Commentary to the Works of Pindar*. Such advice is out of place in an epinician, for continual effort is not discouraged in the odes, but rather overconfidence in one's happiness. It is the point of these lines that struggle manifests the gods' powers, and therefore frequent participation in the games could not be construed as dangerous or hubristic. The reading I prefer, therefore, is καταβαίνει, with δαίμων as subject. ἐν should be omitted.

This leaves the problem of how best to understand μέτρῳ καταβαίνει and how these words are to be fitted onto the preceding part of the sentence. Some give καταβαίνει a transitive meaning (an unparallelled usage) and translate either "Another man the daemon *brings down to moderation* by his hands" or "Another man the daemon *brings down below the level of his hands*" (taking ὑπὸ χειρῶν μέτρῳ as a single phrase). See, for example, W. J. Slater, *Lexicon to Pindar*, ad καταβαίνω and μέτρον, and, again, see Farnell's discussion.

Better than this, it seems to me, is to keep καταβαίνω intransitive, and translate "Tossing now one man on high, and casting down another below his hands (ἄλλοτ' ἄλλον ὕπερθε βάλλων, ἄλλον δ' ὑπὸ χειρῶν) the daemon proceeds (καταβαίνει) according to measure (μέτρῳ)." See R. W. B. Burton, *Pindar's Pythian Odes*, pp. 187-88. He says that *metrōi* is "practically synonymous" with *kairōi*. If so, the daemon here to an extent resembles Hesychia, who also acts *kairōi sun atrekhei*.

34. On *ephāmeros*, see Matthew Dickie, "On the Meaning of ἐφήμερος," pp. 7-14.

35. Lefkowitz, "Pindar's Pythian 8," pp. 209-21.

36. On Alcmaeon as "neighbor," and, in general, on gods and heroes as "neighbors" of poet or athlete, see second section of chapter 4.

37. See Burton, *Pythian Odes*, pp. 184-86 for a discussion of the many difficulties in this passage and a salutary warning against dogmatism in dealing with them. In my translation, I take κατά .. βλέπειν as a tmesis, and ἁρμονία as essentially a musical term, meaning "scale" or "mode." If we suppose that Pindar refers to the musical scale for its qualities of proportion and order, it is an easy extension to "sense of proportion" or "propriety." I have understood this propriety to be Pindar's own, offered as proof that the celebration has been just. Pindar asks Apollo to look upon (*katablepein*) this, to ensure that the gods' regard (*opis*) not be jealous (verses 71-72).

The use of *katablepein* and *opis*, both referring to acts of seeing by the gods, suggests some such connection between the two sentences.

38. The MSS have ἄφθιτον; ἄφθονον is attested by the scholiast. The latter is certainly to be preferred, for verses 73 ff. work better as a justification for a prayer that the gods' favor be ungrudging, than that it be eternal. That is, the gods' regard should be without jealousy, because the victory has not obscured their part in attaining it.

39. On archaic notions of *alatheia*, see most recently Bruno Snell, *Der Weg zum Denken und zur Wahrheit*, Hypomnemata 57, pp. 91-104, and the bibliography he cites on pp. 91-92, note 2.

40. See Farnell, *Critical Commentary*. He writes that the personification of Olympia occurs nowhere else in surviving Greek literature. (The genealogy of Olympia found in *Et.Mag.*p.623.16, however, indicates that the personification must have been found in some other, now lost, author.)

41. See Anna H. Komornicka, "Quelques remarques sur la notion d' ἀλάθεια et de ψεῦδος chez Pindare," pp. 235-53, and above, note 39.

42. Critics have by and large understood the two snakes to refer to the Aeacids Achilles and Ajax, who failed to destroy the walls. See, for example, Farnell, *Critical Commentary*. See also D. E. Hill, "Pindar, Olympian VIII, 37-46," *Classical Review* 77 (1963): 2-4, and A. J. Beattie, "Pindar, Ol. VIII, 45-46," *Classical Review* 69 (1955): 1-3. There is no warrant for this in the text; Apollo interprets the omen as indicating only that the Trojan wall is vulnerable in that zone constructed by Aeacus. The concluding formula (*hōs emoi phasma legei*, 43) suggests that Apollo's interpretation has with this reached its conclusion. What he goes on to say about the Aeacids who will destroy the wall, therefore, is no longer an interpretation of the omen.

43. The MSS gives τετράτοις, "fourth." Neoptolemus and Epeius, Aeacids who had a hand in the destruction of Troy, belong to the fourth generation only if Aeacus himself is the first generation "of the sons of Aeacus" (45). We may accept this strange expression, and understand Apollo to say that Aeacus and his descendants cooperate in the taking of Troy: Aeacus, by making its walls vulnerable, and his descendants, by overpowering those walls; cf. Hill, "Olympian VIII, 37-46," *CR* 77: 2-4). The other solution is to understand the "first generation" as a reference to Telamon, who also destroyed the walls. If Telamon is the first generation, however, Neoptolemus and Epeius are the third. Ahrens consequently proposed an emendation, the supposed Aeolic τερτάτοις ("third") for the MSS τετράτοις. Although the form is nowhere else attested, see Peter von der Mühll, "Weitere Pindarische Notizen," *Museum Helveticum* 21 (1964): 50-51, for evidence in support of it.

44. *Nem.* 3.1-12; *Ol.* 10.1-12; *Isth.* 1.1-10, 8.5-14.

45. *Ol.* 9.35-40; *Nem.* 3.26-32, 5.16-18.

46. On the *poikilia* of the odes and the poet's work as "weaving" or "plaiting," see *Pyth.* 1.81, 9.76-77, 10.53-54; *Nem.* 7.77-79. On proportion and order in the odes, see *Ol.* 13.43-48, 93-98; *Pyth.* 1.42-45, 81, 8.29-34, 9.78-79; *Nem.* 1.18, 4.33-34, 7.52-53, 104-5, 10.19-22; *Isth.* 1.60-63. See Paola Angeli Bernardini, "Linguaggio e programma poetico in Pindaro," *Quaderni Urbinati di Cultura Classica* pp. 80-97.

47. Cf. *Nem.* 3.76-79, 4.93-96.

48. Cf. *Ol.* 10.91-93; *Pyth.* 3.114; *Nem.* 4.6-8, 7.11-16, and 8.48-50; *Isth.* 4.40. Cf. Schadewaldt, on the "Sieg-Lied" motif, in *Der Aufbau*, p. 277, note 1; p. 278, note 1; and pp. 298 ff.

49. On Pindar as a skilled worker, see most recently Gian Franco Gianotti, *Per una Poetica Pindarica*, pp. 85-127. On poetry as a craft with rules to be mastered, see L. E. Rossi, "I Generi Letterari e le loro Leggi Scritte e non Scritte nelle Lettere Classiche," pp. 69-94, and Angeli Bernardini, "Linguaggio," pp. 80-97.

50. Cf. *Isth.* 8.16a; *Nem.* 4.7-8, 10.1-2; *Pyth.* 6.2, 9.89a-90; *Ol.* 9.21-29; *Isth.* 5.21. On the Graces and their importance in Pindar's odes, see Hermann Gundert, *Pindar und sein Dichterberuf*, pp. 30-76 and Gianotti, *Per una Poetica Pindarica*, pp. 68-83.

51. Some examples of prayers introduced by the request to hear are *Il.* 1.37-41, Archilochus 108W, Theognis 13-14, Solon 13.1-2W, Anacreon 14.8.G. On the conventions of Greek prayers, see Eduard Norden, *Agnostos Theos*, pp. 143-76.

52. On the epic poet and the Muse, see, for example, James Redfield, "The Proem of the *Iliad:* Homer's Art," pp. 95-110 and Marcel Detienne on "La Mémoire du poète," in *Les Maîtres de Vérité dans la Grèce Archaïque*. See also the interesting discussion by Pietro Pucci in *Hesiod and the Language of Poetry*. In Chapter 3 I discuss the different relations that epic and lyric poets have with the Muses.

53. See Andrew W. Miller, "Thalia Erasimolpos: Consolation in Pindar's Fourteenth Olympian," pp. 225-34.

54. *Kleos*, "renown," is basically "that which is heard." See Gregory Nagy, *Comparative Studies in Greek and Indic Meter*, pp. 244-52.

55. The chorus is said to be on the banks of the Asopus. The scholiasts (Dr. III 1c, pp. 41-42) offer several suggestions for the location of this Asopus: in Nemea (near the site of the games), on Aegina (the victor's homeland) or in Boeotia. See Farnell, *A Critical Commentary*, and Hartmut Erbse, "Pindars Dritte Nemeische Ode," pp. 272-91, for arguments that the Boeotian Asopus must be the reference here, and that the chorus is described as visiting the poet in his homeland.

56. See Gretchen Kromer, "The Value of Time in Pindar's Olympian 10," pp. 420-36, on the ambiguity of song. On time and its relation to victory and song, see further Charles Segal, "Time and the Hero: The Myth of *Nem.* 1" pp. 29-39, and Gerber, "What Time Can Do," pp. 30-33, and Paolo Vivante, "On Time in Pindar," *Arethusa* 5 (1972): 107-31. On archaic perceptions of time in general, see Fraenkel, *Wege und Formen*, pp. 1-22.

57. Richmond Lattimore, "The First Elegy of Solon," pp. 161-79.

58. Hamilton, *Epinikion*, pp. 42ff.

59. "Mortal life drives on four virtues; it bids us mark that which is beside us," *Nem.* 3.74-75. The identity of the four virtues has caused problems. Farnell, at pp. 71-76, has suggested that the canon of four virtues is referred to, which is established in Plato and seems to be adumbrated in Aeschylus, *Septem* 610. Erbse, "Pindars Dritte," objects that an allusion to the four canonical virtues is not pertinent here in the ode. It is better to suppose that the three virtues are those appropriate to child, man, and ancient, and the fourth a virtue that includes them all and is valid throughout one's lifetime.

60. Arist. *EN* 1.12.1101b10-1102a4, and 3.7.1114a23-29.

61. H. Jurenka, in "Des Simonides Siegeslied auf Skopas in Platons Protagoras," pp. 865-75, argued, in fact, that the poem was an epinician. On the conventional elements in the poem, see Hugh Parry, "An Interpretation of Simonides 4 (Diehl)," pp. 297-320, and Matthew Dickie, "The Argument and Form of Simonides 542 PMG," pp. 21-33.

62. Leonard Woodbury, "Simonides on ἀρετή," pp. 135-63, argues for a distinction in the poem between necessity (associated with *einai*) and freedom (associated with *genesthai*). Parry, "An Interpretation," pp. 306-7, develops a suggestion by Jurenka, "Des Simonides," p. 866, and finds a distinction drawn "between the momentary demonstration of *aretē* on specific occasions, which certainly falls within the compass of human achievement, and a permanent . . . condition of perfection which can be the happy state only of the gods."

63. See M. L. West, *Hesiod: Works and Days.*

64. Much of the scholarship of the poem has been devoted to reconciling the different statements. See Ulrich von Wilamowitz-Moellendorff, *Sappho und Simonides,* pp. 159-91, and the review of scholarship in Walter Donlan, "Simonides, Fr. 4D and *P. Oxy.* 2432," pp. 71-95. See also W. J. M. F. Kegel, *Simonides;* P. E. Easterling, "Alcman 58 and Simonides 37" pp. 41-43; and the discussions by Fraenkel, *Dichtung und Philosophie,* pp. 396-403 and A. W. H. Adkins, *Merit and Responsibility,* pp. 165-68, 196-97, 355-59.

65. On the troublesome question of the reference of *autōn* in 75, see Richard Hamilton, "Solon 13.74ff. (West)," pp. 185-88.

66. Lattimore, "The First Elegy of Solon," pp. 178-79, says that *atē d'ex autōn anaphainetai* (75) does not mean that *atē* arises from all wealth, whether good or bad. "In the two lines preceding this," he says, "Solon has been speaking specifically of new wealth piled up by greedy rich men." However, there is nothing in those lines to warrant limiting the reference to "greedy rich men." Solon says "no term of wealth is visible for men" (71), and there seems no reason to confine "men" to "evil men."

67. Hildebrecht Hommel, "Solon, Staatsmann und Dichter," in Gerhard Pfohl, ed., *Die Griechische Elegie,* pp. 236-62 denies that the first elegy is a single poem; 33ff. is the work of the young Solon, while 1-32 are from the older Solon, with his matured understanding of *dikē.* Walter Nestle, "Solon und die Odyssee," in the same collection, pp. 205-13, writes that archaic poets were not bothered by such contradictions. Karin Alt, "Solons Gebet zu den Musen," p. 404, discusses the contradictions existing within the poem as a deliberate attempt to catch the full complexity of the world.

68. On Solon's treatment of *tisis,* see Werner Jaeger, "Solon's Eunomia," in his *Five Essays,* pp. 77-99, and Gregory Vlastos, "Solonian Justice," pp. 65-83.

69. I owe this example to Parry, "An Interpretation," pp. 297-320. One might also compare fr. 122.9 (SM): "With necessity, everything is beautiful" (*sun d'anagkāi pan kalon*). That is, the poet does not condemn as *kakon* or *aiskhron* anything imposed by necessity.

CHAPTER 2

1. On the powers of victory to overwhelm death, see *Ol.* 8.70-73, and on the importance of toil and training, see *Ol.* 8.59-66; see the discussion of this poem in chapter 1.

2. The familiarity of the distinction is owing to the influential works of Claude Lévi-Strauss, but, as James Redfield points out, it is at least as old as Aristotle. Redfield's book, *Nature and Culture in the Iliad,* is a fine example of the fruitfulness of the distinction for a reading of Greek poetry. See also Pietro Pucci, "Lévi-Strauss and Classical Culture," pp. 103-17, and Charles P. Segal, "The Raw and the Cooked in Greek Literature: Structure, Values, Metaphor," pp. 289-308.

3. For a review of the scholarship on Perses and his dealings with Hesiod, see M. L. West, *Hesiod: Works and Days,* pp. 33-40. I have adopted the interpretation of Michael Gagarin, "Hesiod's Dispute with Perses," pp. 103-11. In citing Hesiod, I have used the texts of M. L. West in his commentaries to the two poems.

4. On the ambiguities attending sex, as presented by Hesiod, see Pietro Pucci's chapter on Pandora in *Hesiod and the Language of Poetry.*

5. Michael Gagarin, "Dikē in the Works and Days," pp. 81-94. In response to

Gagarin, see Matthew Dickie, "*Dikē* as a Moral Term in Homer and Hesiod," pp. 91–101, and D. B. Claus, "Defining Moral Terms in *Works and Days*," pp. 73–84. On the dearth of *bios* and its origins, see the interesting article of Hans Neizel, "Pandora und das Fass. Zur Interpretation von Hesiod, Erga 42–105," pp. 387–419.

6. The pioneering study in typical scenes is Walter Arend's *Die Typische Scenen bei Homer* (Berlin, 1933), a study whose significance for Milman Parry's work on oral, traditional verse was pointed out by Parry himself; see *The Making of Homeric Verse*, pp. 404–7. A. B. Lord has defined the "theme" as a "recurrent element of narration or description in traditional oral poetry." In "Composition by Theme in Homer and Southslavic Epos," pp. 71–80, Lord writes that the theme is not a matter of word-for-word repetition; it is a protean thing, constantly adaptable to the particular song or situation a poet is narrating.

On Hesiod as an oral, traditional poet see A. Hoekstra, "Hésiode et la tradition orale," pp. 193–225; Berkeley Peabody, *The Winged Word*; G. P. Edwards, *The Language of Hesiod in its Traditional Context*; and P. Walcot, "The Composition of the Works and Days," pp. 1–19. In *Works and Days*, the typical scene of the female's descent from heaven does not serve to forward an ongoing narrative, as in the Homeric epics. The recurring structure with different characters in the several occurrences is used rather to analyze a perennial condition.

7. See D. B. Claus, "Defining Moral Terms," pp. 73–84; K. J. McKay, "Ambivalent ΑΙΔΩΣ in Hesiod," pp. 17–27; Jacques Peron, "L'Analyse des Notions Abstraites dans les Travaux et les Jours d'Hésiode," pp. 265–91, with bibliography cited on p. 268, note 4. See also Jurgen Blusch, *Formen und Inhalt von Hesiods Individuellen Denken*, chapter 3.

8. R. M. Frazer, "Pandora's Diseases, *Erga* 102–104," pp. 235–38, distinguishes the diseases that are part of the normal order and another class of diseases sent directly by the gods. The first class is distinguished by the fact that these diseases are *automata* and silent; those of the second class—most especially, plagues—are directly caused (by gods) and noisy. Frazer's argument is suggestive, but the distinction drawn nowhere emerges clearly in the text of the poem; the distinction between the two classes, if such exists in fact, is never emphasized by Hesiod.

9. Hesiod's works have often been taken as expressions of a new moral earnestness in the Greek spirit. See, for example, Friedrich Solmsen, *Hesiod and Aeschylus*, pp. 87–96, and Luciana Bona Quaglia, *Gli "Erga" di Esiodeo*, pp. 237–42. Dieter Kaufmann-Bühler, in "Hesiod und die Tisis in der *Odyssee*," pp. 267–95, discusses the different presentations of *tisis*, or retribution, in Hesiod and the *Odyssey*. He concludes that it is only Hesiod who presents retribution as secure and based on merit. While Hesiod's description of *tisis* undoubtedly distinguishes him from the tragic, aristocratic world of Homer, it seems unwarranted to attribute such differences to an evolution in Greek consciousness. It is more plausible, though not without difficulties of its own, to see a distinction between an "aristocratic" and "peasant" ethic, but this distinction must not be seen as absolute. Aristocrats and peasants were both members of Greek society.

It should be possible, then, to trace relationships between these two descriptions, to view them as parts of a single system of beliefs. The ethic urged by Hesiod does not deny or ignore the ambiguity and danger of the world. As I argue, the ethic is rather an attempt to respond to these conditions, and to construct a workable community within the considerations of the mortal condition. We may call this a "peasant" ethic inasmuch as it concerns day-to-day living and its maintenance. In other, less circumscribed situations, however, the realities of flux and uncertainty will assert themselves more forcefully. We may call the attitude that stresses uncertainty and *pathos* "aristocratic" inasmuch as the higher echelons of society are freed from the concerns of subsistence and can afford to undertake more ambitious projects.

See Josef Kühn, "Eris und Dike: Untersuchungen zu Hesiods "Εργα καὶ Ἡμέραι," pp. 259-64, section II, on *dikē*, for an interesting comparison of the "peasant" Hesiod and the more aristocratic Homer. See also Walter Donlan, "Tradition of Anti-Aristocratic Thought in Early Greek Poetry," pp. 145-54; Jesper Svembro, *La parole et le marbre*, chapter 2; Peter W. Rose, "Class Ambivalence in the Odyssey," pp. 129-49; and Marcel Detienne, *Crise Agraire et Attitude Réligieuse chez Hesiod*. See below, note 10.

10. I disagree with Pucci's argument in *Hesiod and the Language of Poetry* that Hesiod's text subverts the moral distinctions the poet draws. Pucci would argue, for example, that the moralist's attempt to distinguish absolutely between a good strife and an evil strife is doomed by the stubborn residue of similarity between the two, which exists by virtue of their both being, in the final analysis, strife. I have argued, however, that the ethic is a response to the world, not a denial of its contradictory mode; the ethic represents an attempt to construct a stable, predictable culture within the instabilities of the world.

11. To ask "what is it that men learn" is misleading. The hymn can be distorted by arguing that since Agamemnon learns nothing, it can be no profound *mathos* that Aeschylus refers to. See for example, J. D. Denniston and D. Page, *Aeschylus: Agamemnon*, pp. 85-86; Hugh Lloyd-Jones, "Zeus in Aeschylus," p. 62; and Michael Gagarin, *Aeschylean Drama*, pp. 139-50. On the other hand, E. R. Dodds, "Morals and Politics in the *Oresteia*," pp. 19-31, stresses rather the different kinds of relevance *pathei mathos* has for the several characters.

12. David C. Young, *Three Odes of Pindar*, Mnemosyne Supplement 9, pp. 28 ff. See also J. H. Barkhuizen, "A Note on Pindar Pyth.III.8-60," *Acta Classica* 13 (1970): 137-39.

13. Mary R. Lefkowitz, *The Victory Ode*, gives a thorough treatment of the pattern of verbal repetitions in the ode. She points out, for example, that when Peleus and Cadmus are described *"estasan orthan kardian,"* this "dramatically restates how Asclepius the healer stood some men straight with incision (*estasen orthous*)" (p. 153). See also Young, *Three Odes*, p. 54, who points this out. Both stress the continuity of motifs (e.g., song, fire, medicine) throughout the poem.

14. See both Lefkowitz and Young for the importance of the motif of proximity and distance in the poem.

15. The text presents problems. σάος, accepted by Snell-Maehler, is not found in the MSS, which give ὅς. Young (*Three Odes*, pp. 56-58) prefers ὅς, and gives a persuasive reading of the whole passage. Even without σάος, these lines are a reflection on the mutability of men's fortunes.

16. The development in *Pyth.*3 from evils caused by the person's own folly to evils structured into human existence is similar to a number of other poems already considered. For example, in the first part of *Pyth.*8, those who were overwhelmed by Hesychia and Apollo were the unjust. In the latter parts of the ode, however, there is no suggestion that defeat is due to moral defect (cf. 76-87); Pindar stresses rather men's subjection to the *daimon*, who exalts and abases. The movement from a "moral" to a "tragic" view of evils can be traced in Solon 1 and, as I argued, in the Simonides scolion as well (see excursus to chapter 1).

17. On the function of the Poseidon myth in the poem, and the reasons for Pindar's rejection of the traditional story about Pelops, see Adolf Köhnken, "Pindar as

Innovator: Poseidon Hippios and the Relevance of the Pelops Story in Olympian 1," pp. 199-206.

18. On danger and its importance for making deeds memorable, cf. *Ol.* 5.15-16, 6.9-11, and *Pyth.* 4.71; cf. *Nem.* 8.20-21.

19. On the famous opening priamel, which reviews several instances of the best, see Tilman Krischer, "Die logischen Formen der Priamel," pp. 79-91. The narrative consisting of two "panels" (the Tantalus story, pp. 36-64, and the Pelops story, pp. 65-89) seems to compare implicitly the two heroes, by way of locating the "best" life for men. In the final address to Hieron, too, Pindar emphasizes the constituents of the best life ("The good which lasts always, day to day, comes as the highest for all mortals," 99-100) and the fact that Hieron enjoys the best of lives ("The ultimate peaks for kings," 113-14).

20. The MSS give δυσφροσυναν or δυσφροσύνας, neither of which fits the meter. *P. Oxy.* 17.2092 preserves αφροσυν[. J. van Leeuwen, *Pindarus' Tweede Olympische Ode,* in his text of the poem, writes ἀφροσυνᾶν παραλύει. Jean Defradas, in "Sur l'Interprétation de la Deuxième Olympique de Pindare," pp. 131-43, accepts this and offers arguments in support. These seem to me to have been conclusively refuted, however, by Jean Carrière, "Sur l'Olympique II de Pindare, A Propos d'un récent examen," pp. 436-43. Carrière supports Snell's text.

21. Pindar's account of the underworld has been studied for its apparent connections with Orphic or Pythagorean cults. Cf. Nancy Demand, "Pindar's Olympian 2, Theron's Faith, and Empedocles' Katharmoi," pp. 347-57. She argues that the passage is indebted to a peculiarly Acragantine religion. Other treatments include Erich Thummer, *Pindars Religiosität,* pp. 121-30; R. Hampe, "Zur Eschatalogie in Pindars Zweite Olympischen Ode," pp. 46-65; Friedrich Solmsen, "Two Pindaric Passages on the Hereafter," p. 503-6; and Ileana Chirassi Colombo, "La Salvezza nell' Aldilà nella Cultura Greca Arcaica," pp. 23-39. Leonard Woodbury, in Pindar *Ol.* 2.61-62," pp. 597-616, writes on the equinox and its connotations of justice. The appropriateness of the passage in an encomium is demonstrated by Gian Franco Gianotti, in "Sull' *Olimpia* Seconda di Pindaro," pp. 26-52. He argues, moreover, that no part of Pindar's description necessarily comes from Orphic or Pythagorean sources.

22. Gianotti (previous note) ingeniously argues that ἐστρίς ἑκατέρωθι μείναντες (68-69), normally taken as a reference to metempsychosis, is intended merely as a description of the impossible; the isles of the blessed, like the land of the Hyperboreans in *Pyth.* 10, are precisely where the mortal person cannot go. This is unconvincing. Pindar says, "Whoever dared to keep his soul away from injustice, while staying three times on each side . . . " It is unlikely that Pindar would suggest that the just life is an impossibility.

23. On the ode as recompense, see for example, *Ol.* 7.16; *Pyth.* 1.58-59, 2.14; *Nem.* 1.70, 7.15-16; *Isth.* 3.1-8. In *Isth.* 1.47-51, Pindar sets forth in a priamel the wages that are appropriate for different pursuits, and he compares the laborer's striving to avoid hunger with the athlete's search for glory or *kudos.* The passage shows that insofar as victory demands recompense, it exists within the considerations of morality as much as does the Hesiodic peasant's attempt to sustain himself.

24. On the narrative and structural problems prescribed by this episode, see Wilhelm Mattes, *Odysseus bei den Phäaken;* Francis R. Bliss, "Homer and the Critics: The Structural Unity of *Odyssey* Eight," pp. 53-73; and Charles P. Segal, "The Phaeacians and the Symbolism of Odysseus' Return," pp. 17-64. See also Bernard

Fenik, *Studies in the Odyssey*, pp. 102-3, and Cedric H. Whitman, *Homer and the Heroic Tradition*, p. 289.

25. On suggestions of Phaeacian hostility in the story, see G. P. Rose, "Unfriendly Phaeacians," pp. 387-406.

26. The text in 24.196-97 runs:

τῷ οἱ κλέος οὔ ποτ᾽ ὀλεῖται
ἧς ἀρετῆς, τεύξουσι δ᾽ ἐπιχθονίοισιν ἀοιδὴν . . .

οἱ could refer either to Odysseus or Penelope. I interpret it as referring primarily to Odysseus, whose fame will not die because Penelope has welcomed him back home and has acknowledged him as her husband and the head of his household. See Gregory Nagy, *The Best of the Achaeans*, pp. 36-39. On the connections between the themes of Penelope's reception of Odysseus and encomiastic praise, see Sheila H. Murnaghan, *Anagnorisis in the Odyssey*.

27. Georges Dumézil, *Servius et la Fortune: Essai sur la fonction sociale de louange et de blâme et sur les éléments indo—européens du cens romain*. See also his *Idées Romaines*, pp. 103-24.

28. Cf. Bruno Gentili, "Aspetti del Rapporto Poeta, Committente, Uditorio nella Lirica Corale Greca," pp. 70-88; Gian Franco Gianotti, *Per una Poetica Pindarica*, p. 136.

29. See Adolf Köhnken, *Die Funktion des Mythos bei Pindar*, who devotes a chapter to *Nem.* 4 and demonstrates the symmetry of the opening and close. See also Gilles Maloney, "Sur l'Unité de la Quatrième Neméenne de Pindare," p. 176, who points out that the poem opens with song as the comforter of struggle and concludes with the poet as himself a struggler.

30. For a review of scholarly opinions on this difficult passage, see Jacques Peron, *Les Images Maritimes de Pindare*, pp. 91-100. The Greek text at 36-37 reads:

ἔμπα, καίπερ ἔχει βαθεῖα ποντιὰς ἅλμα
μέσσον, ἀντίτειν᾽ ἐπιβουλίαις ·

I translate, following the interpretation of the scholiast (Dr.IIIp.74; 58c), "Come, even though the deep briny sea is in between. . . ." Cf. Lewis R. Farnell, *A Critical Commentary to the Works of Pindar*. Interpreted this way, the passage refers to the sea between Pindar on the mainland at Thebes and Timasarchus on Aegina. Pindar addresses himself, "Even though you are not on Aegina, nonetheless put forth an effort on the victor's behalf." Thus, *Nem.* 4 resembles *Pyth.* 3.77-79 and *Nem.* 3.1-5, where Pindar describes himself as being at home. The poet's references to being at home, far from disrupting the encomium of the athlete's victory, seem to be instances of a commonplace, whereby the poet comments on the victory from a distance. By stating that he is at home, Pindar enunciates a point of view from which he will offer his praise. See second section of chapter 4 on the poet and his home.

31. I have retained the traditional interpretation of *hekati*; see W. J. Slater, *Lexicon to Pindar* s.v. ἕκατι. H. Maehler, "Zu Pindar, *N.* 4.22," *Hermes* 101 (1973): 380-82 argues that *hekati* means "by the will of . . .," as in Homer. Maehler also argues that it would be tactless for Pindar to say that Thebes crowned the athlete because of the mythic ties between Thebes and Aegina, since this would imply that Timasarchus had not deserved to win on his own merits. But to say that someone is well disposed toward someone else and therefore happily greets the person's achievements in no way belittles what that person has accomplished. Furthermore, the next sentence, introduced by *gar*, is offered as an explanation of what Pindar meant in 22. "For coming as a friend among friends he saw a hospitable city . . ." This explains why the Thebans crowned Timasarchus willingly (*ouk aekontes*, 21). In this context, it is much simpler to understand *Aiginas hekati* as another reference to the ties binding the two cities,

rather than the causes of Timasarchus's victory. Cf. *Isth.* 8.16 ff. for another passage where Pindar bases his recognition of and tribute to a victory on grounds of Thebes' and Aegina's kinship.

32. Köhnken, *Funktion*, p. 198, shows how this brief myth is a heroic projection of the guest-friendship between Thebes and Aegina.

33. Köhnken, *Funktion*, pp. 205-9. See following note.

34. Cf. Maloney, "Sur l'Unité," p. 181, who discusses the double reference of the poem, which praises both athlete and poet alike. Köhnken, *Funktion*, pp. 206-13, deemphasizes the poet's role as much as possible, since he wishes to establish that Pindar is not offering a personal defense here. So, for example, when Pindar says ἐμοὶ δ' ὁποίαν ἀρετὰν ἔδωκε Πότμος ἄναξ (41-42), Köhnken sees it as an example of the "indefinite first person," whereby the poet says *egō* to refer to any good man. (On the "indefinite first person" see Hermann Fraenkel, *Dichtung und Philosophie*, p. 543, note 12 and p. 587, and Young, *Three Odes*, pp. 58-59).

The whole passage, on Köhnken's interpretation, is transitional; in it, Pindar turns away from the Telamon myth and urges his lyre to defend the athlete. The passage for Köhnken is encomiastic—that is, centered upon the victor, not the poet. The "indefinite first person," however, while it may have relevance to all good men, must not be used to argue away the poet's presence. When Pindar says "I," it may not exclude others, but it must include at least the one who says it. Hence it seems mistaken to deny that Pindar is in fact discussing himself, and presenting himself as a struggler like the heroes and the athlete.

35. On the "community" of poet and athlete, see Hermann Gundert, *Pindar und sein Dichterberuf*, pp. 32-39.

36. See note 30.

37. See Maloney, "Sur l'Unité," p. 176, on the pervasive water images in the poem.

38. David C. Young, "Pindar, *Nemean* 7: Some Preliminary Remarks (1-20)," pp. 633-43.

39. René Girard, *Violence and the Sacred*, p. 49.

40. This is not to say that Agamemnon and Clytaemnestra are presented as being of a just character. That *dikē* is not synonymous with "just character" in the *Oresteia* is argued by Gagarin, *Aeschylean Drama*, pp. 66 ff; see, more recently, Suzanne Saïd, *La Faute Tragique*, pp. 152-78, and John Gould, "Dramatic Character and 'Human Intelligibility' in Greek Tragedy," pp. 43-67 and especially 58-61.

41. This has been frequently pointed out. See, for example, Karl Reinhardt, *Aischylos als Regisseur und Theologe*, pp. 79 ff., 85 ff.; cf. Bruno Snell, *Aischylos und das Handeln im Drama*, pp. 112-14, who shows a similar movement from confident assertion to doubt and anxiety in the speeches of the several *dramatis personae*. In quoting from the plays, I have used the Oxford text, edited by Denys L. Page (Oxford, 1972).

42. See *A* 1431 ff. for Clytaemnestra's claim to have worked justice, and *A* 1505 ff. for the chorus's assertion that she is herself responsible.

43. There is an interesting contradiction in statements made in the *Oresteia* about the dead. On the one hand, murder is irrevocable, because death is absolute (e.g., *A* 1019-21; *C* 48; *E* 647-48). As the chorus says, "Once the dark mortal blood falls before a man to the earth, who could call it back by incantations?" (*A* 1019-20). On the other hand, the dead Agamemnon is supplicated by Orestes and Electra to help them in their vengeance (*C* 324-26, 479-80, 489); he clearly remains an active force.

44. See Reinhardt, *Aischylos*, pp. 80-83, on the significance of victory in *Agamemnon*. Verses 551 ff. may be suggestively compared with Simonides 542 P. In

551–53, the messenger says that the same thing is both praise- and blameworthy; the reason for this is that only the gods live a life without sorrows (553–54). This parallels Simonides' assertion that only a god can be unfailingly *agathos;* if one is *philomōmos,* there is always subject matter for his blame, because humans are necessarily *kakoi* or *agathoi* as the gods ordain. From this, the messenger concludes that people should simply ignore the past and ill fortunes. It has sometimes been thought that Simonides draws the same conclusion; see, for example, Ulrich von Wilamowitz-Moellendorff, *Sappho und Simonides,* pp. 159–91. This seems to me unlikely; see above, excursus to chapter 1.

45. See above, note 41.

46. There are other motifs that appear both in the first and second parts of the lyric, but in radically different senses. Thus, *kharis* in 371 refers to the qualities of charm or grace in the sacrosanct; cf. Eduard Fraenkel, *Aeschylus: Agamemnon.* In 417, however, *kharis* appears again, but now in reference to the statues of Helen, which remind Menelaus of his unfaithful wife. In both passages, the *kharis* is roughly treated (cf. *kharis patoith',* 371–72; *ekhthetai kharis,* 417), but the effect is quite different. The earlier passage suggests an outrage of justice, while the latter describes the forlorn king's despair, which has cost so much to soothe. *Mataios,* too, appears in the first part (387) in a description of inexorable justice, and again later (421), in the lines on Menelaus's deceptive dreams of Helen. The debasing of *kharis* and *mataios* from the sacred to the erotic spheres complements the thematic movement of the ode from the divine causation of Troy's fall to the human and equivocal causes. Several studies have been devoted to the systems of imagery in the *Oresteia.* See, for example, Anne Lebeck, *The Oresteia: a Study of Language and Structure.*

47. On covert, ambiguous references to the Atreids in the choral songs, see Bernard Knox's study of *A* 717 ff., "The Lion in the House," pp. 17–25.

48. *Nikē* is one of the common motifs running through the *Oresteia,* and it plays an important part in all the crucial passages in the trilogy—e.g., the hymn to Zeus, *A* 160–83, especially 169, 173, 174, and Clytaemnestra's persuasion of Agamemnon (*A* 941–42). In *C, dikē* is frequently described as a victory or as causing victory (cf. *C* 148, 497–99, 868); yet *nikē* has a more sinister aspect in the play as well (*C* 600, 1017). In *E,* the judicial hearing is called an *agōn* or contest (*E* 677, 743; cf. *A* 1377), and the decision involves victory for one or the other side (432, 477, 741). *Nikē* also looms large in Athena's final persuasion of the Eumenides (*E* 903, 974, 1009).

49. *A* 785–87, and 799 ff. The use, throughout this passage, of typically encomiastic sentiments is noteworthy. Cf. *A* 785–87, and *Pyth.* 1.42–45; *A* 790–92 and *Nem.* 1.53–54; *A* 805–6 and the several passages throughout the odes, where Pindar asserts his good will. See below, on the significance of *nikē* in the *Oresteia.* On song as a motif, see J. A. Haldane, "Musical Themes and Imagery in Aeschylus," pp. 33–41.

50. *A* 131–37, 140–45. On Artemis's anger and its cause, see William Whallon, "Why is Artemis Angry?" pp. 78–88, and John J. Peradotto, "The Omen of the Eagles and the ΗΘΟΣ of Agamemnon," pp. 237–63.

51. See Hugh Lloyd-Jones, "The Guilt of Agamemnon," pp. 187–99, and Denniston and Page, *Aeschylus: Agamemnon,* pp. xxiii ff. They argue that Agamemnon had no other choice but to sacrifice his daughter.

52. See, for example, Dodds (above, note 11) and Snell (above, note 41), p. 143. K. J. Dover, "Some Neglected Aspects of Agamemnon's Dilemma," pp. 58–69, argues that the question of Agamemnon's freedom is irrelevant and not answerable from the text; he lays stress rather on the dramatic consistency and interest of Agamemnon as a character.

53. See excursus to chapter 1, on this passage from Hesiod.

54. See above, note 50. See also the discussion of Orestes in Richard Kuhns, *The House, the City and the Judge.*

55. It is disputed whether Athena's vote is part of the tie, or whether it breaks the tie. See Michael Gagarin, "The Vote of Athena," pp. 121-27, who offers persuasive arguments for Hermann's view that Athena's vote for acquittal produces the tie. Sidgwick took the opposite view (viz., that Athena breaks a tie produced purely by human votes), and wrote in a note on this passage that unless we suppose this, we have the majority of judges against Orestes, and Athena "interfering" (Sidgwick's word) to turn a majority into a minority. This is not quite fair, for Athena, if indeed she does cast a vote, is thereby a part of the jury, and so can scarcely be said to "interfere" with it.

If Hermann's view be accepted, we have a presentation of the jury as a cooperative venture by god and man, and signifying a grand reconciliation. On the other hand, the text does not absolutely compel us to agree with Hermann, and it would make good sense, too, to have Athena interpreting an ambiguous vote as meaning acquittal. In this way, the vote and its decision would continue the concern in the trilogy with ambiguous omens and their interpretation (e.g., *A* 122-38); that is, a vote which could mean either acquittal or condemnation is decisively interpreted as signifying acquittal.

56. On *tethmos*, see Gundert, *Pindar*, p. 63, and 135, note 303. On the question of artistic canons and "laws" in archaic lyric, see L. E. Rossi, "I Generi Letterari e le loro Leggi Scritte e non Scritte nelle Lettere Classiche," pp. 69-94, and Claude Calame, "Réflexions sur les Genres Littéraires en Grèce Archaïque," pp. 113-28.

57. Gagarin, *Aeschylean Drama*, pp. 80-86, discusses the reconciliation as expressed in the recurring imagery. Gagarin notes, for example, how *erōs* "which is thoroughly evil in the first two plays (*A* 341, 743, 1478; *C* 597, 600) is at the end directed toward the achievement of glory" (*E* 865). We might also note the use of *erōs* in *E* as that which joins men and women together; cf. *E* 215 ff. and note 46 above. *Erōs* goes from being a fatal drive in the individual to a force reconciling individuals.

58. On the ode as welcoming back the athlete to the community and securing a happy *nostos* for him, see Chapter 4.

59. Karl Meuli, "Der Ursprung der Olympischen Spiele," in *Gesammelte Schriften* II (Basel, 1975), 881-906 (=*Antike* 17 [1941], 189-208); Louis Gernet, *Droit et Société dans la Grèce Ancienne*, pp. 9-18.

CHAPTER 3

1. Emile Benveniste, *Le Vocabulaire des Institutions Indo-Européens*, s.v. φίλος. I.335-53. See also Hermann Gundert, *Pindar und sein Dichterberuf*, pp. 32-40. Cf. *Ol.* 10.12; *Pyth.* 1.60, 2.17, 4.1 on the poem as a work of friendship.

2. E.g., *Ol.* 1.16 ff., 2.93 ff., 13.1-3; *Pyth.* 10.64; *Nem.* 7.61-62; *Ol.* 4.4; *Pyth.* 2.17; *Nem.* 1.19 ff.

3. E.g., *Ol.* 6.83-87; *Nem.* 4.22 ff., *Isth.* 1.1 ff., 3.1-3, 8.16 ff.; *Pyth.* 5.74-76.

4. On passages where references are ambiguous between poet and athlete, and, in general, on ambivalence in the odes see Thomas K. Hubbard, *Language and Mediation in Pindar and Heraclitus: A Semiotic Inquiry.* On *Nem.* 1 in particular and the connections between poet and athlete, see Peter Rose, "The Myth of Pindar's First Nemean: Sportsmen, Poetry, and Paideia," pp. 145-75, and G. A. Privitera, "Eracle nella Prima 'Nemea'," pp. 28-51.

5. S. Radt, "Pindars Erste Nemeische Ode," *Mnemosyne*, pp. 154–60 has collected the various solutions to the problems presented by 24. In my translation, I have accepted Hermann's interpretation (see Radt, p. 156)—that is, I take Khromios to be the subject of λέλογχε, with ἐσλούς as the direct object, and μεμφομένοις as dative of interest. Perhaps by using λαγχάνειν, a word often used of winning a victory (e.g., *Ol.* 10.61; *Pyth.* 8.88; *Nem.* 3.31, 9.45), Pindar suggests that the good men (*esloi*) who defend the victor are an award for his excellence (in hospitality, as in the games).

6. It would be mistaken to understand the first-person in 31 ff. ("I do not love to hide and have great wealth . . . ") as a example of the "indefinite first-person," without any particular reference to the speaker—i.e., the poet. Nor again does the first-person introduce purely private thoughts, unrelated to the interests of the victor. Pindar refers to himself in the role of *laudator* and excellent man; the attitudes and prerogatives of this "first person" ally him with the victorious athlete. See chapter 2, note 34.

7. Pindar does not explicitly refer to any of his own labors. However, the *gar* in 32 (*koinai gar erkhont' elpides* . . .) serves to explain the previous sentence, in which Pindar sets forth his own hopes ("to fare well and be esteemed in doing good to my friends"). The reason he entertains such hopes, he says, is that "the hopes of much-laboring" men are all alike. Hence, Pindar seems to present himself as one who toils, just as the athlete does.

8. For *luō*, cf. *Ol.* 4.20, 10.9; for *lutron*, cf. *Ol.* 7.77; *Isth.* 8.1; for *lutērios*, cf. *Pyth.* 5.106.

9. E.g., *Nem.* 8.42–44. Jacob Stern, "The Myths of Pindar's *Nemean* 10," pp. 125–32 points out the connection between 78 and 54 (καὶ μὰν θεῶν πιστὸν γένος). The loyalty of mortals is distinguished from that of the gods in that the former involves *ponos*. Stern also argues that the loyalty of the gods is not necessarily motivated by the justice of men. Idas and Lynceus are blasted by Zeus's thunderbolt, but this does not imply that they were evil; it means no more than that they had been abandoned by the gods (cf. 72).

10. This is not to say that Castor and Polydeuces "equal" the athlete and poet, or even that they are "analogous" to each other. Privitera, "Eracle," pp. 28–51, suggests that the mythic narrative and present occasion be seen as similar functions of a single system of ethics and values, and that any analogies or equivalences between the occasion and the myth be regarded as secondary features. Thus, to point out that Pindar prays to Zeus on Theaios's behalf (29–30)—just as Polydeuces does for Castor—is valid, but this connection must not be made too rigid. A poet celebrating a victor and asking Zeus's favor on the victor's ambitions evinces a loyal willingness to toil on the victor's behalf; the necessity of celebration and fellow toilers is a part of the system of values that informs the odes. This loyalty also finds expression, on the heroic plane, between Polydeuces and Castor.

11. See C. Daremberg and Edm. Saglio, *Dictionnaire des Antiquités Grecques et Romaines*, pp. 294–98, s.v. *Hospitium*, for more on the guest-host relationship in the Greek world.

12. On the question of money, see Gian Carlo Gianotti, *Per una Poetica Pindarica*, pp. 3–16; Gianotti argues that references to the mercenary aspects of song must be appreciated in the context of the ties binding poet and athlete, and celebrations of the victor's liberality. See also Gundert, *Pindar*, p. 36, and below, on *Isth.* 2. The question of Pindar's mercenary relationship to the athlete is similar to the question of the significance of gifts in the warrior society described in the *Iliad*. Achilles insists on "payment" in gifts and the material recognition of his work; he refuses to fight because he has been denied payment. On the other hand, as is made clear by

his rejection of Agamemnon's gifts in *Il.* 9, he does not "sell" his services to others. Thus, his cooperation with Agamemnon is partly a matter of payment, but not wholly so. See D. B. Claus, "*Aidōs* in the Language of Achilles," pp. 13-28. Similarly, the poet receives money for his efforts, but the relationship between poet and athlete cannot, for all that, be reduced to a purely mercantile one.

13. On these lines, see D. E. Gerber, *Euterpe*, whose translation I have used.

14. See Max Treu, "Sappho," cols. 1235-36, for a review of the controversy. On Sappho's "circle," see R. Merkelbach, "Sappho und ihr Kreis," pp. 1-29; Giuliana Lanata, "Sul linguaggio amoroso di Saffo," pp. 63-79; and Francois Lasserre, "Ornements Erotiques dans la Poésie Lyrique Archaïque," in *Serta Turyniana: Studies in Greek Literature and Paleography in honor of Alexander Turyn*, pp. 20-30. On the connections between Sappho's *thiasos* and institutions of male fellowship, see Bruno Snell, *The Discovery of the Mind*, pp. 68-70.

15. In the Suda, s.v. Σαπφώ, we read of students from Miletus, Colophon, and Salamis.

16. See Denys L. Page, *Sappho and Alcaeus*, pp. 133-40, on the subjects treated in Sappho's odes and the girls addressed in them.

17. See Lanata, "Sul linguaggio," pp. 63-79, and Bruno Gentili, "La Veneranda Sappho," pp. 37-62.

18. Suda, s.v. Σαπφώ.

19. See Max. Tyr. xviii.9, 230H., and cf. Frr. 57, 131, 133, 144, 213 LP.

20. Claude Calame, *Les Choeurs de Jeunes Filles en Grèce Archaïque*, I.368-69.

21. For a review of the discussion concerning homosexuality among Sappho and her companions, and some interesting observations on the connections between sexual passion and the *thiasoi* of young persons, see Calame, *Choeurs* I.427-32 and note 154.

22. Merkelbach, "Sappho," p. 6.

23. On Solon's view of the *polis* as a cooperative system in which any individual's justice does injury to the whole, see excursus to chapter 1, note 68.

24. On *kharis* in Pindar's odes, see the studies of Gianotti, Gundert (above, note 12).

25. On the classification of ancient poetry, see Hans Färber, *Die Lyrik in der Kunsttheorie der Antike*, and A. E. Harvey, "The Classification of Greek Lyric Poetry," pp. 157-75.

26. Cf. *Ol.* 9.47-49; *Nem.* 8.20-21; *Isth.* 5.63; for the poet as one who "finds" song, cf. *Ol.* 1.110, 3.4-6, 9.80; *Pyth.* 1.60, 4.247-48; *Paean* 6.53, 7b10-20; *Nem.* 7.16; Bacch. fr. 5. Paola Angeli Bernardini, "Linguaggio e Programma Poetico in Pindaro," pp. 88-89, understands such passages as references to "il problema dell'atteggiamento del poeta nei confronti della tradizione e della cultura dei suoi predecessori." However, the "newness" of song seems to be one of the defining elements of epinicians (as of much lyric poetry). The "novelty," then, of Pindar's verse has less to do with the individual's confrontation with tradition than with the genre of "persuasive" poetry that deals with current, "new" situations.

27. Cf. *Ol.* 6.90, 7.21, 9.25, 13.100; fr. 70b24; *Pyth.* 4.279, 9.2; *Nem.* 6.57b. See Gundert, *Pindar*, pp. 130-31, note 250.

28. On moderation at the symposium, Theogn. 413-14, 467-96, 627-28, 837-44, Xenophanes 1.17-18. In general, on the traditional motifs of symposiastic poetry, see Giuseppe Giangrande, "Sympotic Literature and Epigram," in *L'Epigramme Grecque*, pp. 91-174, and Karl Bielohlaweck, "Gastmahls- und Symposionslehren bei Griechischen Dichtern," pp. 11-30.

29. Cf. Theogn. 763, 989, 1042, 1047, 1043. Giangrande, "Sympotic Literature,"

p. 101, note 2, refers to the work of P. Kagi on such "Aufforderungen," in "Nach-wirkungen der älteren griechischen Elegie in der Epigrammen der Anthologie" (diss., Zurich, 1917), which I have not seen.

30. On the translation of *ekrinonto* (535), see M. L. West's commentary to the *Theogony*, and Gregory Nagy, *The Best of the Achaeans*, pp. 215-16.

31. See J. Rudhardt, "Les Mythes Grecques Relatifs à l'Instauration du sacri-fice: Les Roles Correlatifs de Promethée et de son Fils Deucalion," pp. 1-15. For a description of Greek sacrifice, see Walter Burkert, *Homo Necans*, pp. 8-20.

32. That the heroes are not presented in a flattering light has not, perhaps, been properly appreciated. Different scholars have tried to explain away almost every indication of disgraceful behavior. Farnell, for example, understands 36 as an apol-ogy for Amphiaraus's flight, as due to a miraculous fear. But Pindar has already attributed sedition and folly (*thrasumēdea*, verse 13) to him; why then would he apologize for his cowardice? C. A. M. Fennell, in *Pindar: The Nemean and Isthmian Odes*, understands 15 as meaning not that "A greater strength put an end to justice," but that "Superior intelligence brought the dispute to an end." But the verse clearly means that in the civil strife Amphiaraus prevailed in strength, and justice was stopped.

33. On *piaino* and verbs of eating in context of blaming, see Nagy, *Best of the Achaeans*, pp. 225-26.

34. The question of gifts and recompense is by this point in the story a dead letter, as far as Achilles is concerned (19.146-53). This suggests that his connections with the Achaeans are now of secondary importance.

35. On the banquet as a sign of reconciliation, cf. *Il.* 1.457-74. The motif is per-haps connected to a mythic motif, wherein one must stay in a place forever, once he has taken something to eat there. So, Persephone was unable to leave Hades for good, once she had been tricked into eating pomegranate seeds (h. hymn Dem. 370-74). See Denys L. Page, *Folktales in Homer's Odyssey*, on the Lotus eaters and other instances of this motif.

36. See my "Pythian 2 and Conventional Language in the Epinicians," pp. 1-12.

37. Cf. C. Carey, "Pindar's Eighth Nemean Ode," pp. 26-42. He shows Hora's applicability both to sex and to athletes and demonstrates the contrast between Aeacus (supreme merit, supremely recognized) and Ajax (supreme merit, supremely unrecognized).

38. Thus, *erōs* is used as an encomiastic theme; it does not indicate an amorous attachment between poet and victor. On the use of erotic motifs in encomiastic poetry, see Peter von der Mühll, "Weitere Pindarische Notizen," *Museum Helveticum* 21 (1964): 168-72, who endorses the argument propounded by F. G. Welcker, *Rheinisches Museum* (1834) (=*Kleine Schriften*, 220ff.) that erotic language is a fea-ture of encomiastic poetry and used by the poet as such, rather than a direct expres-sion of the speaker's feelings. See also Francois Lasserre (above, note 14).

39. On *erōs* as an external force, see Snell's chapter on the "Rise of the Individual in Early Greek Lyric," in *Discovery*.

40. On reciprocity in homosexual relationships, see Francis Cairns, "ΕΡΩΣ in Pin-dar's First Olympian Ode," pp. 129-32.

41. On this narrative, see R. P. Winnington-Ingram, "Pindar's Ninth Pythian Ode," pp. 9-15, and Leonard Woodbury, "Apollo's First Love: Pindar, *Pyth.* 9.26ff.," pp. 561-73. See also Nancy Rubin, "Narrative Structure in Pindar's Ninth Pythian," pp. 353-67.

42. The ode thus resembles those considered in the first chapter. In the first part of *Pyth.* 9, as in the openings to those poems, the glory of the achieved victory is

stressed; the conclusion emphasizes rather the uncertainty and toil involved in victory. *Pyth.* 9 is unusual in its placement of lengthy mythic narratives at both beginning and conclusion, but the strange format turns out to be a means of expressing something central to Pindar's odes and his understanding of victory.

43. Crotty, "Pythian 2," pp. 1-12.

44. See Bruno Gentili's edition of *Anacreon*, vol. 14, and Calame, *Choeurs* I. 421-35. See also K. J. Dover, *Greek Homosexuality*, pp. 185-96. Plut. *Lyc.* 17.1 speaks of the *erastēs - erōmenos* relationship between adult and youth as part of the Spartan educational system. Xenophon (*Symp.* 8.35) denies that there was physical love between the two partners; nonetheless, the fact that these words are used suggests a connection between *erōs* and education.

45. Dr.III.p. 213.1b. Pindar seems to allude to these poets throughout the ode, by quoting or adapting verses of their poetry. Cf. Alcaeus 360P and *Isth.* 2.11; Anacreon 106G and *Isth.* 2.8.

46. Leonard Woodbury, "Pindar and the Mercenary Muse: Isth. 2.1-13," p. 533.

47. For the problems offered by this opening passage, see the article by Woodbury. See also Carlo Pavese, "χρήματ' ἀνήρ ed il Motivo della Liberalità nella Seconda Istmica di Pindar," pp. 103-12, and Frank J. Nisetich, "Convention and Occasion in *Isthmian 2*," pp. 133-56. Pavese argues that the opening description of the mercenary Muse must be referred to topics of wealth and liberality, which are conventional in the odes. See also note 12 above.

48. E.g., Homer, at *Pyth.* 4.277, *Nem.* 7.21, *Isth.* 4.37; Hesiod at *Isth.* 6.67; Archilochus at *Pyth.* 2.55.

49. Cf. however Dithyramb 2, which seems to distinguish an earlier kind of song from a later. Pavese, "Il Motivo," p. 111, suggests that *nun de* be taken very specifically as "on this occasion." The language throughout the opening lines, however, is so general that it seems easier to take the words as introducing a general modern practice rather than a specific occasion.

50. Woodbury, "Mercenary Muse," p. 533.

51. Hesiod, *Works and Days*, pp. 25-26.

52. See Aristotle *EN* 8.1155a32-b16.

53. David C. Young, *Pindar: Isthmian 7, Myth and Exempla* pp. 16-17, has pointed out the careful chronological development of these verses, which provide "a poetic epitome of Theban ancient history."

54. On road images, see O. Becker, *Das Bild des Weges und Verwandte Vorstellungen im Frühgriechischen Denken.*

55. On the motif of liberality in the odes and *Isth.* 2 in particular, see the articles by Woodbury and Pavese (above, notes 46, 47).

56. See the discussion of *eris* in *Works and Days* in chapter 2.

57. See F. M. Cornford, *Principium Sapientiae*, chapter 11, on the importance of separation as a cosmogonic force, both in mythic accounts, such as Hesiod's in the *Theogony*, and in philosophical accounts, such as Anaximander's.

58. On cunning and trickery in Greek myths about cosmogony and divine power, see Marcel Detienne and Jean-Pierre Vernant, *Cunning Intelligence in Greek Culture and Society*, pp. 55-130.

CHAPTER 4

1. The primary MSS of Plato have βιαίων τὸ δικαιότατον, a corruption that seems due to copyists rather than Plato himself. See E. R. Dodds's commentary on the

Gorgias ad 484b1–c3. Knowledge of the poem was increased in 1961 by the publication of a papyrus (*P. Oxy.* 2450) containing extensive fragments of the poem. For a discussion of the papyrus, see Hugh Lloyd-Jones, "Pindar Fr. 169," pp. 45–56 and the bibliographical references cited on pp. 45–46.

2. However, see now Giovanni Pini, "Sul Νόμος ὁ πάντων βασιλεύς di Pindaro (fr. 169 Sn⁴), pp. 185–210.

3. Lloyd-Jones, "Pindar Fr. 169," pp. 45–56.

4. Lloyd-Jones, "Pindar Fr. 169," p. 55. Among recent exponents of the first theory (*nomos* as "custom"), see C. M. Bowra, *Pindar*, pp. 74 ff.; W. Theiler, "Νόμος ὁ πάντων βασιλεύς," *Museum Helveticum* 22 (1965), pp. 69–80; and W. K. C. Guthrie, *A History of Greek Philosophy*, vol. 3 (Cambridge, 1969), pp. 131–34. They defend the view taken by Ulrich von Wilamowitz-Moellendorff in *Pindaros*, p. 462. Martin Ostwald, "Pindar, Nomos, and Heracles," pp. 109–38, argues that *nomos* denotes "the attitude traditionally or conventionally taken to a norm by those to whom it applies." For arguments in support of the second theory (*nomos* as "fate" or "law of the cosmos"), see M. Gigante, *Nomos Basileus*, esp. pp. 72–102; Dodds, *Gorgias, ad* 484b1–c3; and Max Treu, "Νόμος βασιλεύς, alte und neue Probleme," *Rheinisches Museum* 106 (1963): 193–214. See also the treatment of F. Heinimann, *Nomos und Physis*, pp. 68–70, who argues, not persuasively, for Orphic influences in Pindar's conception of *nomos*. For a review of earlier discussions of the fragment, see Gigante, *Nomos Basileus*, 79–92.

5. Aristides II, 70 (Dindorf) and the scholiast *ad loc.* (III, p. 409, Dind.).

6. Cf. above, the excursus to the first chapter, where the scolion by Simonides in honor of the Skopadai is discussed. Simonides, in the role of encomiast, considers the gods' influence over men's lives and concludes that he will praise the man who does not commit wrong willingly. Simonides distinguishes an active and a passive aspect of *aretē* and professes to confine his attention to the active side of it. Pindar seems to do just the opposite. The gods' hostility to Geryon, who acted in a manner worthy of men's praise, again serves to distinguish a passive and active side to excellence, but by refusing to continue with praise for Geryon, Pindar stresses the importance of the passive character of excellence; that is, the one who is not loved by the gods will not be praised. Rather than speak of a "disagreement" between Simonides and Pindar, however, it is better to stress the persisting ambiguity of *aretē*, which confronts any encomiast, and which lends itself to various presentations stressing different sides of it.

7. Such is the interpretation of Gigante and Lloyd-Jones. The concept of a violent, unjustified act that becomes just by virtue of serving "the order of the universe" is a troubling one, and, so far as I can see, unparalleled in Pindar. To the extent that the *Oresteia* offers a parallel, violence in pursuit of a goal seems to compromise the result seriously. Agamemnon killed his daughter in order to carry out Zeus's will that Troy be punished, but the worthiness of that goal does not "justify" Agamemnon's deed. Moreover, Pindar's Heracles is not a straightforward emblem of justice and order in the odes; in *Ol.* 9 he is a *theomakhos*, whose story the poet refuses to continue. There is no need, then, to suppose that he must be a champion of "universal order" in this passage.

8. See chapter 3 on the connections between *Il.* 19 and 24.

9. Cf. Pindar fr. 215.1–2 (SM).

10. Cf. also *Ol.* 6.98 and *Pyth.* 5.22, where Pindar refers to the reception of the returning athlete by the king; and *Nem.* 4.11, where Pindar hopes that his song will be "received" by the Aeginetans. For an interesting treatment of the semantic richness of *dekhomai*, see G. Devereux, "The Exploitation of Ambiguity in Pindaros O.3.27," pp. 289–98.

11. Cf. Michael Nagler, *Spontaneity and Tradition*, pp. 131-66, and Mary Louise Lord, "Withdrawal and Return: an Epic Story Pattern in the Homeric Hymn to Demeter and in the Homeric Poems," pp. 241-48, on Achilles' "return."

12. Cf. Gregory Nagy, *The Best of the Achaeans*, pp. 26-41, for a comparison of Odysseus and Achilles in terms of *nostos*.

13. See, for example, Douglas Frame, *The Myth of Return in Early Greek Epic*. He argues for a solar myth of departure and return as the original from which descends the *nostos* theme in Epic.

14. On Heracles and Eurystheus, Apollod.2.5.1, Diod.Sic.4.12.1; on Theseus, Plut.*Thes*.22.

15. On Orestes, see Aesch.*Cho*.269ff.; on Perseus, see Pindar, *Pyth*.10.46-48 and 12.9-17, and Apollod.2.4.3.

16. On the suitors as violators of hospitality, see *Od*.14.56ff. and 14.80ff. On the kinsmen of the slain and their grievance, see *Od*.24.413ff. See Angelo Brelich, *Gli Eroi Greci*, pp. 225-83, on the darker and even monstrous aspect of the hero.

17. See M. L. Lord (above, note 11) and on the Hittite myth of Telepinus, Walter Burkert, *Structure and History in Greek Mythology and Ritual*, pp. 123-42, and Hans G. Güterbock, "Hittite Mythology," in Samuel Noah Kramer, ed., *Mythologies of the Ancient World*, pp. 143-50.

18. On "liminality" see Mary Douglas, *Purity and Danger*, especially chapters 6 through 8, and Victor W. Turner, "Betwixt and Between: The Liminal Period in *Rites de Passage*," in his *The Forest of Symbols*, pp. 93-111.

19. Arnold van Gennep, *Rites of Passage*, p. 26.

20. Douglas, *Purity and Danger*, p. 96.

21. Works dealing with the problem of initiation rites in Greece include Henri Jeanmaire, *Couroi et Courètes* and Angelo Brelich, *Paides e Parthenoi*. See also Jeanmaire, "La Cryptie Lacédémonienne," pp. 121-50; Pierre Vidal-Naquet, "The Black-Hunter and the Origin of the Athenian Ephebeia," pp. 49-64; and Claude Calame, *Les Choeurs de Jeunes Filles en Grèce Archaïque*.

22. Brelich, *Paides*, pp. 13-112. See also Mircea Eliade, *Birth and Rebirth*, chapters 1 and 2, and Calame, *Choeurs* I.32-38.

23. Thus, this kind of initiation is distinguished from others—for example, shamanistic or mystic—in which the person is initiated into an extraordinary mode of life. See Brelich, *Paides*, pp. 19-25. Jacqueline Duchemin, *Pindare, Poète et Prophète*, pp. 311ff. has also argued for connections between the odes and rites of initiation. Where our approaches differ, essentially, is that Duchemin speaks of a mystic initiation into immortal life as being comparable to the odes, while I compare them, rather, to initiation into the normal life of the community.

24. Vidal-Naquet, "The Black Hunter," pp. 55-56.

25. See Eliade, *Birth and Rebirth*, chapter 2, on the dramatic scenarios connected with initiation rites in Tierra del Fuego, in Africa, and on the Loango coast.

26. Marcel Detienne, *Dionysos Slain*, pp. 20-52.

27. Vidal-Naquet, "The Black Hunter," pp. 49-64.

28. For a reconstruction of the ceremonies, see Walter Burkert, *Homo Necans*, pp. 102-6. In the following section, I have avoided, as too problematical, the question of the Olympian games and their possible origins in local rites of initiation. See however Brelich, *Paides*, pp. 449-56, for a discussion.

29. On the site of the *agōn*, see Paus.8.38.4; on the age of the contests, Paus. 8.2.1. Pindar mentions these games at *Ol*.9.96, 13.107-8; *Nem*.10.45-48.

30. Burkert, *Homo Necans*, pp. 106-8.

31. Paus 3.14.8-9.

32. Xen. *de rep. lac.* 2, 9. See Martin P. Nilsson, *Geschichte der Griechische Religion*, pp. 487 ff.

33. On the Oschophoria, Ludwig Deubner, *Attische Feste*, pp. 142-47, and also H. W. Parke, *Festivals of the Athenians*, pp. 75-81.

34. Plut. *Thes.* 23.3.

35. The Theseus story was associated with the rites probably no later than the sixth century, according to Deubner, *Attische Feste*, p. 142. On the kind of connection that exists between myths and rituals, see Brelich, *Gli Eroi Greci*, pp. 59-66.

36. Plut. *Thes.* 22.2. ff. and 23.2 ff.

37. See Jacob Stern, "The Myth of Pindar's *Olympian* 6," pp. 332-40, and Carl A. P. Ruck, "On the Sacred Names of Iamos and Ion: Ethnobotanical Referents in the Hero's Parentage," pp. 235-52.

38. On the "nature-culture" polarity in the ode, see E. Robbins, "Cyrene and Cheiron. The Myth of Pindar's Ninth Pythian," pp. 91-104.

39. The motif of the hero's exploit with his companions suggests one aspect of the parallel between athlete and poet. For the poet too goes about the risky venture of encomium together with the chorus of "young men" (*Nem.* 3.5), who are "companions" (*hetairoi, Ol.* 6.87). In *Ol.* 6, the poet, the chorus leader, and the members of the chorus must see if they can "escape with their words from an old reproach—'Boetian swine'," 89-90. See Gundert, *Pindar und sein Dichterberuf*, p. 121, note 137.

40. See the discussion in Brelich's chapter "Iniziazoni Spartane," in *Paides*, of the age categories among Spartan youth. Different ages are distinguished by the different excellences associated with them; cf. *Nem.* 3.72-73.

41. For a discussion of the difficulty of these lines, see Mary Lefkowitz, "Pindar's *Nemean XI*," p. 51, note 19.

42. The ambivalence is found elsewhere in Greek genealogies. In the *Theogony*, children continue their parents and represent various aspects of them; for example, the children of Night (Fate, Death, Sleep, Dreams, Blame, Sorrow, Hesperides, Nemesis, Deceit, Love, Old Age, Strife) specify different facets or associations of Night. On the other hand, children also overthrow their parents (Cronus castrates Uranus; Zeus defeats Cronus) and this subversion by the new generation provides a driving, progressive force to time. See Paula Philippson, "Genealogie als Mythische Form." Similarly, in the *Oresteia*, the generations are in discord with each other: the older generation murders its young, and the younger generation rises up against its elders. At the same time, however, each generation is but a continuation of the curse on the house of Atreus.

43. See Bruno Gentili, "Aspetti del Rapporto Poeta, Committente, Uditorio nella Lirica Corale Greca," pp. 70-88, and "L'Interpretazione dei Lirici Greci Arcaici nella Dimensione del Nostro Tempo," pp. 7-21.

44. I borrow this phrase from Michael E. Cooke, *Acts of Inclusion* (New Haven, 1979), although I use the phrase in a sense different from that which Cooke gives it.

45. Apollod. 1.3.2; Ovid, *Met.* 10.1-85, 11.1-84.

46. Joseph Fontenrose, "The Athlete as Hero," pp. 73-104.

47. Paus. 6.3.8; 7.17.6-7.

48. Paus. 6.9.6-8.

49. Callim. fr. 84-85 Pf., with *diēgēsis.*

50. For a full discussion of the stories of Neoptolemus at Delphi, see Leonard Woodbury, "Neoptolemus at Delphi: Pindar, *Nem.* 7.30 ff.," pp. 95-133, and Joseph Fontenrose, *The Cult and Myth of Pyrros at Delphi.* See also Nagy, *Best of the Achaeans*, pp. 118-41.

51. See Carl A. P. Ruck, "Marginalia Pindarica," pp. 143-53, who argues that we have no good grounds for interpreting the version of Neoptolemus's story found in *Nem.* 7 as a palinode of the version found in the paean. That *Nem.* 7 represented an apology for the "unflattering" portrait of Neoptolemus in the paean was the suggestion of Aristodemus, (Dr.III.p.137 *ad Nem.* 7.150a), and was intended to explain why Pindar lays so much emphasis in *Nem.* 7 on his good will.

52. Adolf Köhnken, *Die Funktion des Mythos bei Pindar*, pp. 50-54 has argued extensively that γε, as proposed by Erasmus Schmidt, should be read in 22, rather than τε, as proposed by Hermann. In this way, he distinguishes Homer's act from Odysseus's lies. For Köhnken, the passage is in praise of the powers of song, which are such as to make even spurious merit (such as Odysseus's) glorious, and are presumably yet more powerful when the poet has a genuinely meritorious theme (such as Ajax and Neoptolemus) to celebrate. Gretchen Kromer, in "Homer and Odysseus in *Nemean.* 7.20-27," *Classical World* 68 (1975): 437-38, argues, on the other hand, for the deliberate ambiguity of the passage. In 22, οἱ could refer to either Homer or Odysseus; each has skills of eloquence that are capable of misleading others. This seems to me a better interpretation of the passage. Consequently, τε, which links the *pseudeis* and *potana makhana* of Homer and Odysseus, should be kept.

53. On the translation of 39-40, see Woodbury, "Neoptolemus at Delphi," pp. 131-32.

54. The identity of the witness is controversial. That the *martus* is Pindar himself has been argued by Lloyd-Jones, "Modern Interpretation," p. 133; Segal, "Pindar's Seventh Nemean," *Transactions of the American Philological Association* 98 (1967): 449; and Tugendhat, "Zum Rechtfertigungsproblem in Pindars 7, Nemeisches Gedicht," *Hermes* (1960): 395, note 1. *Epistatei*, however, in οὐ ψεῦδις ὁ μάρτυς . . . ἐπιστατεῖ, indicates a presiding function (cf. Sophocles *OT* 1028, Plato *Gorgias* 465c-d, *Republic* 443c); frequently the verb refers to discharging the office of overseer (*epistatēs;* cf. the article in *LSJ*). This would refer *martus* to the official *themiskopos* Neoptolemus, rather than the poet. It is to be noted that nowhere else does Pindar ever speak of himself as "presiding" (*epistatein*) over another's deeds.

Farnell (at verses 48-52), who also understands Neoptolemus as the *martus*, correctly explains the force of εὐώνυμον ἐς δίκαν τρία ἔπεα διαρκέσει as referring to the concise praise which follows—that is, "to do fair justice to Neoptolemus three words are enough; namely, no false witness presides over the deeds of Zeus's and your offspring, Aegina." See also the discussion by Ruck, "Marginalia," pp. 143-53.

55. Woodbury, "Neoptolemus at Delphi," p. 132 demonstrates the pattern of this section, in which two pieces of bad luck for Neoptolemus are turned to happy results.

56. See Nagy, *Best of the Achaeans*, p. 118, note 2, and p. 119.

57. Dario Sabbatucci, *Saggio sul Misticismo Greco*, pp. 41-84. See also Marcel Detienne, *Dionysos Slain*, pp. 53-67.

58. See J. Rudhardt, "Les Mythes Grecs Relatifs à l'Instauration du Sacrifice," pp. 1-15.

59. Of course, the episode is not typical, for these are not ordinary horses but explicitly divine horses. Still, that a horse can be divine seems to result from a certain connection between the divine and animal worlds.

60. *Od.* 4.499-510; Apollod. Epitome 5.22-23, 6.6; cf. also Alcaeus 298 P.

61. On Alcmaeon, see Apollod. 3.6.2, 3.7.5; on Pelops, e.g., Hyg. *Fab.* 84.

62. See J. H. Molyneux, "Two Problems Concerning Heracles in Pindar *Olympian* 9.28-41," pp. 301-27, for a discussion of the myth. Molyneux stresses the

importance of the ambiguity and "tension" in the myth: the strength that comes to heroes from the gods can be such as to threaten the divine benefactors. See also Gundert, *Pindar*, p. 49.

63. See above, note 60.

64. On the numerous similarities between these passages, see Michael Simpson, "Pindar's *Ninth Olympian*," pp. 113–24.

65. Köhnken, *Funktion*, p. 183.

66. On the introduction and conclusion of speeches in lyric poetry, see R. Führer, *Formproblem-Untersuchungen zu den Reden in der Frühgriechischen Lyrik*, esp. pp. 61–62.

67. These are suggestions by the scholiasts; *Dr.* II.pp. 80–81, 137a,b, 138, 139a,b. See W. J. Slater, "Pindar's House," pp. 141–52. I agree with Slater that we are not dealing here with a personal reference by the poet to himself; however, I cannot agree that the reference is to a Sicilian cult. To establish this, he argues that statements in the first-person (e.g., 68, 76) refer to the chorus, not to the poet. That seems to create more problems than it solves. See Mary R. Lefkowitz, "ΤΩ ΚΑΙ ΕΓΩ. The First Person in Pindar," pp. 177–253.

68. See, for example, Köhnken, *Funktion*, 79–86; Ruck, "Marginalia," pp. 143–53; W. J. Slater, "Futures in Pindar," pp. 86–94; Erich Thummer, *Pindar: die Isthmischen Gedichte* pp. 94–98; and, of course, E. L. Bundy, *Studia Pindarica*. For a judicious treatment of the limits of Bundy's approach in regard to this poem, see Hugh Lloyd-Jones, "Modern Interpretations," pp. 109–37. See also G. M. Kirkwood, "*Nemean* 7 and the Theme of Vicissitude in Pindar," in G. M. Kirkwood, ed., *Poetry and Poetics From Ancient Greece to the Renaissance*. Alessandro Setti, "Persona e 'Poetica' nella VII Nemea," pp. 405–29, argues that the ode is in fact a response to the criticisms of Aeginetans.

69. On this translation, see Charles Segal, "Two Agonistic Problems in Pindar," pp. 31–45. See also E. D. Floyd, "Pindar's Oath to Sogenes," pp. 139–51.

❀ Bibliography ❀

The abbreviations of journal names are those used in *L'Année Philologique*.

Adkins, A. W. H. *Merit and Responsibility*. Oxford, 1960.

Alt, Karin. "Solons Gebet zu den Musen." *Hermes* 107 (1979): 389–406.

Angeli Bernardini, Paola. "Linguaggio e Programma Poetico in Pindaro." *QUCC* 4 (1967): 80–97.

Barrett, W. S. "Pindar's Twelfth *Olympian* and the Fall of the Deinomenidai." *JHS* 93 (1973): 23–25.

Becker, O. *Das Bild des Weges und Verwandte Vorstellungen im Frühgriechischen Denken*. Hermes Einzelschriften 4. Berlin, 1937.

Benveniste, Emile. *Le Vocabulaire des Institutions Indo-européens*. Paris, 1969.

Bielohlaweck, Karl. "Gastmahls- und Symposionslehren bei Griechischen Dichtern." *WS* 58 (1940): 11–30.

Bliss, Francis R. "Homer and the Critics: The Structural Unity of *Odyssey* Eight." *Bucknell Review* 16 (1968): 53–73.

Blusch, Jurgen. *Formen und Inhalt von Hesiods Individuellen Denken*. Bonn, 1970.

Bona Quaglia, Luciana. *Gli "Erga" di Esiodeo*. Turin, 1973.

Bowra, C. M. *Pindar*. Oxford, 1964.

Brelich, Angelo. *Gli Eroi Greci*. Rome, 1958.

——. *Paides e Parthenoi* I. Rome, 1969.

Bremer, J. M. *Hamartia*. Amsterdam, 1969.

Bundy, Elroy L. *Studia Pindarica*. 2 vols. Berkeley, 1962.

Burkert, Walter. *Homo Necans*. Berlin, 1972.

——. *Structure and History in Greek Mythology and Ritual*. Berkeley, 1979.

Burton, R. W. B. *Pindar's Pythian Odes*. Oxford, 1962.

Cairns, Francis. "ἜΡΩΣ in Pindar's First Olympian Ode." *Hermes* 105 (1977): 129–32.

Calame, Claude. *Les Choeurs de Jeunes Filles en Grèce Archaïque.* 2 vols. Rome, 1977.

——. "Réflexions sur les Genres Littéraires en Grèce Archaïque." *QUCC* 17 (1974): 113–28.

Carey, C. "Pindar's Eighth Nemean Ode." *PCPS* New Series 22 (1976): 26–42.

Carrière, Jean. "Sur l'Olympique II de Pindare, A Propos d'un récent examen." *REG* 86 (1973): 436–43.

Chirassi Colombo, Ileana. "La Salvezza nell' Aldilà nella Cultura Greca Arcaica." *Studii Clasice* 15 (1973): 23–29.

Claus, D. B. "*Aidōs* in the Language of Achilles." *TAPA* 105 (1975): 13–28.

——. "Defining Moral Terms in *Works and Days*." *TAPA* 107 (1977): 73–84.

Cornford, F. M. *Principium Sapientiae*. Cambridge, 1952.

Bibliography

Crotty, Kevin. "Pythian 2 and Conventional Language in the Epinicians." *Hermes* 108 (1980), 1-12.

Daremberg, Ch., and Saglio, Edm. *Dictionnaire des Antiquités Grecques et Romaines.* Paris, 1900.

Defradas, Jean. "Sur l'Interprétation de la Deuxième Olympique de Pindare." *REG* 84 (1971): 131-43.

Demand, Nancy. "Pindar's Olympian 2, Theron's Faith, and Empedocles' Katharmoi." *GRBS* 16 (1975): 347-57.

Denniston, J. D. and Page, Denys L. *Aeschylus: Agamemnon.* Oxford, 1957.

Detienne, Marcel. *Crise Agraire et Attitude Réligieuse chez Hesiod.* Brussels, 1963.

———. *Dionysos Slain.* Translated by Mireille Muellner and Leonard Muellner. Baltimore, 1979.

Detienne, Marcel. *Les Maîtres de Vérité dans la Grèce Archaïque.* Paris, 1967.

——— and Vernant, Jean-Pierre. *Cunning Intelligence in Greek Culture and Society.* Translated by Janet Lloyd. Sussex, 1978.

Deubner, Ludwig. *Attische Feste.* Berlin, 1932.

Devereux, G. "The Exploitation of Ambiguity in Pindaros *O.3.27.*" *RhM* 109 (1966): 289-98.

Dickie, Matthew. "The Argument and Form of Simonides 542 PMG." *HSCP* 82 (1978): 21-33.

———. "*Dikē* as a Moral Term in Homer and Hesiod." *CP* 73 (1978): 91-101.

———. "On the Meaning of ἐφήμερος." *ICS* 1 (1976): 7-14.

Dodds, E. R. *The Greeks and the Irrational.* Berkeley, 1951.

———. "Morals and Politics in the *Oresteia.*" *PCPS* New Series 6 (1960): 19-31. (= *The Ancient Concept of Progress and Other Essays.* 43-63. Oxford, 1973.)

———. *Plato: Gorgias.* Oxford, 1959.

Donlan, Walter. "Simonides, Fr. 4D and P.Oxy.2432." *TAPA* 100 (1969): 71-95.

———. "The Tradition of Anti-Aristocratic Thought in Early Greek Poetry." *Historia* 22 (1973): 145-54.

Douglas, Mary. *Purity and Danger.* London, 1966.

Dover, K. J. *Greek Homosexuality.* Cambridge, Mass., 1978.

———. "Some Neglected Aspects of Agamemnon's Dilemma." *JHS* 93 (1973): 58-69.

Duchemin, Jacqueline. *Pindare, Poète et Prophète.* Paris, 1955.

Dumézil, Georges. *Idées Romaines.* Paris, 1969.

———. *Servius et la Fortune: Essai sur la fonction sociale de louange et de blâme sur les éléments indo-européens du cens romain.* Paris, 1943.

Easterling, P. E. "Alcman 58 and Simonides 37." *PCPS* 200 (1974): 41-43.

Edwards, G. P. *The Language of Hesiod in its Traditional Context.* Oxford, 1971.

Eliade, Mircea. *Birth and Rebirth.* Translated by Williard R. Trask. New York, 1958.

Erbse, Hartmut. "Pindars Dritte Nemeische Ode." *Hermes* 97 (1969): 272-91.

Färber, Hans. *Die Lyrik in der Kunsttheorie der Antike.* Munich, 1936.

Farnell, Lewis R. *A Critical Commentary to the Works of Pindar.* London, 1932.

Fenik, Bernard. *Studies in the Odyssey.* Wiesbaden, 1974.

Fennell, C. A. M. *Pindar: The Nemean and Isthmian Odes.* Cambridge, 1883.

Floyd, E. D. "Pindar's Oath to Sogenes." *TAPA* 96 (1965): 139-51.

Fontenrose, Joseph. "The Athlete as Hero." *CSCA* 1 (1968): 73-104.

———. *The Cult and Myth of Pyrros at Delphi.* Berkeley, 1960.

Fraenkel, Eduard. *Aeschylus: Agamemnon.* Oxford, 1950.

162

Bibliography

Fraenkel, Hermann. *Dichtung und Philosophie des Frühen Griechentums*. 2d ed. Munich, 1962.

———. *Wege und Formen Frühgriechischen Denkens*. Munich, 1960.

Frame, Douglas. *The Myth of Return in Early Greek Epic*. New Haven, 1978.

Frazer, R. M. "Pandora's Diseases, *Erga* 102-104." *GRBS* 13 (1972): 235-38.

Führer, R. *Formproblem-Untersuchungen zu den Reden in der Frühgriechischen Lyrik*. Zetemata 44. Munich, 1967.

Gagarin, Michael. *Aeschylean Drama*. Berkeley, 1976.

———. "Dikē in the Works and Days." *CP* 68 (1973): 81-94.

———. "Hesiod's Dispute with Perses." *TAPA* 104 (1974): 103-11.

———. "The Vote of Athena." *AJP* 96 (1975): 121-27.

Gennep, Arnold van. *Rites of Passage*. Translated by Monica B. Vizedom and Gabrielle L. Caffee. Chicago, 1960.

Gentili, Bruno. "Aspetti del Rapporto Poeta, Committente, Uditorio nella Lirica Corale Greca." *Studi Urbinati* 39 (1965): 70-88.

———. "L'Interpretazione dei Lirici Greci Arcaici nella Dimensione del Nostro Tempo. Sincronia e Diacronia nello Studio di una Cultura Orale." *QUCC* 8 (1969): 7-21.

———. "La Veneranda Sappho." *QUCC* 1 (1966): 37-62.

———, ed. *Anacreon*. Rome, 1958.

Gerber, D. E. *Euterpe*. Amsterdam, 1970.

———. "What Time Can Do (Pindar, *Nemean* 1.46-7)." *TAPA* 93 (1962): 30-33.

Gernet, Louis. *Droit et Société dans la Grèce Ancienne*. Paris, 1955.

Giangrande, Giuseppe. "Sympotic Literature and Epigram." In *L'Epigramme Grecque*. Fondation Hardt 14. Geneva, 1968.

Gianotti, Gian Franco. "Sull' Olimpia Seconda di Pindaro." *RFIC* 99 (1979): 26-52.

———. *Per una Poetica Pindarica*. Turin, 1975.

Gigante, M. *Nomos Basileus*. Naples, 1956.

Girard, René. *Violence and the Sacred*. Translated by Patrick Gregory. Baltimore, 1977.

Gould, John. "Dramatic Character and 'Human Intelligibility' in Greek Tragedy." *PCPS* 204 (1978): 43-67.

Gundert, Hermann. *Pindar und sein Dichterberuf*. Frankfurt, 1935.

Güterbock, Hans G. "Hittite Mythology." In *Mythologies of the Ancient World*, edited by Samuel Noah Kramer. Garden City, 1961.

Haldane, J. A. "Musical Themes and Imagery in Aeschylus." *JHS* 85 (1965): 33-41.

Hamilton, Richard. *Epinikion*. The Hague, 1974.

———. "Solon 13.74ff. (West.)" *GRBS* 18 (1977): 185-88.

Hammond, N. G. L. "Personal Freedom and Its Limitations in the *Oresteia*." *JHS* 85 (1965): 42-55.

Hampe, R. "Zur Eschatalogie in Pindars Zweite Olympischen Ode." In Ἑρμηνεία: *Festschrift zum 60 Geburtstag O. Regenbogen dargebracht*. Heidelberg, 1952.

Harvey, A. E. "The Classification of Greek Lyric Poetry." *CQ* 49 (1955): 157-75.

Heinimann, F. *Nomos und Physis*. Basel, 1945.

Hoekstra, A. "Hésiode et la tradition orale." *Mnemosyne*, 4th series 10 (1975): 193-225.

Hommel, Hildebrecht. "Solon, Staatsmann und Dichter." In *Die Griechische Elegie*, edited by Gerhard Pfohl. Wege der Forschung 129. Darmstadt, 1972.

Hubbard, Thomas K. "Language and Mediation in Pindar and Heraclitus: A Semiotic Inquiry." Ph.D. dissertation, Yale University, 1979.

Bibliography

Jaeger, Werner. *Five Essays.* Translated by Adele M. Fiske. Montreal, 1966.

Janni, Pietro. "Σώτειρα e σωτήρ in Pindaro." *Studi Urbinati* 39 (1965): 104-9.

Jeanmaire, Henri. *Couroi et Courètes.* Lille, 1939.

——. "La Cryptie Lacédémonienne." *REG* 26 (1913): 121-50.

Jones, John. *Aristotle and Greek Tragedy.* London, 1962.

Jurenka, H. "Des Simonides Siegeslied auf Skopas in Platons Protagoras." *Zeitschrift für die österreichischen Gymnasien* 57 (1906): 865-75.

Kaufmann-Bühler, Dieter. "Hesiod und die Tisis in der Odyssee." *Hermes* 84 (1956): 267-95.

Kegel, W. J. H. F. *Simonides.* Groningen, 1961.

Kirkwood, G. M. "*Nemean 7* and the Theme of Vicissitude in Pindar." In *Poetry and Poetics from Ancient Greece to the Renaissance,* edited by G. M. Kirkwood. Ithaca, 1975.

Knox, Bernard. "The Lion in the House." *CP* 47 (1952): 17-25.

Köhnken, Adolf. *Die Funktion des Mythos bei Pindar.* Berlin, 1971.

——. "Perseus' Kampf und Athenes' Erfindung (Bemerkungen zu Pindar, Pythien 12)." *Hermes* 104 (1976): 257-65.

——. "Pindar as Innovator: Poseidon Hippios and the Relevance of the Pelops Story in Olympian 1." *CQ* 68 (1974): 199-206.

Komornicka, Anna H. "Quelques remarques sur la notion d' ἀλάθεια et de ψεῦδος chez Pindare." *Eos* 60 (1972): 235-53.

Krischer, Tilman, "Die logischen Formen der Priamel." *Grazer Beiträge* 2 (1974): 79-91.

Kromer, Gretchen. "The Value of Time in Pindar's Olympian 10." *Hermes* 104 (1976): 420-36.

Kühn, Josef. "Eris und Dike: Untersuchungen zu Hesiods Ἔργα καὶ Ἡμέραι." *Würzburger Jahrbücher für die Altertumswissenschaft* 2 (1947): 259-64.

Kuhns, Richard. *The House, the City, and the Judge.* Indianapolis, 1962.

Lanata, Giuliana. "Sul linguaggio amoroso di Saffo." *QUCC* 1 (1966): 63-79.

——. *Poetica Pre-Platonica.* Florence, 1963.

Lasserre, François. "Ornements Erotiques dans la Poésie Lyrique Archaïque." In *Serta Turyniana: Studies in Greek Literature and Paleography in honor of Alexander Turyn.* Urbana, 1974.

Lattimore, Richmond. "The First Elegy of Solon." *AJP* 68 (1947): 161-79.

Lebeck, Anne. *The Oresteia: a Study of Language and Structure.* Cambridge, Mass., 1971.

Leeuwen, J. van. *Pindarus' Tweede Olympische Ode.* Assen, 1964.

Lefkowitz, Mary R. "The Influential Fictions in the Scholia to Pindar's Pythian 8." *CP* 70 (1975): 173-85.

——. "Pindar's Nemean XI." *JHS* 99 (1979): 49-56.

——. "Pindar's Pythian 8." *CJ* 72 (1976-77): 209-21.

——. "ΤΩ ΚΑΙ ΕΓΩ: The First Person in Pindar." *HSCP* 67 (1963): 177-253.

——. *The Victory Ode.* Park Ridge, New Jersey, 1976.

Lesky, Albin. "Decision and Responsibility in the Tragedy of Aeschylus." *JHS* 86 (1966): 78-85.

——. "Die Göttliche und Menschliche Motivation bei Homer." *Stzbr. Heidelberger Akad. Philo-Hist. Kl.* 45 (1961).

Lévi-Strauss, Claude. *La Pensée Sauvage.* Paris, 1962.

Lloyd, G. E. R. *Polarity and Analogy.* Cambridge, 1966.

Bibliography

Lloyd-Jones, Hugh. "The Guilt of Agamemnon." *CQ* 12 (1962): 187-99.

———. *The Justice of Zeus*. Berkeley, 1971.

———. "Modern Interpretation of Pindar." *JHS* 93 (1973): 109-37.

———. "Pindar Fr. 169." *HSCP* 76 (1972): 45-56.

———. "Zeus in Aeschylus." *JHS* 76 (1956): 55-67.

Lord, A. B. "Composition by Theme in Homer and Southslavic Epos." *TAPA* 82 (1951): 71-80.

———. *Singer of Tales*. Cambridge, Mass., 1964.

Lord, Mary Louise. "Withdrawal and Return: An Epic Story Pattern in the Homeric Hymn to Demeter and in the Homeric Poems." *CJ* 62 (1967): 241-48.

Maloney, Gilles. "Sur l'Unité de la Quatrième Neméenne de Pindare." *Phoenix* 18 (1964): 173-82.

Mattes, Wilhelm. *Odysseus bei den Phäaken*. Würzburg, 1958.

McKay, K. J. "Ambivalent ΑΙΔΩΣ in Hesiod." *AJP* 84 (1963): 17-27.

Merkelbach, R. "Sappho und ihr Kreis." *Philologus* 101 (1957): 1-29.

Meuli, Karl. "Der Ursprung der Olympischen Spiele." In *Gesammelte Schriften* II. Basel, 1975. (=*Antike* 17 [1941]): 189-208.

Miller, Andrew W. "Thalia Erasimolpos: Consolation in Pindar's Fourteenth Olympian." *TAPA* 107 (1977): 225-34.

Molyneux, J. H. "Two Problems Concerning Heracles in Pindar *Olympian* 9.28-41." *TAPA* 103 (1972): 301-27.

Murnaghan, Sheila H. "Anagnorisis in the Odyssey." Ph.D. dissertation, University of North Carolina, 1980.

Nagler, Michael. *Spontaneity and Tradition*. Berkeley, 1974.

Nagy, Gregory. *The Best of the Achaeans*. Baltimore, 1979.

———. *Comparative Studies in Greek and Indic Meter*. Cambridge, Mass., 1974.

Neizel, Hans. "Pandora und das Fass. Zur Interpretation von Hesiod, Erga 42-105." *Hermes* 104 (1976): 387-419.

Nilsson, Martin P. *Geschichte der Griechische Religion*. 2d ed. Munich, 1955.

Nisetich, Frank J. "Convention and Occasion in Isthmian 2." *CSCA* 10 (1977): 133-56.

———. "The Leaves of Triumph and Mortality: Transformation of a Traditional Image in Pindar's Olympian 12." *TAPA* 107 (1977): 235-64.

Norden, Eduard. *Agnostos Theos*. Stuttgart, 1956.

Ostwald, Martin. "Pindar, Nomos, and Heracles." *HSCP* 69 (1965): 109-38.

Page, Denys L. *Folktales in Homer's Odyssey*. Cambridge, Mass., 1973.

———. *Sappho and Alcaeus*. Oxford, 1955.

Parke, H. W. *Festivals of the Athenians*. London, 1977.

Parry, Hugh. "An Interpretation of Simonides 4 (Diehl)." *TAPA* 96 (1965): 297-320.

Parry, Milman. *The Making of Homeric Verse*, edited by Adam Parry. Oxford, 1971.

Pavese, Carlo. "χρήματ' ἀνήρ ed il Motivo della Liberalità nella Seconda Istmica di Pindaro." *QUCC* 2 (1966): 103-12.

———. "Le Olimpiche di Pindaro." *QUCC* 20 (1975): 65-121.

———. "Semantematica della Poesia Corale Greca." *Belfagor* 23 (1968): 389-430.

Peabody, Berkeley. *The Winged Word*. Albany, 1975.

Peradotto, John J. "The Omen of the Eagles and the ΗΘΟΣ of Agamemnon." *Phoenix* 23 (1969): 237-63.

Bibliography

Peron, Jacques. "L'Analyse des Notions Abstraites dans les Travaux et les Jours d'Hésiode." *REG* 89 (1976): 265-91.

------. *Les Images Maritimes de Pindare.* Paris, 1974.

Pfohl, Gerhard, ed. *Die Griechische Elegie.* Wege der Forschung 129. Darmstadt, 1972.

Philippson, Paula. "Genealogie als Mythische Form." *Symb. Osl.* suppl. 7 (1936).

Pini, Giovanni. "Sul Νόμος ὁ πάντων βασιλεύς di Pindaro (Fr. 169 Sn[4])." *SIFC* 46 (1974): 185-210.

Privitera, G. A. "Eracle nella Prima 'Nemea'." *GIF* 24 (1972): 28-51.

Pucci, Pietro. *Hesiod and the Language of Poetry.* Baltimore, 1977.

------. "Lévi-Strauss and Classical Culture." *Arethusa* 4 (1971): 103-17.

Radt, S. "Pindars erste nemeische Ode." *Mnemosyne* Fourth Series 19 (1966): 148-74.

Redfield, James M. *Nature and Culture in the Iliad.* Chicago, 1975.

------. "The Proem of the *Iliad:* Homer's Art." *CP* 74 (1979): 95-110.

Reinhardt, Karl. *Aischylos als Regisseur und Theologe.* Bern, 1949.

Robbins, E. "Cyrene and Cheiron. The Myth of Pindar's Ninth Pythian." *Phoenix* 32 (1978): 91-104.

Rose, G. P. "Unfriendly Phaeacians." *TAPA* 100 (1969): 387-406.

Rose, Peter W. "Class Ambivalence in the Odyssey." *Historia* 24 (1975): 129-49.

------. "The Myth of Pindar's First Nemean: Sportsmen, Poetry, and Paideia," *HSCP* 78 (1974): 145-75.

Rossi, L. E. "I Generi Letterari e le loro Leggi Scritte e non Scritte nelle Lettere Classiche." *BICS* 18 (1971): 69-94.

Rubin, Nancy. "Narrative Structure in Pindar's Ninth Pythian." *CW* 71 (1977-78): 353-67.

Ruck, Carl A. P. "Marginalia Pindarica." *Hermes* 100 (1972): 143-69.

------. "On the Sacred Names of Iamos and Ion: Ethnobotanical Referents in the Hero's Parentage." *CJ* 71 (1976): 235-52.

Rudhart, J. "Les Mythes Grecs Relatifs a l'Instauration du Sacrifice: Les Roles Corrélatifs de Prométhée et de son Fils Deucalion." *MH* 27 (1970): 1-15.

Sabbatucci, Dario. *Saggio sul Misticismo Greco.* Rome, 1965.

Saïd, Suzanne. *La Faute Tragique.* Paris, 1978.

Schadewaldt, Wolfgang. *Der Aufbau des Pindarischen Epinikion.* Reprint from 1928. Darmstadt, 1966.

Schlesinger, Eilhard. "Pindar, Pyth.12." *Hermes* 96 (1968): 275-86.

Segal, Charles P. "The Phaeacians and the Symbolism of Odysseus' Return." *Arion* 1, no. 4 (1962): 17-64.

------. "The Raw and the Cooked in Greek Literature: Structure, Values, Metaphor." *CJ* 69 (1973-74): 289-308.

------. "Time and the Hero: The Myth of Nem.1." *RhM* 117 (1974): 29-39.

------. "Two Agonistic Problems in Pindar." *GRBS* 9 (1968): 31-45.

Setti, Alessandro. "Persona e 'Poetica' nella VII Nemea." In *Studia Fiorentina Alexandro Ronconi Oblata.* Rome, 1970.

Simpson, Michael. "The Chariot and the Bow as Metaphors for Poetry in Pindar's Odes." *TAPA* 100 (1969): 437-73.

------. "Pindar's *Ninth Olympian.*" *GRBS* 10 (1969): 113-24.

Slater, W. J. "Doubts about Pindaric Interpretation." *CJ* 72 (1976-77): 193-208.

------. "Futures in Pindar." *CQ* 63 (1969): 86-94.

Bibliography

——. *Lexicon to Pindar.* Berlin, 1969.

——. "Pindar's House." *GRBS* 12 (1971): 141-52.

Snell, Bruno. *Aischylos und das Handeln im Drama.* Philologus suppl., vol. 20, No. 1. Leipzig, 1928.

——. *The Discovery of the Mind.* Translated by T. G. Rosenmeyer. New York, 1960. Harper Torchbooks.

——. *Der Weg zum Denken und zur Wahrheit.* Hypomnemata 57. Göttingen, 1978.

Solmsen, Friedrich. *Hesiod and Aeschylus.* Ithaca, 1949.

——. "Two Pindaric Passages on the Hereafter." *Hermes* 96 (1968): 503-6.

Stern, Jacob. "The Myth of Pindar's *Olympian* 6." *AJP* 91 (1970): 332-40.

——. "The Myths of Pindar's *Nemean* 10." *GRBS* 10 (1969): 125-32.

Strohm, Hans. *Tyche. Zur Schicksalsauffassung bei Pindar und den Frühgriechischen Dichtern.* Stuttgart, 1944.

Svembro, Jesper. *La parole et le marbre.* Lund, 1976.

Thummer, Erich. *Pindar: die Isthmischen Gedicte.* 2 vols. Heidelberg, 1968.

——. *Pindars Religiosität.* Innsbruck, 1957.

Treu, Max. "Sappho." In *RE.* Suppl. 11, cols. 1222-40.

Turner, Victor W. *The Forest of Symbols.* New York, 1967.

Verdenius, W. J. "Pindar's Twelfth Olympian Ode, A Commentary." In *Zetesis. Album amicorum door vrieden en collega's aangeboden aan Prof. Dr. E. de Strycker.* Antwerp, 1973.

Vidal-Naquet, Pierre. "The Black Hunter and the Origin of the Athenian Ephebeia." *PCPS* New Series 14 (1968): 49-64.

Vivante, Paolo. "On Time in Pindar." *Arethusa* 5 (1972): 107-31.

Vlastos, Gregory. "Solonian Justice." *CP* 41 (1946): 65-83.

Walcot, P. "The Composition of the Works and Days." *REG* 74 (1961): 1-19.

West, M. L. *Hesiod: Works and Days.* Oxford, 1978.

Whallon, William. "Why Is Artemis Angry?" *AJP* 82 (1961): 78-88.

Whitman, Cedric H. *Homer and the Heroic Tradition.* Cambridge, Mass., 1958.

Wilamowitz-Moellendorff, Ulrich von. *Pindaros.* Berlin, 1922.

——. *Sappho und Simonides.* Berlin, 1913.

Winnington-Ingram, R. P. "Pindar's Ninth Pythian Ode." *BICS* 16 (1969): 9-15.

Woodbury, Leonard. "Apollo's First Love: Pindar, *Pyth.* 9.26ff." *TAPA* 103 (1972): 561-73.

——. "Neoptolemus at Delphi: Pindar, *Nem.* 7.30ff." *Phoenix* 33 (1979): 95-133.

——. "Pindar and the Mercenary Muse: *Isth.* 2.1-13." *TAPA* 99 (1968): 527-42.

——. "Pindar Ol. 2.61-62." *TAPA* 97 (1966): 597-616.

——. "Simonides on ἀρετή." *TAPA* 84 (1953): 135-63.

Young, David C. "Pindaric Criticism." *Minnesota Review* 4 (1962): 584-641 (=Calder, W. M. and Stern, J., eds. *Pindaros und Bakchylides*, Wege der Forschung, 134. Darmstadt 1970. 1-95.)

——. *Pindar: Isthmian 7, Myth and Exempla.* Leiden, 1971.

——. "Pindar, *Nemean* 7: Some Preliminary Remarks (1-20)." *TAPA* 101 (1970): 633-43.

——. *Three Odes of Pindar.* Mnemosyne suppl. 9. Leiden, 1968.

Index of Sources

Numbers printed in roman type refer to pages in this book; numbers printed in italic type refer to ancient sources.

Index of Subjects

172

THE JOHNS HOPKINS UNIVERSITY PRESS

Song and Action
This book was composed in IBM Baskerville medium text
type by Horne Associates, Inc., with Weiss roman display
type from a design by Susan P. Fillion. It was printed on
50-lb. Sebago Eggshell Cream Offset paper and bound in
Kivar 5 cloth by Universal Lithographers, Inc.